Modernity and Ethnic Processes in India

Modernity and Ethnic Processes in India

Editor
D.V. KUMAR

RAWAT PUBLICATIONS
Jaipur • New Delhi • Bangalore • Hyderabad • Guwahati • Kolkata

ISBN 978-81-316-0639-1

Published by
Prem Rawat for **Rawat Publications**
Satyam Apts, Sector 3, Jawahar Nagar, Jaipur 302 004 (India)
Phone: 0141 265 1748 / 7006 Fax: 0141 265 1748
E-mail: info@rawatbooks.com
Website: www.rawatbooks.com

New Delhi Office
4858/24, Ansari Road, Daryaganj, New Delhi 110 002
Phone: 011 2326 3290

Also at *Bangalore, Hyderabad, Guwahati* and *Kolkata*

Typeset by Rawat Computers, Jaipur
Printed at Chaman Enterprises, New Delhi

Contents

Acknowledgements

I sincerely wish to thank the North-Eastern Hill University and the Indian Council of Social Science Research (North-Eastern Region) for extending financial assistance for organising a national-level seminar on "Modernity and Ethnic Processes in India". Articles in the present volume are revised versions of papers presented in the seminar. The seminar was organised under the SAP-DRS Phase III of the University Grants Commission.

I am extremely thankful to the contributors for having taken deep interest in revising their papers in the light of discussions in the seminar. I only had to gently remind them once or twice for submitting the revised papers on time. They did it with a lot of enthusiasm and without any more reminder from my side.

I am thankful to my colleagues I. Lanu Aier, C.L. Imchen, A.K. Nongkynrih, B. Panda and Rekha M. Shangpliang for providing an excellent atmosphere in which I could pursue my research interests.

I would be failing in my duty if I do not acknowledge the help I received from Rawat Publications and especially Pranit Rawat throughout.

A volume of this kind would not have been possible if proper environment was not available at home. I would like to thank my wife Radhika and children Lahari and Pranay for enabling me to concentrate on my work at home too.

Contributors

T.N. Madan is Emeritus Professor (Sociology) at the Institute of Economic Growth, Delhi, and Distinguished Senior Fellow (Adjunct), Centre for the Study of Developing Societies, Delhi. A Fellow of the Royal Anthropological Institute, London, he was conferred an honorary doctorate by the University of Paris (Nanterre) in 1993 and received the Lifetime Achievement Award of the Indian Sociological Society in 2008. His most recent publications include *Sociological Traditions: Methods and Perspectives in the Sociology of India* (2011) and *Sociology at the University of Lucknow: The First Half Century* (2012). His current research interests include the sociology of religion and the history of sociology in India.

T.K. Oommen is presently Professor Emeritus at the Jawaharlal Nehru University, New Delhi. During his distinguished career, he held very important positions such as the President of the International Sociological Association and also of the Indian Sociological Society. He has been a Visiting Professor at the University of California, Australian National University, Institute of Advanced Studies (Budapest) and so on. He has published extensively. Some of the books which received wide acclaim include *Citizenship, Nationality and Ethnicity: Reconciling Competing Identities* (1997), *Pluralism, Equality and Identity: Comparative Studies* (2002) (to mention only a couple of them). He also won prestigious awards in the field of Sociology such as V.K.R.V. Rao Prize in Sociology (1981), G.S. Ghurye Prize in Sociology and Anthropology (1985) and the Swami Pranavananda Award in Sociology (1997). He was also a member of the Prime Minister's High Level Committee (2004–2006) for the study of Social, Economic and Educational Status of the Muslim Community in India. He was conferred the Padma Bhusan, the second highest civilian award in 2008.

Ravindra K. Jain is an anthropologist, retired from Jawaharlal Nehru University (JNU), New Delhi. He is a leading international authority on the Indian Diaspora. Prof. Jain held the Chair of Social Anthropology (1979–2002) and was Dean, School of Social Sciences (1992–94) at JNU. He has taught sociology and social anthropology in all parts of the world including the prestigious appointment as University Lecturer in the Social Anthropology of South Asia and Fellow of Wolfson College at Oxford University, UK (1966–74). He was elected to the THB Symons Fellowship in Commonwealth Studies and in that capacity held a Visiting Professorship at the Australian National University, Canberra (1995–96). R.K. Jain is the author of several internationally reputed publications, including *South Indians on the Plantation Frontier in Malaya*, (1970); *Text and Context: The Social Anthropology of Tradition*, (editor) (1977); *Indian Communities Abroad: Themes and Literature,* (1993); *The Universe as Audience: Metaphor and Community among the Jains of North India*, (1999); *Between History and Legend: Status and Power in Bundelkhand,* (2002). The G.S. Ghurye Award winning publication, entitled *Indian Transmigrants: Malaysian and Comparative Essays*, (2009) has been brought out in an updated edition in 2011 by Strategic Information and Research Development Centre, Petaling Jaya, Malaysia. His latest publication is *Nation, Diaspora, Transnation: Reflections from India* (2010). He has contributed over a hundred research papers in journals and books of higher learning.

Avijit Pathak is Professor, Centre for the Study of Social Systems, School of Social Sciences, Jawaharlal Nehru University, New Delhi. He is deeply engaged with issues of modernity and identity. Some of his books which have received wide acclaim are *Indian Modernity: Contradiction, Paradoxes and Possibilities* (1998), *Social Implications of Schooling* (2002) and *Modernity, Globalization and Identity: Towards a Reflexive Quest* (2006). Apart from the above, he has published articles in leading academic journals.

Ananta Kumar Giri is currently on the faculty of the Madras Institute of Development Studies, Chennai, and has worked and taught in many universities in India and abroad, including University of Kentucky, USA; Aalborg University, Denmark and University of Freiburg,

Germany. He has an abiding interest in social movements and cultural change, criticism, creativity and contemporary dialectics of transformations, theories of self, culture and society, and ethics in management and development. Giri has written numerous books in Oriya and English. Some of his major works are *Global Transformations: Postmodernity and Beyond* (1998), *Conversations and Transformations: Toward a New Ethics of Self and Society* (2002), *A Moral Critique of Development: In Search of Global Responsibilities* (co-editor, 2003), *Sociology and Beyond: Windows and Horizons* (2011), *Philosophy and Anthropology: Border-Crossing and Transformations* (co-editor, forthcoming) and *Pathways of Creative Research: Towards a Festival of Dialogues* (editor, forthcoming).

D.V. Kumar is Associate Professor, Department of Sociology, NEHU, Shillong. His research interests include modernity, ethnicity, development and social change. He has widely published on these issues. His other major works include *Modernisation and Ethnicity* (2006) and *Social Change and Development* (editor) (2012), apart from articles in some of the leading academic journals.

V. Bijukumar is currently Assistant Professor, Department of Political Science, North-Eastern Hill University, Shillong. His areas of research interests include comparative politics, democratic theory, political economy and development. His latest publication is *Reinventing Congress: Economic Policies and Strategies Since 1991* (2006). He has also published a number of articles in academic journals.

Manish Thakur is an Associate Professor at the Public Policy and Management Group, Indian Institute of Management, Calcutta. He was also a Fellow at the Indian Institute of Advanced Study, Shimla. His areas of interest are political and agrarian sociology. His most recent publication is *Indian Village: A Conceptual History* (2014).

I. Lanu Aier is Professor, Department of Sociology, NEHU, Shillong. He has been examining issues related to politics and religion. He has also been engaged with a critical interrogation of ethnic relations. His other major work is *Contemporary Naga Social Formation and Ethnic Identity* (2006).

Rekha M. Shangpliang is presently Assistant Professor, Department of Sociology, NEHU, Shillong. Her main research interests concern the sociology of environment, politics of ecology and livelihood issues. She has authored the book *Forest in the Life of the Khasis* (2010) and she also has a number of research papers in journals and edited books to her credit.

Esita Sur is Assistant Professor, Department of Political Science, Scottish Church College, Kolkata. She is currently pursuing her research on Muslim Women: Issues of Agency and Backwardness. She has widely published on issues related to Muslim women.

G. Amarjit Sharma is Assistant Professor of Political Science at Nambol L. Sanoi College, Government of Manipur, Manipur. He has published in journals such as *Eastern Anthropologist, Man in India and Oriental Anthropology*. His areas of research interests include ethnicity, political anthropology of state and society, politics of land and territoriality, civil society activism and conflict studies.

Nandini Basistha is currently Junior Research Fellow attached to Rajiv Gandhi Chair in Contemporary Studies, University of Allahabad. Her research interests include ethnic identity and politics of separatism.

Introduction

Modernity and Ethnic Processes in India

Modernity, backed by tremendous political and intellectual support, spread across the globe in a relatively 'unproblemmatical' manner. Both in terms of reach and intensity, there are a few phenomena which are comparable to modernity. There is hardly any society which has remained immune to the influence of modernity and the degree to which it has impacted different societies is quite profound. Modernity has had a deeply critical impact on the social structures and cultural institutions across the globe. What modernity is and how one negotiates with it are the questions which have been dealt with elsewhere (Kumar 2008). I would, therefore, refrain from pursing it further. Briefly recapitulating the basic argument, I would say that modernity can be looked at in three important ways which are different but not contradictory to one another (Callinicos 1999: 297). First, modernity can be looked as a philosophical idea. As an idea it represents a radical rupture with the past. It privileges progress, science, optimism and universality. It critiques superstitions, blind faiths and pessimism. It encourages us to adopt alternative ways of looking at world and its possibilities. Secondly, modernity can also be looked at as a form of society which would be characterised by distinctive economic, political and social characteristics. Economically, for example, there would be increasing mechanisation of production (use of inanimate sources of energy), a shift from agriculture to industry, growth of urbanisation as workers need to move from place to place where industries are located (Levy 1966). In the social sphere, a modern society has come to be associated with important shifts in values and institutional devices. In terms of value orientations, as Talcott Parsons (1964: 339–57), there would be a shift from particularism to universalism, ascription to achievement and so on. Thirdly, modernity can also be looked at as an experience, an experience which is full of contradictions. On the one hand, it promises many things: progress, advancement, removal of ignorance, power, joy, etc. On the other hand, it seeks to destroy everything we have and are known by. It introduces an element of uncertainty, risk and confusion (Berman 1982: 15). Scholars like Riggs would also like to look at modernity as essentially ambivalent. For him modernity combines both positive and negative consequences. In his own words, 'we view "melodies" as beautiful and "maladies" as ugly. Yet both apply with equal force to the consequences of modernity' (1998: 270). They are others who, much before Riggs, tried to problematise modernity by focusing on the destructive and alienating consequences of modernity. Be that as it may, we leave it at that as we are here concerned with exploring the linkages between modernity and ethnic processes in India.

Coming back to the question of interrogating the relationship between modernity and ethnic processes, when modernity spread everywhere, it came in contact with different socio-economic and political realities prevalent in different societies. One of such realities was ethnicity. Ethnicity refers to the consciousness of ethnic identity. De Vos, in fact, defines it as 'subjective, symbolic or emblematic use by a group of people – of any aspect of culture in order to differentiate themselves from other groups' (1975: 16). Brass would like to contend that ethnicity is to ethnic category what class consciousness is to class (1991: 45). Scholars such as Oommen made considerable amount of effort to distinguish between an ethnic group and a nation (1988, 1997). We will not pursue it here as Oommen's article in this volume also is engaged with that. Ethnicity, expressing itself in terms of ethnic mobilisation, ethnic movements and in some cases ethnic conflicts, was something which was noted. This has been observed not only in the relatively 'underdeveloped' areas of the world but also in 'progressive' and' modern' societies. Eruption of violent ethnic conflicts in different parts of the world such as Northern Ireland, Kosovo, Cyprus, Rwanda and nearer home Sri Lanka made sociologists, in particular, sit up and reflect on the relationship between modernity and ethnicity. Going by the dominant sociological literature on the question of ethnic consciousness, both Marxists and 'liberals' (to follow the conventional categorisation) have argued that ethnicity would decline in its significance in conditions of modernisation (Balibar and Wallerstein 1991; Diamond and Plattner 1994; Kupchan 1995; Miles 1984).

Marxists would contend that the inevitable development of class consciousness, which is taken as an expression of modernity, would strike at the very root of ethnicity. Ethnicity and nationalism are viewed as retrogressive forces which are essentially ideological weapons in the hands of the capitalist class to weaken the class-based movements and perpetuate the socio-economic, political and cultural domination of the capitalist class (See Tishkov 1997). They, however, argue that ethnic attachments will gradually give way to class solidarity. The very logic of capitalism demands that particularistic attachments, such as ethnic relations, would be weakened in the context of intensification of class contradictions as capitalism develops. Though there are some Marxists such as Gilroy (1987), Solomos and Back (1995) who take a more reasoned position that ethnic attachments would continue and they should be viewed as being autonomous from class relations. But such voices are still feeble within the overall Marxist scholarship.

As far as liberals are concerned, the argument is contextualised in terms of economic, political, social and cultural spheres. In the economic sphere, particularistic attachments are rendered redundant in view of the principle of meritocracy. Occupations are acquired on the basis of merit rather than birth. Similarly, in the political sphere, principles of liberty, equality and justice which are considered universalistic in spirit will undermine the dominance of any one ethnic group. In the social sphere, it is argued that formal associations supplant allegiance found on kinship and communal membership ascribed at birth. One of most perspicuous positions taken on ethnicity is that of Durkheim who viewed 'race' and ethnic origin as declining facts of the modern social order, precisely because both were rooted in birth (see Fenton 1999). Similarly, Weber would argue that the development of rationality and scientific outlook, as reflected in the privileging of reason over faith and belief in the modern world would lead to the emasculation of 'traditional' social bonds, of which ethnic attachments are a prime example (ibid.). The growth of rationality would strike at the very root of traditional structures, as he would emphasise. Most American scholarship influenced by Karl Deutsch (1953) on the question of impact of modernisation on ethnicity assumes that modernisation leads to a loss of ethnic identity. He popularised the thesis that social changes associated with modernisation will result in a shift from particularistic to universalistic identities because of mass communication systems, mass public educational system, spatial and social mobility.

The euphoria demonstrated by both Marxists and liberals (who otherwise fundamentally differ on the theoretical and methodological issues connected with the understanding of social reality) on the question of decline of ethnic consciousness appears to have evaporated in the context of spectacular manifestations of ethnicity in the contemporary world. One can rationalise them in terms of inadequate modernisation in the case of traditional societies. But how would one explain them in case of even the 'modern' and advanced societies? Modernity which was expected to have struck a blow to ethnic identities seems to be in a state of helplessness.

India, too, has had its share of protracted ethnic and cultural movements. These occurred even in those areas which were supposed to have become quite progressive and advanced. One recalls the situation in Punjab in the 1980s when one of the most powerful identity-based movements took place. Tamil Nadu, too, had seen its own share of ethnicity-based movement. Some of the studies conducted in cities such as Bengaluru observed that people continue to think along ethnic lines, however modern they may be otherwise (Kumar 2006). When one moves towards the North-East, one realises that some of the most protracted ethnic/national movements took place even in the context of political modernisation having been activated (see Kumar 2009, 2010). In the present times also, demands continue to be structured around issues of identity. Ethnic/national identities continue to assume a prominent place in the discussions on the nature of socio-economic and political changes which are sought to be introduced.

How one explains this apparent 'paradox' is the question which has been engaging the attention of the scholars for quite some time now. Many explanations have been offered. One such explanation, for example, offered by some scholars is that the very logic of modernisation reaffirms the need for an identity. Modernisation with its accent on homogenisation seeks to subvert everything that does not fit into its framework and ridicules different forms of social and ethnic cohesions. It regards itself as the first claim to universality that leaves no one out of its domain. There is only one legitimate structure of power, morality and truth. All others are invalid. The end result of such a hegemonic world view is the creation of a sense of rootlessness and restlessness among groups which then crave for what they regard as 'authentic' identity. Thus, modernisation ironically reasserts and consolidates ethnicity. Apart from such an explanation, one also needs to search for more sociologically grounded explanations to account for this 'paradox'. This volume would endeavour to dwell on the relationship between modernisation and ethnicity by not only critically examining various theoretical formulations available but moving beyond them in an attempt to arrive at more meaningful and satisfactory explanations. It would also seek to contextualise these explanations in concrete empirical situations.

T.N. Madan, in his keynote address delivered at the seminar, sets the ball rolling by making certain general and suggestive remarks about the topic modernisation and ethnic processes in India. The general style of presentation (in tune with what a keynote address is expected to be) explains the fact that one does not find usual references at the end of the article. He deals at length with the grand narrative of contemporary times, that is globalisation. He examines some of the important consequences of globalisation in terms of not only weakening of the nation-state but also strengthening of ethic consciousness and identities. The sense of loss of certainty of identities caused by the process of globalisation has ironically led to the consolidation of group identity which is visible not only in India but also elsewhere. He contends that globalisation as a process offers a number of challenges, one of which is reconciling the local with the global.

T.K. Oommen in his cogently argued article refers, to begin with, to the enormous confusion that is found about the interchangeable use of the terms ethnicity and nationality. For him nations were essentially cultural entities till they constituted themselves into states as it happened in Western Europe, thus losing their cultural significance. But nations should be viewed as groups of people who share a moral claim over a homeland (original or adopted) and a language. Ethnic groups need to be viewed as groups who are dislocated from their original homelands. It is the disjuncture between territory and culture which creates 'ethnies'. The whole burden of his argument is that concepts have their own historicity which needs to be appreciated. Decontextualising them would mean 'draining them of their meaning content'. Then he goes on to explore four different axes (structural differentiation, rationalisation, history-making project and modern life) around which the notion of modernity is articulated. Finally, examining the relationship between modernity and ethnicity and nationality, he says that the assertion that modernity has supplanted ethnic and nationalist consciousness needs to be critically interrogated. There are rich empirical variations which need to be factored into any examination of the relationship among them.

Ravindra K. Jain's article on hierarchy, hegemony and dominance: politics of ethnicity in Uttar Pradesh 1995, written in the context of the growing power of BSP in the 1990s, would actually help us revisit the political scenario that was prevalent in the UP then. The rise of BSP was an extremely sociologically interesting phenomenon which was sought to be captured by him in an analytically insightful manner. In his article, he argues that Weber's theory of ethnicity and Gramsci's concept of hegemony can illuminate trends in UP politics – particularly the rise of the BSP in the 1990s. The former hierarchical caste system characterised by 'integral hegemony' has been transformed into one of ethnicised status groups and 'minimal hegemony', a process that has been primarily political. Under this scenario a counter-hegemonic regime becomes a theoretical possibility, but this depends upon the advent of a revolutionary ideology and leadership. He looks at the ethnicisation of politics (led by BSP) which was caused not only by caste composition but also structural factors like uneven economic development which in a sense provides the macro setting. Ethnicity, for Jain, was like a sliding-scale concept always responding to realpolitik as witnessed in UP. The substantive reality of caste transforming itself into ethnicised status-groups in UP has been brought out in a highly insightful manner by Jain.

Avijit Pathak, in his deeply engaging article, interrogates the grand narrative of modernity which has captured the imagination of social scientists in general and sociologists in particular. The immense relevance of this article lies in the fact that it virtually sets the tone for the rest of the articles which, in their own ways, seek to link the issue of ethnic identity with that of modernity. Avijit Pathak looks at both the empowering aspects of modernity which, as he says, is here to stay as we can not go back in history and its alienating and debilitating aspects. On the one hand, it (modernity) offers us freedom, freedom to question oppressive social practices and traditions and customs and has enhanced our reflexivity. On the other hand, it seeks to delegitimise alternative modes of thinking and identities which have given a source of security and psychological solace for the people and in the process making them feel alienated and nervous. The enhancement of risk in a modern society has been pointed out like other sociologists such as Anthony Giddens have done before. The essential point that emerges from this article is that there is a great need to engage with modernity in a critical, creative and reflexive manner.

Ananta Kumar Giri, in his article, writes about how ethnic mobilisation in India followed the modernist logic nation-state. The same process is visible in many parts of the north-east India also. At the same time, the history of multi-directional cultural exchange and flows also need to be recognised. This is where the notion of transmodernity (which has been taken from Ernique Dussel, an American philosopher) is found to be useful. Transmodernity refers to the creative engagement between tradition and modernity and at the same time going beyond the limit of both of them. Transmodernity enables cultures to respond from the perspective of their own cultural experiences. It also offers the possibility of rethinking ethnicity and, in fact, can lead to post-ethnic consciousness 'where ethnic groups are not only interested in maintaining their boundary but in boundary-crossing inter cultural dialogues and communication'.

D.V. Kumar argues that nationalism and ethnicity have become key categories to make sense of what is happening around us not only in the so-called Third world countries but also the modern and 'progressive' societies in the West. In our contemporary world system, it has been increasingly observed that ethnic and nationalist conflicts have become a major force. One only had to look around to see the enhanced salience of ethnic and nationalist conflicts. They have come to be associated with modernity. What modernity appears to have done is it has changed the nature and character of inter-ethnic cultural differences and made them assume the shape of ethnicity and nationalism. His article looks at the dynamics of ethnicity and nationalism in the context of enhanced process of modernisation.

V. Bijukumar uses intersectionality as an analytical tool in theorising identity and oppression in a society. He says that as an approach intersectionality seeks to examine the multiple forms of discrimination faced by some social groups. Intersectionality has emerged as a compelling critique of universal identity created by modernity. It contends hat no social group is homogeneous. On the contrary, one can find different categorisations within the group thereby thwarting group identity. Though some communities appear to be homogenous from outside, internally one can find tensions between different categories. The emergence of ethnicity in the process of modernisation evoked a mixed response from various scholars in social sciences. Ethnicity is viewed as the manifestation of intersectionality created by modernity. Intersection of various categories leads to oppression and multiple forms of discrimination. When social groups face multiple forms of discrimination due to the onslaught of modernity, identity formation begins. Modernisation as a process emerged out of the western Enlightenment, reaffirms its commitment to establish a universal identity. When modernisation reaffirms its commitment to universal identity, the emergence of intersectional identities are breaking the universal identity and forming separate identity distinct from others. The assertion of ethnic identities can be seen in the context of protest against the modern nation-state dominated by single identity. Enlightenment modernity seeks to subvert everything that do not fit into its framework and ridicules the different forms of social and ethnic identities. Modernity leads to intersectionality which is manifested in ethnicity. However, in all kinds of society, modernity is not leading to intersectionality. When the values of modernity are not internalised by all sections of the society, ethnicity manifests as an intersectional phenomenon. In other words, ethnicity is gaining strength in the process of modernisation due to intersectionality. He further argues that modernity has created multiple forms of exploitation – class, regional and religious. Ethnicity is the outcome of multiple forms of oppression and discrimination faced by a community. Ethnic group in most cases is a minority group based on racial, linguistic, religious discrimination. He concludes by saying that most of the ethnic assertions are due to the perception and projection of the modern nation-state as being discriminatory and oppressive in ethnic terms.

Manish Thakur's paper is quite relevant from the perspective of the main theme of the volume. The important role that ethnic-based associations play in constructing identity is highlighted in this article. Specifically, his paper examines the role of Malayalee associations in representing the Keralite migrants to the host community and the everyday state in Goa.

Rather than uncritically privileging the given cultural distinctiveness of a migrant community, it carefully unpacks the everyday politics of representation and its implications for civil society. Based on fieldwork, the paper highlights ethnicity as a meticulously crafted and constructed identity form and suggests that ethnic associations do not always work as pressure groups solely concerned with the articulation of particularistic interests, which may however be treated as a contentious issue. The very logic of an ethnic association suggests that 'particularistic interests' do get articulated more often than not.

Lanu Aier discusses the role of the Naga Club in the emergence of Naga ethnic identity. He says that for most Naga tribesmen, the Naga Club is the central institution, instrumental for the emergence of a Naga ethnic identity, out of the social conglomeration of several tribal groups then in the Naga hills in the early part of the twentieth century. Based upon oral history, this paper reconstructs how similarities of socio-cultural constructs of different tribes, who were living under a common rule by an alien colonial power, were used by the Naga Club to form the basis of a common Naga ethnic identity. In course of time, Naga ethnic politics assumed divergent dimensions which continued even after independence. Contemporarily, he says that one can witness the involvement of various Naga insurgent groups, which is a reflection of Naga ethnicity. The continued search for independence by these various groups is underpinned by a heightened sense of ethnic identity among the Nagas.

Rekha M. Shangpliang's paper deliberates on the issue of appropriate utilisation of forest resources, whether they need to be used for the development of the country or the ecological balance and the dependence of the people on them needs to be kept in view. This has been a deeply contested issue. The ill-conceived policies of the government have done irreparable damage to the ecological balance and sustainability of resources. This paper makes an attempt at focusing on the forest management policies of the government and their impact on the life of the people bringing about socio-economic development and conflict in Khasi and Jaintia Hills ever since the colonial rule.

Esita Sur examines the relationship between modernity and ethnicity in contemporary India. She argues that ethnicity is a multi-faceted phenomenon based on physical appearance, subjective identification, cultural and religious affiliation, stereotyping as well as social exclusion. In words of Durkheim, all societies need some kind of 'collective effervescence' to affirm their unity and identity but Weber argued that modernity exhausted the possibilities of cultural renewal and meaning. In India, we have found that after independence, under the framework of a liberal democratic polity, in spite of having individual rights, communities and collective identities have remained powerful and continued to claim their recognition and rights. She located her discussion in the context of the growth of Muslim identity as ethnic identity in post-colonial India. While addressing this question, the relationship between the ethnic identity makers and modernity has been given special attention. This paper also tries to address the role of the modern state and other institutions to nurture and manipulate ethnic identities under the purview of liberal democracy.

Amarjit Sharma's paper discusses the modernity of Meitei traditional polity in Manipur that uses and transforms traditional scheme of life and territory. A section of valley dwelling Meiteis revive a cultural core around an ancient political centre (Kangla, the centre of ancient Meitei state) to strengthen affinity with the surrounding hill tribes. This occurs in the context of movements for the greater territorial identities of hill tribes that challenges age-old perception of an organic polity. The key argument of this paper is that there are not only different routes of modernity but also differential ways of using tradition; it is not merely that tradition gets itself transformed in modern context. However, this modernity encounters the state government's secular policy that attempts to convert sacred sites of the ancient polity into heritage sites. This has threatened to end the revival of tradition and spatial and temporal aspects of the collective imagination (of hills valley union) among people in the valley of Manipur.

Nandini Basistha tries to establish a close link between modernity and ethnicity by examining the nation-building process of the Rajbangshis which she says has taken place through movements such as Kshatriyaisation, Hitasadhani and later Uttarakhand. Before that she dwells at length on the growing phenomenon state versus community conflict which has been explained differently by different scholars. She spends some time trying to explain these various theoretical perspectives.

As one can see, the articles in the book try and deal with the central dialectic of the volume, that is the relationship between modernity and ethnic processes in India both at conceptual/theoretical and empirical levels by examining the concrete situations obtaining in different parts of India.

References

Balibar, E. and I. Wallerstein. 1991. *Race, Nation, Class: Ambiguous Identities*. London: Verso.

Berman, M. 1982. *All That is Solid Melts into Air: The Experience of Modernity*. London: Verso.

Brass, P. 1991. *Ethnicity and Nationalism: Theory and Comparison*. New Delhi: Sage Publications.

Callinicos, A. 1999. *Social Theory: A Historical Introduction*. Cambridge: Polity Press.

Deutsch, Karl W. 1953. *Nationalism and Social Communication*. New York: John Wiley.

De Vos, G. 1975. 'Ethnic Conflict', in George De Vos and Lola Romanucci-Ross (eds), *Ethnic Identity: Cultural Continuities and Change*, California: Mayfield Publishing Co., pp. 102–32.

Diamond, I. and M.F. Plattner. 1994. *Nationalism, Ethnic Conflict and Democracy*. London: John Hopkins University Press.

Fenton, S. 1999. *Ethnicity, Racism, Class and Culture*. London: Macmillan.

Gilroy, P. 1987. *There Ain't No Black in the Union Jack*. London: Hutchinson.

Kumar, D.V. 2006. *Modernization and Ethnicity*. Delhi: Mittal Publications.

——. 2006. 'Modernization and Ethnicity: Interrogating Theoretical Perspectives', *The Eastern Anthropologist*, 59 (3–4): 341–56.

——. 2008. 'Engaging with Modernity: Need for a Critical Negotiation', *Sociological Bulletin*, 57 (2): 240–54.

——. 2009. 'Explaining the Mizo Ethnicity: The Relevance of Oppositional Approach', *Man in India*, 89 (1–2): 37–50.

——. 2010. 'Ethnicity, Famine and the State', *The Eastern Anthropologist*, 63 (3–4): 461–78.

Kupchan, A. (ed.) 1995. *Nationalism and Nationalities in the New Europe*. New York: Cornell University Press.

Levy, Jr M.J. 1966. *Modernization and the Structure of Societies*, Vols I and 2. Princeton, NJ: Princeton University Press.

Miles, R. 1984. 'Marxism Versus the 'Sociology of Race Relations?'', *Ethnic and Racial Studies*, 6 (5): 217–37.

Oommen, T.K. 1988. 'Nation, State and Ethnicity: Towards a Conceptual Clarification and an Empirical Explication', *Social Action*, 38: 333–43.

——. 1997. *Citizenship, Nationality and Ethnicity: Reconciling Competing Identities*. Cambridge: Polity Press.

Parsons, T. 1964. 'Evolutionary Universals in Society', *American Sociological Review*, 29 (3): 339–57.

Riggs, F.W. 1998. 'The Modernity of Ethnic Identity and Conflict', *International Political Science Review*, 19: 269–88.

Solomos, J. and I. Back. 1995. 'Marxism, Racism and Ethnicity', *American Behavioral Scientist*, 88 (3): 407–20.

Tishkov, V. 1997. *Ethnicity, Nationalism and Conflict in and after the Soviet Union: The Mind Aflame*. London: Sage Publications.

1

Ethnicity in an Era of Globalisation

T.N. MADAN

The cultural region loosely called the North-East, comprising seven states of the Republic of India, is of immense historical, cultural anthropological and sociological interest. It is also, of course, of great political and strategic importance. Culture, society and politics are intertwined here in complex patterns and the history of the region is read in different ways by its peoples, some of whom, such as the Ahom, the Nagas and the Meities, are indigenous, while others, like the Bodos and the Mizos came in centuries ago from the north or the east, but are today as indigenous as anyone else. The peoples of the North-East speak different languages, follow different religions, exhibit different lifestyles, and combine tradition and modernity in distinct, creative ways. Regrettably, but perhaps inevitably, the region also has been a theatre of ethnic conflict during the last half century, where both militancy and negotiations have been employed to settle issues of entitlement to political and economic power among competing groups.

In view of what I have just said, one would have expected that there would be an informed interest in the North-East in other parts of India. This, alas, is limited and usually focused on episodes of inter-ethnic group strife or violence against the agencies of the state. There is insufficient knowledge about the history and cultures of the region and little understanding of its problems. Persons hailing from the North-East are sometimes negatively stereotyped as strangers, who look, dress, and eat differently, even in places like Delhi, the national capital. This is regrettable and deeply disturbing. Difference should be the reason for and the means of mutual appreciation, not mutual discrimination or hostility.

It has been well said, I think, that an age is defined by the problems it faces and even more by the manner in which people cope with them. We are now in the second decade of the twenty-first century, and know fairly well what all demands our attention now and in the foreseeable future. We still have not completed the agenda of the Millennium Development Goals – we still have a backlog of significant tasks, such as alleviation of poverty, provision of health care for all, and achieving universal literacy, to complete. Time does not stay still, however, and new challenges keep emerging from the ongoing processes of social, economic, technological and political changes, or become more formidable than before. Thus, there is the promise and the potentially threatening nature of double-edged technologies, the resurgence of religiosity for good or evil, and the onrush of globalisation with its positive and negative aspects.

Globalisation confronts us today primarily as a cluster of economic processes comprising inter-country flows of financial, technological and human resources. Everywhere one form or another of democratic governance is being crafted. In today's globalising world, attachment to the idea of the nation-state is weakening, and inter-state formations – most notably the European Union and, in our part of the world, the South Asian Association for Regional Cooperation (SAARC) – are being forged. Trade drives foreign policy as is evident in the evolving relations between China and India, and India and Pakistan. Politically and economically, countries are being compelled to look outwards as the most effective way of serving national interest. Such a perspective may have seemed paradoxical in another time but makes perfect sense in a globalising era. Moreover, our time has seen the movement of peoples across countries and continents as students, opportunity seekers, or political refugees on an unprecedented scale. And when people travel as transients or migrants, they carry considerable cultural baggage with them.

What I am driving at is that globalisation has a cultural dimension also. Alongside the various 'flows' I mentioned a little while ago, there are cultural flows too. We are witness to much cultural homogenisation which is hegemonic in character since the West remains dominant as the principal source of modern culture, so called. Education, art, architecture, cinema, music, sartorial styles, and so on, everywhere exhibit the influence of the West in some measure. But there are counter flows also of which the counter-culture movements of the 1960s in Europe and the US were an early manifestation. Thus, while the proficiency of the educated peoples of the world in the English language is increasing, we today read, write and speak many Englishes.

In other words, homogenisation goes hand in hand with hybridisation in the domain of culture. Fusion in art forms is the order of the day, as it were. Japanese methods of management are being adopted in the US, and the professional skills of Indian workers have been lauded in the UK. While homogenisation does often entail much cultural loss, hybridisation arguably is a process of enrichment. Numerous processes of give and take are work in progress and no final assessments or outcomes are yet discernible; they, perhaps, never will be.

Globalisation too has brought us gains and losses, provided solutions to old problems but also generated new problems. Its consequences are not entirely intended or foreseeable, and this creates anxieties. As we are pulled out of our regional or national cultural moorings, we begin to feel increasingly concerned about our individual and collective identities. A sense of collective identity, we know, is strongest within relatively closer, well defined, and stable boundaries. The classical sociological distinction between 'community' (Gemeinschaft) and 'association' (Gessellschaft) comes to one's mind, within the associated types of values and relationships, but the scales of interaction are vastly different now. It may well be broad minded to think of the world as a 'global village' and of ourselves as world citizens, but identities so broadly defined are vague and betoken a sense of alienation from lived, day-to-day reality and of loss of the self.

One feels emotionally insecure. One wants to speak in one's primary, childhood tongue with those who share it with us even when one meets them abroad, away from home. Migrants are known worldwide to cling to traditional cuisines, wear traditional clothes on formal occasions, and even wake up to elements of one's ancestral faith when confronted with other forms of religiosity. This is, for instance, true of Hindu migrants to the US, where they encounter the Christian faith even in secular settings: even that best known symbol of American culture, the dollar bill, proclaims trust in God!

The sense of loss of identity often leads to practical action to recover it. Multiculturalism as a careful revision of the old, uncritical idea of cultural relativism, which cultural anthropologists raised to the level of a doctrine about a hundred years ago, is today's preferred ideology. All cultures must be recognised as valuable but not insulated. In the US, the famous melting pot has been almost thrown away; Americans today come in many skin colours and in many cultural shades, and they want to stay like that, different but also together, and assert their rights as equal citizens of the republic.

In practical terms, multiculturalism goes hand in hand with ethnic assertiveness. In the last two decades, membership of the United Nations (UN) has gone up from 151 to 191 primarily as a consequence of the secession of ethnic communities from larger multi-ethnic states, whether in the territories of the old Soviet Union, or in eastern Europe, or in Africa. In many instances, this may have been by objective criteria a good thing to happen, but it has more than often been accompanied by ethnic fratricide and ethnic cleansing. Our memories of what happened in, say Bosnia or, nearer home, Sri Lanka, or for that matter in Kashmir from where the Pandits were forced into exile in 1989–90, need hardly to be refreshed. Ethnic violence has scarred the North-East too.

What, then, is ethnicity all about? It first describes a state of being, an awareness of collective identity constituted by apparent physical resemblance attributed to putative common descent, (as among the Mizos or the Nagas), attachment to a territory conceived as native land (for example, *Shonar* Bangla), common language, (as in all the linguistic states), shared cultural heritage and, most importantly, cultural pride (for example, Gujarati *swabhiman* or Marathi *manoos* about which we hear a great deal these days). Second, ethnicity envisages a wide range of actions to construct or bolster identity and protect the political and economic interests of the ethnic group. The internal plurality of ethnic identity – its multi-stranded character – makes it a more effective basis of mobilisation for action than, say, class because of the manoeuvrability it offers.

Ethnic groups were, of course, the stuff of classical ethnography, externally identified and observed, and described in languages other than their own in terms of presuppositions rooted in the ethnographer's own culture. By convention rather quickly established, ethnic groups were non-European or non-Western, preliterate, preindustrial, and so on, with small populations and remote habitats. Ethnographers did not wholly disregard self characterisations of the peoples described, but such characterisations were regarded as inadequate or incoherent, and even suspect. Thus, if non-Western bodies of knowledge did not make sense in terms of Western forms of rationality, they were simply dubbed as prelogical and even worthless. You, here in the North-East, know all this very well, and I need not say more about it.

Times have changed. The peoples of Africa, Asia, the Pacific, and South America have come into their own in the last half century. They make their own assessments of their cultural legacies, construct their own economies and polities, decide upon appropriate forms of governance, and, most important of all, decide how they will be described or represented. The power of description has been snatched from 'alien' hands, old categories of representation have been rejected, revised, or reinvented. The so-called Negroes of the US, who were later redesignated as Blacks, conveying various shades of stigmatisation, ranging from the blatant to the shame faced, are today proudly, by self description, African Americans.

We are witness to the transformation of embattled into empowered selves. Insofar as these transformative exercises are not forms of retreat but of recovery and assertion, as long as they are not expressions of hostility but of the resolve of co-existence, they bode well for the future. Ethnification is, obviously, double edged too: if it binds people of a kind together it should be welcome, but if it divides these people from others in violent ways, it should not be welcome. Moreover, the aspiration to become a nation-state is not always feasible, as, for instance, when a people are scattered and share their habitat with other people. Federalism and multiculturalism show the way to a peaceful future, and peace is the first precondition for balanced, sustainable development, which is what the North-East needs urgently. The responsibility for this does not rest on the shoulders of the peoples of the region or the union and state governments alone, it is a national responsibility.

It is clear, then, that ethnicity is about who one is and about what one may do for the preservation of one's cultural heritage and in promotion of one's political and economic interests. Ethnicity has a substantive dimension as also an instrumental one. It is about a sense of self or identity and it is about strategising for a better future. It conceives of arenas of action where ethnic groups may appear as antagonists, and the state may not be seen by everyone as a neutral umpire but itself as an antagonist. It is thus that, in my limited understanding of what has been going on in the North-East for half a century, the Ahom and the Bodo, or the Naga and the Meitei – each group reading the history of the region differently, constructing different pasts – compete with one another and also challenge the state.

The goals are usually clear with the appearance of unchangeability, but the strategies must be flexible. Such flexibility is the key to success, as we know so well from the events that unfolded in Bengal in the mid-twentieth century and East Pakistan later. As you know, Muslims in the province asserted the religious component of their identity in the 1940s, saying they were Muslims who happened to be Bengalis, because that seemed to be the best way to protect their Islamic way of life and their economic interests. The experience of being the eastern 'wing' of Pakistan, dominated by Pathans and Punjabis, led them to revise their self representation and present themselves to the world as Bengalis culturally and linguistically who happen to be Muslims. This switching of self representations, using religion as the marker of identity in a given set of circumstances but replacing it by language when religion had failed to protect cultural distinctiveness and deliver political power and material benefits, is an excellent, historical example of what ethnicity is all about. The face is one, in a manner of speaking the masks are many. Ethnicity is the name of an open ended game and, it must be noted, the outcomes are contingent, never certain. The Bengalis got their Bangladesh, Sri Lankan Tamils have not gotten their Eelam.

By way of concluding remarks, let me offer a couple of general and rather simple observations on some of the courses that ethnic movements may follow, and the responses that the state may make. Two obvious options are open to the aggrieved ethnic communities, and two to the state. The Mizos tried insurgency but eventually settled for negotiations. Mizoram is today the most peaceful of the North-Eastern states. Kashmiri Muslims also opted for the gun in 1989–90, and raising the slogan of *azadi* (independence) pursued the path of militancy for more than a decade and a half. What was at stake, according to the leaders of the secessionist movement, was not only economic and political interests but also cultural identity, Kashmiriyat. Recent developments seem to indicate that they are now coming round to the idea of peaceful settlement although not as yet to the negotiating table. The Tamil Tigers of Sri Lanka, whom I just mentioned, fought one of the longest and bloodiest wars for a state of their own, thousands upon thousands died, but they failed in the end. In the concluding stages of the war, the Sri Lankan state too had the blood of just too many innocent people on its hands.

The two options open to the state obviously are the path of enforced integration, imposed from above, and the path of accommodation such that the state rests on and accommodates ethnic identities rather than treads over them. Many years ago, sometime in the early 1970s (if I remember right), Surajit Sinha, who was the Director of the Anthropological Survey of India, told me of his encounter with a Naga young man at a seminar on national integration. Everybody seemed to be convinced that the Nagas must be made to see the wisdom of joining the 'national mainstream'. Having heard the monotonous rhetoric for what obviously seemed to him a long while, the young man stood up to acknowledge that joining the mainstream did, indeed, seem to be a good idea, but asked with some passion if someone would tell him where the mainstream flows. He waited a while for an answer, and then declared, 'it flows here in Nagaland!' His declaration was understandably greeted with stunned silence. That says it all, and provides, too, an answer to the question of what ethnicity in a globalising era is all about: it is about reconciling the local and the global, and reaping two harvests instead of one, as it were.

2

Nationality, Ethnicity and Modernity

Clearing the Ground

T.K. OOMMEN

Although the terms nationality, ethnicity and modernity are in wide currency in contemporary social science, I am afraid there exists enormous confusion particularly because the first two are often inter-changeably used and the third is believed to be undermining them fast. Therefore, it is necessary to begin our discussion by specifying the contexts out of which these notions emerged. However, I do not intend to define these concepts but only to unfold their historicity with the hope that clarity will be achieved in that process.

In the hoary past, there were no states in the modern sense of the term; indeed stateless societies continue to exist even today. Human societies were then constituted into 'nations'. A nation being '... a people, a folk, held together by some or all of such more or less immutable, characteristics as common descent, territory, history, language, religion, way of life, or other attributes that members of a group have from birth onward' (Peterson 1975: 181).

It is clear that the concept of the nation was essentially cultural in content and it encapsulated a variety of attributes; nationhood was a product of the conjoint existence and interaction of these attributes. But as nations started to constitute themselves into states, as political entities, in Western Europe, following the maxim, one-nation one-state, a new socio-political formation emerged and the hyphenated term 'nation-state' came into vogue. However, it is often forgotten that the nation-state implies a process and it is possible and historically true that the process can even be reversed. Not only that a nation can be constituted into a state, but a state can dismantle and destroy nations. Further, a state can accelerate the process of endowing a people with nationhood. It seems, the eclipse of the nation as a cultural entity is almost complete and it has invariably come to mean a political entity. Yet, it is necessary to place the notion in its historical context so as to understand the difference between nation and state.

While a nation may constitute itself into a state, the state covers an immense variety of political structures – kingdoms, empires, city states, principalities, republics, federations. And, the state only implies establishing successful claim within a territory which gives it the monopoly of legitimised use of physical force (Weber 1948).

That is, the state and nation need not be conterminous. And the term nation connotes society in the sense in which social anthropologists and sociologists have been using the term. But the difficulty arises (in multi-nation states) when a society is designated as a nation by the people concerned, with the intention of establishing a sovereign state. Thus, if one were to speak of Tamil, Kashmiri, Sikh, Naga or Mizo society in India there cannot be any objection. But the moment the term nation is invoked to refer to these societies; considerable alarm is expressed precisely because it is believed to be a threat to the territorial integrity of the Indian state and involves change of citizenship status to a section of its population. And those who assign the label 'nation' to their 'society' usually imply this.

It was only by the end of World War I the idea that every nation should have its own state and every citizen in this state should have full political rights got crystallised. And, by the 1940s, citizenship became a sacred right everywhere which in turn legitimised the need to regulate foreign migration. Today, single citizenship is a near-universal principle although some states do permit dual citizenship partly because there is no provision for renouncing citizenship (once a Greek, always a Greek!).

Ethnicity emerged through interaction between different peoples; it was initially a product of conquest, colonisation and immigration. That is, ethnicity implies dislocation from one's original country, region, or nation, that is, homeland. In contrast, the nation inevitably alludes to a people belonging to a specific territory whose moral claim to political authority over it is perceived as legitimate. That a whole nation can be uprooted from its territory and rendered into an ethnie (a French word which alludes to a people without a common territory and citizenship) only points to the historical process and possibility of one category being transformed into another. When this happens in the immediate temporal vicinity we are horrified and perturbed. But when it is a matter of the distant past we are reconciled and undisturbed. It is my contention that it is the rupture between territory and culture which creates ethnicity. What deserves our attention is the process through which a nation dissolves into an ethnic group and an ethnie crystallises into a nation. This is so because an ethnie endowed with legitimate political authority over a territory usually leads to the formation of a nation-state. Thus, the link between nation, ethnicity and state is clear.

Most discussions of ethnicity focus on a wide variety of attributes of ethnic groups – religion, sect, language, region, caste, race, colour, culture, etc. These attributes singly or in different combinations are used to define ethnic groups. While it is widely acknowledged that the saliency of these attributes varies under different circumstances, rarely does one come across any discussion and specification of the crucial or independent variable. Methodologically, it is not even possible to specify the crucial attribute because what is crucial is determined by the context. Therefore, it is not so much the attributes of ethnicity which are important, but the property of the situation in which they obtain and operate. No particular attribute of ethnicity can assume eternal importance, which varies with historical circumstances and existential conditions. In contrast, the concepts of homeland and territory are crucial in the case of a nation. Even if all other attributes are present together, a nation does not come into being unless it establishes moral claim over a territory which in turn provides it with the potential to state-formation.

The 'ethnification' of a nation takes place precisely when it does not have the resources for state formation, namely a homeland and legitimate political authority over it. What I am suggesting is that ethnie, nation and state should be viewed in a processual relationship. When an ethnie acquires moral claim over a territory it becomes a nation and when a nation secures political jurisdiction over that territory it becomes a state. Pursuantly, to be an ethnie is to operate within a nation-state or to be dispersed into several of them. By the same token to be an ethnie is to be in the periphery and to be a nation is to be in the centre of the polity. If a state has different nations in its territory that state is a multinational state.

Hardly any author, with the exception of Anthony Smith, refers to the notion of 'ethnie'. Smith lists six characteristics of an ethnie. These are: a collective name, a common myth of descent, a shared history, a distinctive shared culture, an association with a specific territory, and a sense of solidarity (1986: 24). There are two main difficulties with this characterisation. First, the sixth characteristic is a product of the first five features, which conjointly produce a sense of solidarity; to invoke the product also as a defining feature does not accord well with the rest of the features. The second difficulty is that this characterisation fits the concept of nation equally well, although Smith may respond by saying that an ethnie becomes a nation only when it acquires its own state. Such a position creates several problems, but will suffice for the present to note that nation and ethnie share all the features listed by Smith, except territory. That is, if and when an ethnie identifies itself with a territory, it becomes a nation. An ethnie is a cultural collectivity which lives outside its ancestral territory, actual, (e.g., European Jews) or imagined, (e.g., gypsies). The settlers of the New World who nurse a sojourner attitude also constitute an ethnie. When they adopt the territory into which they have immigrated as their homeland they become a nation. However, to become nationals in the territory into which a group migrates is not simply a matter of that group's choice, but also its acceptance by the earlier inhabitants. This was clearly evident in the case of German Jews.

It is possible to identify at least five different senses in which an ethnic group and ethnicity are conceptualised (see Roosens 1989). First, an ethnic group is conceptualised as a relatively small one, sharing a common culture with and tracing its descent to a common ancestor, the tribe being the favourite example cited. But in today's world, societies and groups are not insulated by descent and kinship. They are constantly exposed to alien influences through migration and colonisation, as well as through the mass media. This changing context has invested ethnicity and ethnic groups with new meanings, and most writers do not use these concepts in their original sense. As Gordon has noted, 'Ethnicity, as representing a special ancestral identification with some portion of mankind... disappeared entirely' (1964: 24), although some argue that ethnicity should be defined in terms of common descent, that is, race (Francis 1976). Second, an ethnic group is viewed as a self-defined group based on subjective factors, which are chosen by the members from their past history or present existing conditions. The cultural traits so selected provide for the creation and maintenance of a socio-cultural boundary vis-à-vis other ethnic groups with whom they interact (Barth 1969). Third, ethnic groups are viewed as interest groups competing for benefits from the welfare state (Glazer and Moynihan 1975). Racial, religious and linguistic groups are included in this definition, which views ethnicity as a resource used by deprived immigrant groups. Fourth, ethnicity is considered as an identity-seeking instrument by the peoples of multi-racial and multi-cultural societies. In this latter case ethnicity is not always instrumentally oriented (Horowitz 1985). Fifth, ethnicity is conceptualised as a device through which people seek a profound psychological unity, often based on common origin that is, sharing common blood, actual or fictitious (see Devos and Ross 1975).

A few interesting points about these conceptualisations may be noted. One is the nature of the societies where the studies were done and the disciplinary orientations of the authors, which have clearly influenced their conceptualisations. The first definition is based on the classic field work situation of social and cultural anthropology that is, the isolated tribal societies. Although the authors of the second and the fifth definitions are also anthropologists, their places of study are vastly different. Barth did his work in Afghanistan where different tribes lived in the same geographical area, which perhaps prompted the salience of boundary maintenance in his definition of ethnicity. In contrast, the psychological orientation is brought forth by those authors who did their work in complex multi-cultural situations in which the minority ethnic groups were experiencing a deep psychological insecurity. The third definition is formulated by sociologists in the context of multi-ethnic United States of America. They document the way in which successive immigrant groups use their ethnic identity as a resource to improve their material conditions through democratic bargaining. Horowitz, instead, having undertaken a comparative study across Asia, Africa and the Caribbeans, finds ethnicity to be a feature even of those groups that are native to the soil – that is, nationals.

Further, definitions one and five recognise the phenotypical similarity of the ethnic group (common descent, blood), while definitions two and four focus on other dimensions of identity. The locus of definition three is on material pay-offs. If definition three is geared to emphasise the instrumental dimension, definition four concentrates on the symbolic aspect. It is clear that each author is impressed by the specificity of his particular empirical location and emphasises it, reminding us of the famous Indian fable of five blind men trying to understand the shape of an elephant. This is so much the case that Roosens has written. In his own words, 'the term 'ethnic identity' can, for example, refer to origin, uniqueness, passing on of life, 'blood', solidarity, unity, security, personal integrity, independence, recognition, equality, cultural uniqueness, respect, equal economic rights, territorial integrity and so on, and these in all possible combinations, degrees of emotional content, and forms of social organisation.... It is impossible for ethnic identity to mean anything without the existence of ethnic groups or categories, for it is a relational construct' (1989: 19).

It is necessary at this juncture to advert briefly to the controversy between the primordialists and constructionists that is frequently alluded to in current social science writings. The intellectual ancestry of primordialists can be traced to Weber. Those who pursue this perspective treat ethnicity as a latent phenomenon present everywhere, which is invoked by deprived communities at an opportune moment when they experience an erosion of existing privileges, or when they attempt to overcome long-standing denials of privileges. This contextual invocation of ethnicity does not satisfy the constructionists, who insist that ethnicity and its cultural content is invariably the result of particular historical conjunctures (see, for example, Anderson 1983; Hobsbawm and Ranger

1983). It is suggested that identities such as Yoruba, Zulu and so on (in the African context) are nineteenth-century European creations (see Comaroff 1991: 666–67). It is also the case that identities such as European and Hindu are creations, the first by the Greeks and the second by the Muslims. The important point here is not who has 'created' these identities and when, but why these labels stuck, while others, (e.g., barbarians, primitives) did not. I would suggest that it is because they struck a familiar chord, fulfilled an emotional need and provided a shorthand device to communicate certain aspects shared alike by all the people under reference, be it a common homeland, religion, language or civilisation. Thus, some of the constructed identities become acceptable precisely because they contain a primordial element, which is construed as 'sacred' by the collectivity concerned. The posited dichotomy between the primordialists and the constructionists is, therefore, a false one.

We need concepts to make sense of the complex and often confusing empirical reality. But the ways in which ethnicity is defined has led to contrary results. What we need is a reformulation, and this is to be done vis-à-vis nationality. Both ethnicity and nationality are identities, but their bases differ; even in democratic states, they are often invoked by states to confer or deny equality.

The terms ethnic and ethnicity are most favoured and popular in the US, as they should be, because they aptly capture and convey the social situation there; the US is a conglomeration of varieties of people 'uprooted' or 'dislodged' from different nations. As Yancey et al. correctly observe, 'ethnicity may have relatively little to do with Europe, Asia or Africa, but more to do with the requirements of survival and the structure of opportunity in this country, that is, the United States of America (1976: 401). But the equivalent concepts that are suited to describe the overall situation in Europe are nation (and nationality), given the strong attachment people have to their homelands. This is equally true of Asia, although of course these terms are scarcely used. And this reluctance should be understood in terms of the prevailing situation in Asian countries. Most Asian states incorporate several nations, and the process of state formation is not yet complete, nor the states stable, largely because of their multinational composition. Therefore, to assert one's identity in national terms is to spell danger to the state. National identity within the sovereign state is often de-legitimised to uphold the integrity of the state. Further, assertions of identity based on religion, language, region, tribe, and so on are viewed as 'communal', 'parochial', and even 'anti-national'.

The term nation-state is coined out of the limited West European experience. Terms such as 'ethno-nationalism' have also been in circulation for quite some time (see, for example, Connor 1994; Richmond 1987) to refer to nationalisms based on primordial loyalties. Similarly,

Worsely writes, 'nationalism is also a form of ethnicity but it is a specific form. It is the institutionalisation of one particular ethnic identity by attaching it to the state. Ethnic groups do not necessarily act together except when they have special interest to secure. When those interests are to obtain a state of its own (or part of a State) the group becomes a nationality' (1984: 247).

This conceptualisation, too, suffers from several difficulties. First, it attributes a specificity to ethnic groups which in fact is common to all groups. No group action, whatever may be the basis of constituting it, takes place unless it has a special interest to pursue. Second, it shares with other conceptualisations the false assumption that the linkage between nation and state is axiomatic. Third, while it recognises instrumental ethnicity, it denies symbolic ethnicity. It seems to me that it is the combination of instrumental ethnicity emanating out of material deprivation, and symbolic ethnicity based on the anxiety to preserve one's cultural identity, that gives birth to the motive force for state formation. Deprivations emanating out of inequality or denial of identity in isolation will not lead to the crystallisation of the demand for a separate state. However, such a demand is plausible only if the ethnic group can constitute itself into a nation, the prerequisites of which are common territory and language.

In order to get rid of the prevailing confusion we need to conceptualise ethnicity as interactional, as against an attributional notion. We must view ethnicity as a product of conquest, colonisation and immigration and the consequent disengagement between culture and territory. It is the transformation of the 'outs' into the 'ins' that leads to the process of ethnies becoming nations.

It is important to remember, however, that once a multi-national or poly-ethnie state emerges and consolidates, it becomes a reality-in-itself. The co-existence and interaction between the different nations or ethnic groups produce certain emergent properties which gives a new meaning and a collective self-definition to the constituent units. That is, just as state can dismantle or divide nations as I have noted above, it can also weld and fuse together different nations as in India. National States such as India are products of such a historical process; they should not be confused with nation-states.

II

India is a multinational state but that does not mean that ethnies do not exist in India. Given the vast size, cultural diversity, disparity in development between regions and freedom of migration ensured through single citizenship, ethnies do emerge and exist. But most ethnies in India do have and are identified with a nation (their homeland) within the country except in the case of such small religious groups as Zoroastrians,

Jews and Baha'is who sought asylum in the country due to religious and/or political persecution in their original homelands or linguistic groups such as Sindhi or Urdu – speakers, products of migration whose numbers depleted. Thus, there are two types of ethnies in India: those who do not lay any claim on a particular part of India as their homeland, such as Jews, Baha'is, Zoroastrians, Sindhi or Urdu speakers and those who do such as Tamils outside Tamil Nadu, Bengalis outside West Bengal but live outside their specific homeland. Pursuantly, it is possible and necessary to distinguish between those who are nationals and ethnies simultaneously and those who are ethnies exclusively.

It is instructive to note here that in all Indian languages the distinction between *desh* (homeland) and *videsh* (foreign land) and consequently that between natives and foreigners is clearly made. In fact, fellow-Indians belonging to cultural zones other than one's own are often referred to as 'foreigners' (see, Oommen 1982: 41–64). *Desh* implies not merely a territory but also a people, language, style of life, pattern of culture; in fact a nation in the European sense of the term. That is, political-administrative units and folk-regions are not conterminous and the concept of *desh* is essentially anchored to the notion of the cultural homeland. In so far as a person is within one's own *desh,* s/he is an insider; his/hers is a 'national' identity. But should s/he cross the boundaries of this region, s/he becomes an outsider, an ethnie.

One may identify several situations wherein national identity becomes salient in the Indian context. (1) The demand for a distinct homeland, either a sovereign state, (e.g., the demand for Khalistan by a section of the Sikhs) or a political-administrative unit within the Indian state, (e.g., Gorkhaland for Nepalis, Jharkhand state for the tribes of Central India). (2) The demand for expulsion of 'outsiders' when the entire state is engulfed by migrants from other states or neighbouring countries, (e.g., Assam and Tripura). (3) The demand for the expulsion of *videshis* ('foreigners') belonging to other folk-regions within the state, (e.g., Chotanagpur tribal demand to expel fellow Biharis of the plains) or from other states (Bengalis or Marwaris), all of whom are designated as Dikus, (4) The demand to expel those who do not belong to the same cultural region although they are from the same linguistic state, (e.g., the demand for the expulsion of Andhras from Telangana region). (5) The demand to expel migrants from other linguistic states who come to work and reside in metropolitan centres (e.g., mobilisation against Tamils in Bombay and Bangalore).

What is common to all these situations is the strong identification of the collectivities with specific territories as homelands. Those who belong to the homeland are insiders, they constitute 'a nation', and the outsiders are 'ethnies'. But most ethnies of India also have homelands normally elsewhere within India as noted earlier. This makes the effort by national collectivities to expel ethnies easier and often appear even legitimate. But yet to assert one's identity in national terms is to spell danger to the state (Sovereign and provincial) and, hence, such efforts are de-legitimised and dubbed as parochial, regional, even anti-national (see, Oommen 1986a: 107–28).

The point I want to affirm at this juncture of the analysis is that all concepts which are intended to describe and explain social reality, have emerged out of specific contexts. To assume that they have universal validity is to ignore their historicity; to de-contextualise them is to drain them of their meaning and content. Further, social science concepts often entwine collective consciences and they need to articulate group sentiments. Concepts such as ethnicity and nationality are expressions of the collective conscience of particular people in specific historical contexts. The moment we recognise the historicity of social science concepts we can steer clear through a lot of muddle and confusion. To achieve clarity we need to recognise the following points.

First, most national states as distinct from nation-states have in their territory, population drawn from different racial, religious and linguistic backgrounds. This has occurred through conquest, colonisation and immigration. Second, inter-state (that is sovereign state) migration is an ongoing process, thereby rendering most societies racially and socio-culturally heterogeneous. The migrants begin with several socio-economic disadvantages and usually it requires a cumbersome procedure even to acquire citizenship, not to speak of national identity. Third, many states have multi-racial, multi-religious and/or multi-lingual population and it is extremely difficult to devise appropriate legislations and adequate policies providing for equal opportunity to all citizens due to historical and political reasons. Fourth, even when equality is guaranteed through law to all citizens, racial, religious, and linguistic differences invariably lead to discriminatory treatment to some, due to persisting prejudices. This in practice results in unequal treatment to some citizens in a variety of situations.

It is instructive to recall here that in West Europe (the cradle of modern nation-states) language was the fulcrum on which states were built. Based on this experience, Gellner (1983) argues that modern 'nations' are moulded in their schools where shared national languages are taught and developed. This is very important, according to him, for building nations because unless there exists a common communication medium the industrial societies cannot be sustained. This, in turn, is based on the assumption and argument that the modern nations emerged because of industrialisation. The economy of the industrial society depends on spatially mobile individuals who can sell their skills and labour in an ever expanding market and who can communicate in a common language. Needless to say Gellner's argument is based on the limited experience of the capitalist industrial societies of Western Europe and is not applicable to most other parts of the world and certainly not to India. Further, the argument is an ex post facto rationalisation. European states emerged out of nations; one-nation one-state was the refrain. At any rate, industrialisation followed state formation. Therefore, the argument cannot be sustained either on logical ground, or on empirical evidence.

Indian nationalism is a product of colonialism and not industrialisation; India remains predominantly agrarian even today and yet she has succeeded in building a modern state. The fact that communication in the whole of India (one-sixth of humanity, speaking over 1600 mother-tongues) cannot be undertaken through one language is proved several rounds over. The point I want to make is that neither industrialisation nor a common language are pre-requisites for building a modern state as the Indian experience clearly demonstrates. Any attempt to impose a common language would create stresses and strains the Indian polity will not be in a position to bear; any effort to equate polity with nationality, and citizenship with membership in society is not admissible in the Indian situation.

It is frequently argued that one of the prominent features of the modern state is that it has a legal system which applies uniformly to all its citizens. However, this argument is applicable and sustainable only in those cases wherein nationality and citizenship are conterminous. Understandably, the proposition is not applicable to the Indian situation. Several legal systems co-exist to regulate the behaviour of Indian citizens (see, Baxi 1982). First, the State Legal System (SLS) which applies uniformly to all citizens in the all-India 'secular' contexts. Second, the Religious Legal Systems (RLS) which has two main variants: (a) the RLS anchored to religious texts partly written and partly unwritten and which operate on an all-India basis for those who profess religions of Indian Origin and (b) the RLS applicable to those who profess religions of 'alien origin' which is at least partly applicable to co-religionists everywhere in the world irrespective of their citizenship status. Third, the Folk Legal System (FLS) based on oral traditions as practiced by the people in their specific regional-cultural contexts as exemplified by the tribal and peasant communities.

The point to be noted is that cultural pluralism of India necessitates the recognition and operation of legal pluralism. And, most of the laws in RLS and FLS are not even codified or incorporated into the official SLS. The presence, operation and recognition of different legal systems indicate the possibility of a multi-cultural system functioning within a polity. I hope the message is clear. There is not, and perhaps, there cannot be, a universally valid set of characteristics applicable to nationality.

I have already noted that there is no consensus in the definition of nationality and ethnicity. To complicate matters they are also used interchangeably. For Weber, one of the earliest to define ethnic groups and nationality, the former could be identified by a collectively held belief in their common origin and heritage. This commonality could be anchored to a similar phenotype and/or culture as well as to historical memories of migration and colonisation. But Weber preferred the term nationality (1968: 389). Bell (1975: 157) refers to ethnic groups as culturally defined communal groups. If the content of ethnicity is cultural, there is no need for the concept of nationality, as its content is also cultural. The attempts to define nation and nationality as political entities are not sustainable because they lead to another conceptual conflation, namely, between state and nation, as noted above; furthermore, they are not empirically admissible, as the maxim, attributed to Napoleon – 'to each nation a state, in each state one nation' – has not been realised even in Western Europe, the cradle of the modern nation-state.

Anthony Smith thinks that nationalism emerges from common bonds of religion, language, customs, shared history and common myths of origin, 'in a word, from common ethnicity and common culture' (1979: 43). In a later work he refers to the modern ethnic revival taking the form of nationalism, and defines ethnie or ethnic community as a 'social group whose members share a sense of common origin, claim a common and distinctive history and destiny, possess one or more distinctive characteristics and feel a sense of collective uniqueness and solidarity' (1981: 6). Is it that there is no distinction between nation and ethnie, and hence between nationality and ethnicity? Not quite; ethnie is a passive nation and nationality is active ethnicity because ethnic revival is 'the transformation of passive, often isolated and politically excluded communities into potential and actual nations, active, participant and self-conscious in their historic identities' (ibid.: 24). Thus, nations often grow out of and are constructed from ethnic materials. Notwithstanding important differences of both kind and degree between nationalism and ethnic sentiment, there is also considerable overlap between them, 'which is reflected in the lack of clarity surrounding the concepts themselves' (ibid.: 85). My contention is that, in spite of overlaps between these concepts, there is a qualitative difference between them which can be located in the territorial dimension.

As Smith conflates nations and states, it is understandable, although not acceptable, that he considers ethnie as an isolated and politically excluded community. Connor also considers ethnicity as passive nationalism, thereby leaving nation without any anchorage. He writes, 'self-differentiating ethnic groups are... nations, loyalty to the ethnic group, therefore should logically be called nationalism. We can describe the nation as a self differentiating ethnic group... . It is therefore the self-view of one's group, rather than the 'tangible' characteristics that is the essence in determining the existence or non-existence of a nation' (Connor 1994: 40–43)

The failure to distinguish between nation and ethnie by Connor may be located in the manner in which he defines nation and nationalism. A nation is defined merely or mainly in psychological and emotional terms rather than in terms of any tangible characteristics. There are many others who have taken this line; a short sample follows. Seton-Watson feels that no 'scientific definition' of a nation is possible and all that one can say is: 'A nation exists when a significant number of people in a community consider themselves to form a nation or behave as if they formed one' (1977: 5). He recognises that it is not possible to prescribe this number. However, what is relevant is that people should consider themselves and believe that they constitute a nation. Emerson's characterisation is in the same vein: 'The nation is a community of people who feel that they belong together in the double sense that they share deeply significant elements of a common heritage and that they have a common destiny for the future' (1962: 95), and 'the simplest statement that can be made about a nation is that it is a body of people who feel that they are a nation' (ibid.: 104). According to these authors, it is sufficient that a group of people feels that it constitutes a nation for there to be one. The difficulty is that a wide variety of groups – religious, linguistic, caste, racial, regional, tribal, and so on – may feel that they are nations. But the crucial element that provides for their feelings so as to make them a nation is left unspecified.

Eriksen rightly sees the distinction between nationals and ethnies as that between insiders and outsiders. But, as he attests the familiar position that a successful nation should have its own state, he is constrained to view unsuccessful nationalisms as ethnicities. In his own words, 'many of the ethnies condemned to such a fate eventually vanish through migration, extermination or cultural assimilation' (1991: 265). That is, ethnic groups can survive only if they succeed in establishing their own states. This is simply not true in the case of the New World, where a multiplicity of ethnic groups co-exist in one state. The ambiguity of Eriksen's conceptualisation is evident from the cases he has presented to clinch his argument (ibid.: 268–75). The Sami (Lappish) minority, the First Nation of Northern Norway, becomes an ethnie just because it does not have a state of its own. So do the Trinidad-Indians, the immigrants from the Indian subcontinent. But there is a basic difference between the two peoples under reference: the Samis occupy their ancestral homeland; the Trinidad-Indians are in their adopted homeland. In the first case, in the Sami perspective an outsider has intruded the homeland; in the second case, the

Trinidad-Indians constitute the outsider. Nobody contests the nativity of the Samis, but the native Trinidadians consider the Indians to be an ethnie. That different ethnies can nationalise themselves and co-exist as co-nationals without shedding their cultural identities is illustrated by the Mauritian case presented by Eriksen. The point here again is that it is not the state that is the crucial element in distinguishing nation and ethnie, but the nature of attachment the latter develops to the territory and its acceptance by the original nationals.

I would like to close the discussion on this theme by noting the implications of conflating nation and ethnie. This can be well illustrated with the help of a book entitled: *Ethnic Conflict in the Western World*, edited by Milton Esman (1977). The map identifies twenty-five 'selected ethnic homelands', all of which belong to people without their own sovereign states. Fifteen cases of homelands of those who have their own sovereign states and are majority communities are identified but they are not described as 'ethnic' presumably because they are 'national' homelands. I am making this plausible logical derivation because the ethnic homelands are referred to as minority areas. Therefore, one is entitled to argue that according to the authors contributed to this book an ethnic group is a minority group with a homeland within a multi-national state but not having its sovereign state. Conversely, a nation is a majority group with its own homeland and state.

It is also interesting to note the following from the map: (a) three of the states are without any national homelands – Yugoslavia, Switzerland and Belgium. They have only ethnic homelands; (b) four states – France, United Kingdom, Spain and Italy – have both national and ethnic homelands; (c) ten of the states have only national homelands; (d) no distinction is made between the homelands of those peoples that are divided between two or more states (Basques, Italians, Irish, Germans, French) and whose homelands are exclusively within one state (Scots, Welsh, Bretons, etc.); (e) several of the nations/ethnies are not mentioned, for example those of Finland, Hungary and Rumania; and (f) Czechoslovakia is shown as one common block, presumably because there is only one homeland between the Czechs and Slovaks. This confusion, I suggest, is due to the inappropriate conceptualisation of nation and ethnie, and hence nationality and ethnicity.

Among the numerous authors who have written on ethnic groups and nations, only a few distinguish between the two. Moynihan, for example, holds that, '... it is helpful to distinguish between ethnic group and nation, between ethnicity and nationality. It is a distinction of a degree. The nation is the 'highest' form of the ethnic group, denoting a subjective state of mind as regards ancestry, but also, almost always an objective claim to forms of territorial autonomy ranging from a regional assembly to full blown independence' (Moynihan 1993: 4–5).

Moynihan's definition shares two features of the definitions of others. First, the distinction between nationality and ethnicity is one of degree and not kind. Second, nation and state are conflated, in that nation tends to form its own state. However, he provides a good starting point in terms of the conceptual proposal I am making as nation is viewed as a territorially anchored community.

According to the conceptualisation that I propose, a different perspective emerges. First, all homelands are national, be they ancestral or adopted. Second, there cannot be any ethnic homeland, as ethnicity is a product of dissociation and/or attenuation between territory and culture. Third, some states are mono-national, while others are bi-or multi-national. Fourth, the same national homeland could be divided between two or more states. Fifth, most of the states have ethnies among their populations either because they do not identify the land of their current residence as their homeland, or because even when they do their claim is not accepted. That is, the process of transformation from an ethnie into a nation would occur only when two conditions are met: when an ethnic group adopts the land into which it has migrated as the homeland, and when the earlier inhabitants accept them as co-nationals (this is exemplified in the cases of those Indians who migrated to Fiji, Mauritius, Surinam etc). To conclude, if territory is the crucial element of a nation, attenuation of peoples' association from that territory transforms them into another category, namely, ethnie. This is the rationale behind the distinction between nation/nationality and ethnie/ethnicity.

III

An examination of the classical conceptual baggage of social science unfolds at least four axes around which the notion of modernity is articulated. These are structural differentiation (Emile Durkheim), rationalisation (Max Weber), the history-making project (Karl Marx) and modern life (Georg Simmel) (see Martuccelli 1996: 235–49). What follows is a conceptual exploration of these modernities and how they impinge on nationality and ethnicity.

The notion of structural differentiation gave birth to the dynamics of societal transformation variously conceptualised as a movement from simple to complex, tradition to modern, community to society, sacred to secular, status to contract, folk/rural to urban, to list a few. The mechanisms involved in this transformation are believed to be (a) occupational differentiation and the consequent elaboration of division of labour; (b) diversification and the attendant heterogeneity; and (c) plurality and the gradual evolving of a complex social network and interdependence in the place of the traditional cradle-to-grave arrangement. In this process each society becomes different from the other, less self-sufficient, more specialised and hence increased complementarity between them (Durkheim 1964).

On the other hand, a specific type of social differentiation has laid the foundation for increasing individuation of subjects, the route being organic solidarity brought about through industrialisation. The most compelling element behind this process, it has been argued, is modern technology, so much so that modernisation is conceived as a process in which the progressive displacement of animate energy with inanimate energy occurs (Levy 1966). But for differentiation to occur the intervention through technology is not always a pre-requisite. Thus, differentiation in the West occurred both before the advent of modern technology, (e.g., the bifurcation between state and church) and after it, (e.g., the differentiation between civil society and market). In contrast, in one-party systems, in spite of technological sophistication, structural differentiation did not occur in certain respects. For example, in spite of considerable progress in industrialisation and elaboration of occupational division of labour, both market and civil society remained under the control of the state.

Therefore, while modern technology with its elaborate division of labour and occupational differentiation is common to capitalist and socialist societies, there are basic differences between them. Both are 'modern' but their modernities differ. It is often argued that socialist societies are not fully modern as their political (state) and economic (market) structures are undifferentiated. On the other hand, it may be suggested that technological modernity shared by both capitalist and socialist societies created a convergence between them. This means one can, and perhaps one should, distinguish between the compartmental modernity of socialist systems and the fully-fledged modernity of capitalist systems, which is to say, structural differentiation is not the only critical marker of modernity. This renders structural differentiation as a source of modernity incomplete and inefficient as it can account for only certain dimensions of modernity (cf. Luhmann 1982). This brings us to rationalisation as a source of modernity.

Rationalisation is a process bound up with the disenchantment of the world and its demystification. Accordingly, it is argued that unforeseeable forces no longer interfere in social affairs. The 'good' is defined less in relation to God but more in relation to functioning society. In this rendition of modernity, reason and reality are isomorphic. Understandably, the rationalisation process results in an increasing fit between means and ends. Science and technology, rather than religion or magic become crucial. In this vein of thinking, capitalism is the embodiment of rationality and modern capitalism has its essence in rationality (Weber 1948).

The essential features of rationality of modern capitalism are the calculability furthered by the market place, the purely instrumental orientation of action, a highly technical system of book-keeping and the bureaucratic organisation of firms. Traditional effective constrains wane or vanish as a social world wherein social actors emerge, increasingly, if not exclusively, guided by their instrumental interests. The project of rationality assumes that the individual can evolve, guided by his/her interests, in an intelligible world. Perfection through reason is the guiding principle; and hence God is a dispensable entity. But rationalisation of the world presupposes the depersonalisation of social relations.

However, the fact that functioning 'modern' societies are visited by irrationality, superstition and sentiments is widely acknowledged and recorded which points to the impossibility of a completely rational and hence modern society of this version. The hatred which thrives across religious, linguistic and racial groups and the animosity which prevails across even secular ideological communities in the modern world are not founded in rationality. In fact, human beings are rationalisers rather than rational. This points to the limits of modernity which can be unleashed through the axis of rationality.

It is important to note in passing here the two features shared by the two sources of modernity – structural differentiation and rationalisation. First, both seem to be accounting more for the modernity of capitalist societies and neglect the modernity of socialist societies. Second, both have the displacement syndrome and western epistemological dualism at their core. That is, reality is conceptualised as a duality – traditional/modern, rational/irrational – and it is presumed that in the onward march of social transformation one will displace the other. But available empirical evidence suggests that this is not happening. True, there are partial displacements but there are also partial retentions and occasional accretions. And what is displaced is not always irrational and what is retained and added is not always rational. What we have is a collage of the old and the new, the rational and the irrational.

Both structural differentiation and rationalisation assume the displacement of traditional collectivism with modern individualism. True, modernity cannot be separated from the will of individuals to become an unfettered force in society. In fact, the birth of the individual itself is an indication of modernity. In pre-modern societies, traditional collectivism prevailed. The conscious individual is a creator of history, who interrogates all established social relationships. To do this, the individual should be incessantly in the quest for knowledge not only to meet intellectual curiosity but also to solve practical problems. This voluntarism cannot remain at the individual level; it should generate a new, modern collectivism manifesting in the working class movement and eventuating in a revolution giving birth to a New Society. This is the Marxian project of making history (Marx and Engels 1988).

The two versions of modernity fathered by structural differentiation and rationalisation recognised traditional collectivism but did not yield much space for modern collectivism. In contrast, the version of modernity championed by the history-making project juxtaposed the two antagonistic classes and assumed that social transformation is a function of confrontation between these classes, but this characterisation was not entirely correct even in the case of European societies. There were and are, several non-class, antagonistic social categories – national/ethnic, racial, gender, generational and regional. The existence of these social categories was not adequately recognised in the version of modernity which addressed the project of making history.

However, the salience of working class movements articulating in a myriad form – professional and occupational associations, trade unions and a variety of interest groups – cannot be denied. But their career climaxed in the West in the 1950s and a set of post-class movements – feminist, peace, youth, environmental/ecological, national/ethnic – all of which transcend the class dichotomy and boundaries emerged. These are the New Social Movements. This development was not anticipated by Marx or Marxians but this too has to be reckoned as a project of making history. The New History does not advocate class antagonism but class harmony and the project visualises the harmony of races, sexes and generations as well as the harmony between humans and nature as its ultimate goal.

The old version of the history-making project has been abandoned because of its political authoritarianism. The dictatorship of the proletariat manifested as one-party regimes crystallised as party-states which were totalitarian and all-encompassing. The socialist state became not only the final arbiter but the only adjudicator between contending interests. In this process, it not only prevented the birth of the market but relegated the civil society too to the background (Oommen 1996: 191–202). The project of making history, although begun as a modernist venture, has ended up as an anti-democratic and hence anti-modern project.

I have noted above that neither structural differentiation nor rationalisation adequately recognised modern collectivism. The Marxian project of making history did provide the space for modern collectivism but it recognised only class collectivism and dismissed the collectivism of other varieties as based on false consciousness. In this project of making history in socialist states, the history of non-class categories was cognised as irrelevant and inappropriate. Indeed, an effort was made to banish these inconvenient histories from collective memory and an effort was made to re-invent history in favour of dominant nationalities so as to facilitate their hegemonisation. Russification in Soviet Union, Hanisation in China and Serbianisation in Yogoslavia afford examples of this (Connor 1984). This process had also occurred in capitalist societies, although through a different route, as exemplified by Frenchification in France, Englishisation in the United Kingdom, Spanishisation in Spain, etc. (Oommen 1997). But the relegation of collective memory and identity to the background of a wide variety of categories, including age-groups and gender in homogeneous societies and also of racial, national and religious identities in multi-racial and multi-cultural societies, had prompted these categories to invent their specific histories and insist on their specific identities.

In the absence of a common history, there cannot be a collective conscience or a common vanguard. This is the context of identity politics as against class politics: if in the latter, the society is believed to be polarised into two classes, in the former a wide variety of identities crystallise. If in class politics and its history-making project protest was based on the political economy of exploitation, in the case of identity politics protests focus on the repression of identity too in addition to exploitation (Melucci 1989). If both structural differentiation and rationalisation associated with capitalist modernity produced individual alienation, the loss of non-class collective freedom and the absence of identity-recognition resulted in alienation of collectivities in socialist societies. The break-up of the Soviet Union, Yugoslavia and Czechoslovakia points to the search for a non-class, national identity on the part of marginalised nationalities.

The fourth modernity that I want to discuss relates to modern lifestyle. Modernity implies changes in perceptions of space and time and in the speed of exchange. Modernity involves rapid transactions, life in cities and an accelerated pace of events. Modern life in cities is unsettled and it is constantly in flux. Due to these reasons, barter is not possible and money assumes social importance in three contexts. First, as the symbol of movement and circulation. Second, as the universal equivalent of goods and services transacted. Third, as a universal leveling force. Money empties everything of its particularity, its specific value. Importance is decided in terms of how much money value you command – the neighbourhood you live in, the car you own and the amount of money you can earn. Nothing has an intrinsic value, everything has only money value (Simmel 1990).

Modern lifestyle is made possible through the shrinkage of space and time facilitated through the revolution in transport and communication. From this, the distance to globality itself is short because globalisation ultimately is brought about through a shrinkage in space and time and the ease of exchange. This is further facilitated through money taking new forms, for example, the credit card, wherein even the disadvantages of a multiplicity of currencies are done away with.

All the four classical thinkers recognised the discontents of modernity. Durkheim recognised increasing individuation. Weber warned about depersonalisation. Marx alerted about alienation and Simmel noted the loss of intrinsic worth. Through these processes the community is sentenced to death by modernity, individualism is celebrated and a homogeneity based on similarity in behaviour and attitudes emerges which has no organic base, but is merely aggregative. Social actors are apparently similar viewed in terms of their lifestyles but actually are different in terms of their deeper values. This explains why individuals and groups who share the same lifestyles enter into persisting conflicts based on race, religion or language. Recall the conflicts in Bosnia, Rwanda, Sri Lanka or Kashmir.

Part of the problem here arises from the monistic conceptualisation of modernity as a movement from multiple traditions to singular modernity. Western epistemological dualism and displacement syndrome is at the core of this mode of conceptualisation. It is an either-or paradigm which juxtaposes mind and matter, emperor and pope, church and state, sacred and secular. The fact is that this mode of conceptualisation cannot grapple with the evolving empirical reality even of the West. The co-existence of religious, racial and linguistic plurality along with diverse secular ideologies has become an empirical fact which sits uneasily with the tradition versus modernity paradigm. Further, the ongoing process of transformation also indicates the existence of multiple modernities.

IV

I want to conclude this paper by briefly indicating the intertwinings between the three notions of nationality, ethnicity and modernity. Modernity was originally conceived as a spatial concept in that it was conceptualised as a process which emerged in the West, and that too with one uniform set of attributes, and spread to the rest of the world subsequently wherein it replicated itself. This conceptualisation is interrogated because the contexts out of which modernity emerged in non-western sites varied. This led to the characterisation of modernity as a temporal phenomenon in that all societies/civilisations came to be recognised as having potentiality to evolve their own versions of modernity giving birth to the notion of multiple modernity.

If European nation-states were a product of modern industrialisation, Indian national state was an offshoot of anti-colonial struggles. Further, while European nation-state was visualised as a monocultural entity the Indian national state was consciously designed as a multicultural one encapsulating several nations and ethnicities within it. If all nations are not necessarily attached to sovereign states, if nations are products of *unison* between territory and culture and if ethnicity emerges out of *disjuncture* between territory and culture, modernity will impact on them differently. Further, the idea of multiple modernity often produces different permutations and combinations of nationalities and ethnicities because these modernities impact differently on them. Ignoring the possibility of a rich tapestry of empirical variations the central tendency in social science has been to suggest the eclipse of identities based on nationality and ethnicity with the onward march of modernity. This is not an empirically sustainable position. Therefore, it is high time to examine afresh the inter-relations between nationality, ethnicity and modernity.

(In composing this research paper I have drawn from three of my earlier publications: Oommen 1988: 333–43; Oommen 1997 and Oommen 2001: 1–16.)

References

Anderson, B. 1983. *Imagined Communities: Reflections on the Origins and Spread of Nationalism.* London: Verso.

Barth, F. (ed.) 1969. *Ethnic Groups and Boundaries.* London: Allen and Unwin.

Baxi, U. 1982. *The Crisis of Indian Legal System.* New Delhi: Vikas Publishers.

Bell, D. 1975. 'Ethnicity and Social Change', in Nathan Glazer and D.P. Moynihan (eds), *Ethnicity: Theory and Experience,* Cambridge: Harvard University Press, pp. 141–74.

Comaroff, J. 1991. 'Humanity, Ethnicity, Nationality: Conceptual and Comparative Perspectives in the USSR', *Theory and Society,* 20 (2): 661–87.

Connor, W. 1984. *The National Question in Marxist-Leninist Theory and Strategy.* Princeton, NJ: Princeton University Press.

——. 1994. *Ethnonationalism: The Quest for Understanding.* Princeton, NJ: Princeton University Press.

Devos, G. and L. Romanucci-Ross (eds) 1975. *Cultural Continuities and Change.* California: Mayfield Publishing Co.

Durkheim, E. 1964. *The Division of Labour in Society.* New York: Free Press.

Emerson, R. 1962. *From Empire to Nation: The Rise and Self-Assertion of Asian and African Peoples.* Boston: Beacon Press.

Eriksen, T.H. 1991. 'Ethnicity Versus Nationalism', *Journal of Peace Research,* 28 (3): 263–78.

Esman, M.J. (ed.) 1997. *Ethnic Conflict in the Western World.* Ithaca: Cornell University Press.

Francis, E.K. 1976. *Interethnic Relations: An Essay in Sociological Theory*. New York: Elsevier.

Gellner, E. 1983. *Nations and Nationalities*. Oxford: Basil Blackwell.

Gordon, M.M. 1964. *Assimilation in American Life: The Role of Race, Religion and National Origins*. New York: Oxford University Press.

Glazer, Nathan and D.P. Moynihan (eds) 1975. *Ethnicity: Theory and Experience*. Cambridge: Harvard University Press.

Hobsbawm, E. and Terence Ranger (eds) 1983. *The Invention of Tradition*. Cambridge: Cambridge University Press.

Horowitz, D.H. 1985. *Ethnic Groups in Conflict*. Berkeley: University of California Press.

Luhmann, N. 1982. *The Differentiation of Society*. New York: Columbia University Press.

Martuccelli, D. 1996. 'Alain Touraine's Conceptions of Modernity', in J. Clark and M. Diani (eds), *Alain Touraine*, London: Falmer Press, pp. 235–49.

Marx, K. and F. Engels. 1998. *Manifesto of the Communist Party*. New Delhi: People's Publishing House.

Melucci, A. 1989. *Nomads of the Present*. London: Hutchinson Radius.

Moynihan, D.P. 1993. *Pandemonium: Ethnicity in International Politics*. Oxford: Oxford University Press.

Oommen, T.K. 1982. 'Refugees, Foreigners and Outsiders in the Indian Context', *Sociological Bulletin*, 21 (1): 41–64.

——. 1986(a). 'Insiders and Outsiders in India: Primordial Collectivism and Cultural Pluralism in Nation-Building', *International Sociology*, 1 (1): 53–74.

——. 1986(b). 'Social Movements and Nation-State in India: Towards Re-legitimization of Cultural Nationalisms', *Journal of Social and Economic Studies (NS)*, 3 (2): 107–28.

——. 1988. 'Nation, State and Ethnicity: Towards a Conceptual Clarification and an Empirical Explication', *Social Action*, 38: 333–43.

——. 1997. *Citizenship, Nationality and Ethnicity: Reconciling Competing Identities*. Cambridge: Polity Press.

——. 2001. 'Multiple Modernities and the Rise of New Social Movements: The Case of India', *Indian Social Science Review*, 3 (1): 1–16.

Peterson, W. 1975. 'On the Subnations of Western Europe', in Nathan Glazer and D.P. Moynihan (eds), *Ethnicity: Theory and Experience*, Cambridge: Harvard University Press, pp. 177–208.

Richard, A.H. 1987. 'Ethnic Nationalism: Social Science Paradigms', *International Social Science Journal*, 39 (1): 3–18.

Roosens, E.H. 1989. *Creating Ethnicity*. Newbury Park: Sage Publications.

Seton-Watson, H. 1977. *Nations and States: An Enquiry into the Origins of Nations and the Politics of Nationalism.* London: Methuen.

Simmel, G. 1990. *The Philosophy of Money*, 2 edition. London: Routledge and Kegan Paul.

Smith, A. 1979. *Nationalism in the Twentieth Century.* Oxford: Martin Robertson.

——. 1981. *The Ethnic Revival in the Modern World.* Cambridge: Cambridge University Press.

——. 1986. *The Ethnic Origins of Nations.* Oxford: Basil Blackwell.

Weber, M. 1948. *From Max Weber: Essays in Sociology*. London: Routledge.

——. 1968. *Economy and Society: An Outline of Interpretive Sociology*, Vol. 1. New York: Bedminster Press.

Worsley, P. 1984. *The Three Worlds: Culture and World Development.* Chicago: Chicago University Press.

Yancey, L.W., E. Ericksen and R. Juliani. 1976. 'Emerging Ethnicity: A Review and Reformulation', *American Sociological Review*, 41 (3): 391–403.

3

Hierarchy, Hegemony and Dominance

Politics of Ethnicity in Uttar Pradesh, 1995

RAVINDRA K. JAIN

> '... ethnic membership does not constitute a group; it only facilitates group formation of any kind, particularly in the political sphere. On the other hand, it is primarily the political community, no matter how artificially organised that inspires the belief in common ethnicity' (Weber 1978: 389).

All in all, the notion of 'ethnicity' determined social action subsumes phenomena that a rigorous sociological analysis – as we do not attempt it here – would have to distinguish carefully... . It is certain that in this process the collective term 'ethnic' would be abandoned, for it is unsuitable for a really rigorous analysis. However, we do not pursue sociology for its own sake and, therefore, limit ourselves to showing briefly the diverse factors that are hidden behind this seemingly uniform phenomenon. The concept of the 'ethnic' group ... dissolves if we define our terms exactly (ibid.: 394–95).

According to a rough estimate, the castewise distribution of the population in Uttar Pradesh is as follows: *brahmans* 10 per cent, *thakurs* 6.5 per cent, (other) backward castes 50 per cent and scheduled castes 20 per cent (Sudhir Hindwan, *Pioneer*, 22 July 1995). The Bahujan Samaj Party (BSP) emerged as a by-product of a backlash against the domination of politics in the Hindi heartland by upper caste Hindus, hence the slogan, *'Tilak, tarazu aur talwar, inko maro jute char'* (the diatribe is against brahmans, banias and thakurs). Founded on 14 April 1984, the BSP emerged from Kanshi Ram's DS4 – Dalit Shoshit Samaj Sangharsh Samiti –

which owed its existence to the All-India Backward and Minorities Communities Employees Federation of 1978. In exploring the sociological etymology of the Buhujan Samaj Party, we find that the concept of 'bahujan' refers to majoritarianism. The BSP was conceived originally as a consortium of backward castes and dalits; it was this plank of majoritarianism which provided the ideological and popular base for the alliance between Mulayam Singh Yadav's Samajwadi Party (SP) and the BSP. That this alliance broke up and the latter sprung into action to form the government by itself can be explained by the imperatives of politics (discussed below). It does not detract from the majoritarian agenda of the BSP. To assuage upper caste feelings, Mayawati is said to have spoken of a 'sarvajan-samaj' (all peoples' community) rather than a 'bahujan samaj' (majority community) plank, but this is again to be understood as an input into politics by sloganeering. The concept of 'bahujan', therefore, refers to an essential component of the popular and populist appeal of this party.

We next come to the connotation of the term 'samaj' in exploring what we have called the sociological etymology of BSP. This term refers broadly to what may be called 'community', and in that sense it has a number of meanings which embrace the notions of 'self' and the 'other' as well as socio-cultural pluralism. These ideas of differentiation and co-existence between and among groups, have been examined in a somewhat different context by the anthropologist Michael Carrithers (1991). The context is the analysis of a speech by one Patne, a regional Digambar Jain leader in Maharashtra: 'In constructing (the) congratulatory rhetoric Patne uses the word samaj with ambiguity... he uses it indifferently to refer to Indian Society as a whole throughout India, the Digambaras in particular, and *to the collection of different samajs – Marathas, Jains, Brahmans, Lingayats, etc.,'* (ibid.: 270; italics added). We have italicised the last connotation of the term 'samaj' because this is what aptly characterises the usage by the leaders of the BSP and the SP, who are obviously embarrassed to use the term caste ('jati') and do not, of course, mean class ('varga') by 'samaj'. They are, on the other hand, using the term very much in the last named sense enumerated by Carrithers, a phenomenon well designated by a journalist when he wrote recently that, 'Uttar Pradesh is a melting pot of castes and sub-castes, there being 53 sub-castes among OBCs' (Tavishi Srivastava, *Pioneer*, 16 July 1995). To anticipate somewhat our later argument, this move from caste to ethnicity (a notion which grew up precisely in the circumstances of a 'melting pot' of identities in the US) constitutes the nub of the interface between politics and society in contemporary Uttar Pradesh and, by extension and parallel example, in the whole of the Hindi heartland.

To complete the trio of BSP – the last term 'party' is to be understood in Weberian terms (1978: 938–39). Parties, according to Weber, reside in the sphere of power. The action of parties is oriented toward the acquisition of social power, that is toward influencing social action no matter what its content may be. It is interesting that Weber does not include an 'ideology' as a defining characteristic of 'party'. An association and a clear goal are its only attributes, and the goal may be a cause or 'personal (sinecures, power, and from these, honour for the leader and the followers of the party)'. Usually the party aims at all these simultaneously. To simplify, the Weberian definition of party is closely synchronised with the popular view of politics as 'the art of the possible'. Let us note in passing, though, that according to Weber the sociological structure of parties differs in a basic way according to the kind of social action which they struggle to influence; 'that means, they differ according to whether or not the community is stratified by status or by classes' (ibid.: 939). In our context, it is significant that the community is stratified by caste and, increasingly in the political arena, by ethnicity – the melting pot of castes and sub-castes. It is, thus, the context of status rather than class which is dominant in the case at hand, though a case has recently been made to recognise the underlying class nexus of current politics in UP (Mishra 1995b).

Caste, Ethnicity, Community: Notion of Social Heredity

The idea of consciousness of kind – an essential commonality – among the members of a 'jati' cuts across the so-called hierarchy or system of strata in the cognition of Indians. The main reason for attributing this characteristic to 'Indians' rather than to the Hindus alone resides in the ancillary observation that this consciousness of kind and its basis not only cuts across castes but also permeates what we have seen are 'communities' and shall see further are 'ethnic groups'. The basis unambiguously in the Indian case is a notion of 'social heredity' – known by a number of indigenous terms beginning with the Sanskritic 'sanskar' to the Persianised 'Khandani' (Mayer 1960: 207). This essential idea has been written about in the ethnographic literature in a variety of ways: purity of blood, strict endogamy, a mythological or legendary account of common origin, and so on. In the ethnomethodological theories of the Indian caste system, the same idea is taken up in a highly technical and subtle analysis deriving both from ethnographic sources and textual authority (Marriott and Inden 1973; Marriott 1976) in terms of 'code and substance'. That this descent-based commonality is frequently though not always (Gupta 1992) associated with hierarchy is also well known. A rather spontaneous – and somewhat naïve – expression of the value of social heredity was given recently by the actor Sunil Dutt on the issue of TADA, as it affects his son, in *The Times of India* dated February 28, 1995:

> When you buy a horse or a dog you see their pedigree. Why don't people see the pedigree of a family to judge whether a family can do such a thing

> or not. There should be a reason for becoming a terrorist. I genuinely feel my son cannot be anti-national; he cannot be a desh drohi. Both he and I have always loved the country. Whatever we are today it is because of the love of the people.

The idea of social heredity inheres not only in social structural units like family and caste ('jati') but also in regional, linguistic and religious entities. In the broadly Hindi-speaking northern Madhya Pradesh district of Bundelkhand, I often heard the saying *'jaisa khawe ann, vaisa hoye man'* and *'jaisa piye pani vaisi bole vani'*. The emphasis in the former saying is on hereditary commonality issuing forth from a particular geographical area and its products, and in the latter on a grouping of common language speakers. In regard to religion, one need not belabour the point that not only in Hinduism – the *locus classicus* of 'jati' – is one born with a number of inherited traits, but also in Christianity or Buddhism or Islam one is born as a Christian, Buddhist or Muslim – already inheriting the 'culture' of that religion – without the need for a formal baptism as in most western societies. Even in English society the residual influence of social heredity is found in the oft-cited remark that one begins to belong to the aristocracy ('blue blood') only after at least two generations of inherited wealth and position.

Social Heredity and Holism: Tripartite Caste Divisions

It has been argued, with the help of a number of examples from recorded customs and opinions, that a single agreed upon caste hierarchy even in the sense of a value consensus does not exist in the realm of caste or 'jati' in India (Gupta 1992). There are, nevertheless, two possible objections to the methodology adopted by commentators like Gupta for dismantling the Dumontian scheme. First, Dumont (1970) is concerned with 'the caste system and its implications'. Therefore, the hierarchical paradigm elaborated by Dumont does not lie solely at the emic level as Gupta perhaps unwittingly tries to interpret it (sample his adducing customs and statements as recorded by British officials writing on caste). Second, and following on the first objection, Gupta sidetracks the emphasis on 'holism' – an accompaniment of encompassment in Dumont (ibid.: 340) and an essential feature of values in the caste system according to a number of authors (see, e.g., Singh 1973). The ensemble of castes constitutes a 'system' not only in the etic sense but also emically, as revealed in a number of holistic formulae about 'jati vyavastha' beginning with the four-fold *varna*, but also the tripartite caste divisions, such as Brahman, non-brahman and adi-dravida in Tamil Nadu (Beteille 1965) or dwija, shudra and achhut in much of the Hindi heartland of north India (Lohia 1964: 33). The holistic formulae above are couched in global terms, ie, they exhaust the universe of 'jati' in India, but as is well known there are sub-global holistic formulae within the world of 'jati'. Thus, in the *Ardhakathanka* or Banarasidas, the 17th century autobiography of a merchant in north India, we find the couplets: '*Charon baran basain tis bich: basain chhatis pauni kul nica. Babhan, chhatri, bais apar, sudra bhed chhatis prakara*'. In this case not only are the four *varnas* mentioned as constituting the population of Jaunpur town, but also the 36 'paunis', that is castes of the *sudra varna*. Thirty-six was a conventional number. During my fieldwork among the Jains of Baraut in western UP (1994), I was repeatedly told that the number of castes in the town was 36. There are the '3 ½ *ghar*, 13 *ghar* and 1 ¼ lakh *ghar*' among saryupari Brahmans of UP (Dumont 1970: 122); the 'navnat' among the banias of Gujarat (Banks 1992: 54–58); the three 'kuri', 13 'kuri' and 36 'kuri' among the rajputs of Bundelkhand (Jain 1975); and similar formulae among the artisans castes (of Gupta 1992: 127 on '*nabashakhas*' which he interprets literally). These sub-global formulae are perfect examples of the synecdoche of global holism – as one literary writer in Hindi wrote at the outstanding academic success of the son of a prominent literary friend of his, 'the fragment of a sun is also a sun' (*suraj ka tukra bhi to suraj hota hai*). Incidentally, this metaphor is a good example of the representation of social heredity and holism in Indian values.

As a backdrop to our exploration of ethnicity and politics in Uttar Pradesh, we are more concerned to understand the tripartite holistic formula for caste in north India. Writing in August 1956, Lohia estimated that there were about seven crore *dwiji* or 'janeudhari', 17 crore *shudra*, and five crore harijan or *acchut* in India as a whole (1964: 33–34). Two features of the characterisation of caste by Lohia need to be noted. First, as the most numerous of the caste divisions he writes extensively about the shudra, and the steps needed for their amelioration. The overwhelming attention given to the *shudra* is, thus, reminiscent of the long list of 36 'paunis'[1] given by Banarsidas in seventeenth century northern India. In this lie the seeds of present-day 'majoritarianism' of the deprived castes (read OBCs). Second, Lohia depicts the shudra and the *harijan* as 'lifeless and personality-less' due to their exploitation by the *dwija*. It is noteworthy that in a political context the categories *shudra* and *harijan* do not figure as comprising distinct castes, each with a parallel and rival ideology, as Gupta tries to show on the analogy of the jat (1992: 133); they are, rather, as *categories* seen to be infected by a common malaise. It is not, in this context at least, an example of evoking parallel and rival hierarchies as the matrix for distinct ideologies providing springs of action; rather *both* ideology and value are subsumed in what, following Gramsci (Femia 1987), one may call the hegemony of the dwiji castes. In the framework of hegemony as technically elaborated by Gramsci, ideology and value are not separated (Gupta 1992: 119–20) but show an interface and dovetailing.

Hierarchy and Hegemony

There is a sophisticated social anthropological discussion of the caste system as constituting the hierarchical universe; this discussion emphasises the 'fit' between ideology and values in the Indian system of hierarchy (Dumont 1970). In Dumont's 'ouvre', the implications of the hierarchical value system as implicated in the Indian caste system are carried much further to contrast the Indian hierarchy with egalitarian values in western societies and, indeed, to provide an illuminating discourse on the place of values in societies with a capital 'S' (Dumont 1982). In our present discourse, we do not question Dumont's valuable contribution to the study of values; in fact, we find his insistence on the nexus between values and ideology most instructive for our analysis. And yet on the subject of the conscious acceptance of the notion of 'hierarchy' by members of the caste hierarchy all the way through from top to bottom, there is ample empirical evidence to suggest modifications in Dumont's position. Before coming to Dumont's position on the conscious acceptance of the notion of hierarchy, however, we might look at some of the views advanced by Indian scholars such as N.K. Bose (1953, 1975). Andre Beteille has pointed out, 'Bose frequently used a classification based on the three traditional qualities or *gunas* of *sattva* (purity), *rajas* (valour) and *tamas* (darkness) (Bose 1975: 171). Three instances of Bose's use of this classification may be noted. While discussing the ideal Vaishnava view that is 'above the bounds of custom or convention (*sanskara*)', Bose alludes to the 'man of the world' cultivating 'the best moral qualities (*sattva guna*) and suppresses the lower traits in his character (Rajas and Tamas *gunas*) (Bose 1953: 13). From this brief allusion, one may deduce that Bose regards the capacity for all three 'gunas' to be present in every human being.

However, in another context, the social heredity aspects of the distribution of 'gunas' is explicitly stated by Bose. 'The differences among the *varnas* are due to differences in the proportions of the three qualities or *gunas* of *sattva* (purity), *rajas* (valour) and *tamas* (darkness). The division into *varnas* is not confined to human society; it is widely known that even lands or temples are classified into Brahmin, *kshatriya* and so on' (1975: 91). Further, in his perception of the changes occurring in Indian society consequent upon the advent of British rule, Bose again uses the 'guna' scheme which shows, by implication that the author accepts that schemes as underlying and explaining not only the statics but also the dynamics of society:

Apart from class exploitation, the Indian productive system also became a victim of inertia. It may be that men's fundamental self-interest has again found room for expression under the influence of western capitalism and is now destroying the inertia of the old arrangements. One poison can be destroyed only by another. *The quality of darkness that is there in the inertia of the caste system is being destroyed by a combination of the forces of darkness and valour* (ibid.: 169; italics added).

It is obvious that Bose regards westernisation also in terms of the immanence of 'guna' theory; the qualities of 'rajas' and 'tamas' elements in contemporary caste systems. The theory of 'guna' advocated by a scholar like Bose, who combined Gandhian and Marxist elements in his thought, is a clear reflection of a long heritage of the acceptance of hierarchy as a natural (though divinely ordained) condition of Indian society. Apropos widespread acceptance of this view of hierarchy, it is worth quoting Mencher (1974: 470–71):

> There appears to be considerable agreement on this point of view, which appears in 'writing as early as the laws of Manu... probably written soon in the early centuries AD. It is well documented in early... and later colonial reports.... Though the wording of it may vary, this point of view tends to emerge in conversation with unsophisticated high-caste people (It is usually masked or unconscious among the more sophisticated) as well as in anthropological writings.

Since Dumont's notion of hierarchy in India is also based on ethnographic observation of high-caste groups and views expressed in sanskritic textual sources, and furthermore, ideology for him is 'conscious ideas' expressed by ideologues (Dumont 1970; Cort 1990), one may at first brush club his views with those in other 'anthropological writings' alluded to by Mencher. While this point of view emerges from the study of the high castes, only one study of an untouchable community in South India (Moffatt 1979) is regarded as 'the chief explication of Dumont's theory of hierarchy as inevitable and acceptable in India' (Zelliot 1992: 337).

We shall take up the point about the 'inevitability and acceptability' of Dumont's theory of hierarchy in India as a whole, especially (a) concerning contemporary developments in caste and politics in India, and (b) the fact that untouchables and *sudras* are fighting their battles using hierarchy as their instrument. The last point has not only baffled but intimidated the traditional powerholders in the caste hierarchy – the imputation that dalit and the 'mandalised' politics of the shudras and the harijans in north India is 'casteist', is being fought on a caste basis, representing a 'revival of caste'. Indeed, writers on the caste system as the key institutional feature of Indian society are taking a 180 degree turn and licking their own wounds now that the *shudras* and *harijans* have turned their own guns (those of the traditional high castes) against them (the high castes). Let it be noted here, as Moffatt (1979: 26–27) has pointed out contra Berreman, who mistakenly thought that Dumont's model represented the caste system as idyllically free of strife and conflict (Berreman 1971: 18–19):

> India emphasises (hierarchy) upon the point that situations tending to equally are unstable and conflict is called for to solve them by the establishment of a gradation. This might well be the basic reason why dispute is so endemic in India: however developed it might, the system has not succeeded in establishing a perfect gradation of the whole of social life (Dumont 1957: 18).

Moffatt adds, 'Therefore hierarchy ... is not a term intended to deny the existence of dispute, but rather to frame the matters that are appropriately the subject of dispute' (1975: 26–27). Indeed, the space provided for conflict has completely reversed itself as between high and low castes under modern political pressures in the Hindu heartland – and this particularly with regard to the 'other backward classes' (OBCs or *shudras*), especially in the states of Bihar and Uttar Pradesh.

To the extent that struggles for equality in the Indian hierarchical system are generated by political processes and these later are not 'encompassed' by the ritual opposition between the pure and the impure in the Dumontian model, 'hierarchy' does not provide an accurate explanatory framework for the kind of struggles (dispute or conflict) that characterise the current confrontation between the *dwiji* and *shudra*/dalits in north India (Let us remember that the locus of conflict in the Dumontian hierarchical model is about gradations of statuses within the caste system). We, therefore, need another concept to analyse and interpret the current conflict in which a commonality of values (social heredity) coexist with jockeying for power, most manifest in the middle reaches of the traditional caste system. This concept is provided by the notion of 'hegemony' as developed by Gramsci, and the social transformation in evidence is from a ritually regulated caste system to an upsurge of 'ehnicity' as understood in a modified version of Weber's classic statement about this phenomenon.[2]

Gramsci on Hegemony and Weber on Ethnicity

As implied in Bose's use of the 'guna' theory and most of the evidence mustered by Dumont, the cognition of hierarchy is natural (as part of the nature of the phenomenal world) for the 'dwija' castes. In Moffatt's argument, the same world-view is naturally followed by the untouchables of Tamil Nadu – a stand sought to be validated by an internal structural analysis of the caste system. The critics of such an internal structural analysis nevertheless make a legitimate point concerning the limitations of structuralism – that it tends to reduce political economy to culture (of the postmodernist critiques of structuralism in Marcus and Fischer 1986). Equally, forcefully, it can be argued that in a reverse direction there is a tendency for culture to be reduced to political economy as in orthodox Marxism – a tendency vigorously sought to be corrected by later day Marxists like Gramsci (Femia 1987; for an Indian example, see Chakrabarty 1989).

It is to Moffatt's credit that while concluding (1979: 290–304) an internal structural analysis of the caste system in the Tamil Nadu of Endavur, with particular reference to its untouchable community, he first undertakes a wide-ranging comparison of his findings with those of other analyses in both south (Gough and Mencher) and north (Berreman, Kolenda and Cohn) India. The structure and world-view of untouchable communities in the latter category of works are seen to rest on a set of 'disjunctive models'. One set of these disjunctive models analysed untouchables as those at some distance from a single dominant high-caste culture (the out-caste image); another set saw them as possessors of alternate cultural and social systems, whose characteristics were somehow controlled by the untouchables' position at the bottom of the Indian social order (the models of diversity). Moffatt's model, on the other hand, is based on continuity and consensus. Second, Moffat compares and contrasts the analytical model of caste with that of race in Dumontian terms (Dumont 1970: 239–58). Third, in the last two paragraphs of his book, Moffatt explicitly states that his description and analysis, being confined to the internal caste structure of Endavur and its untouchables, needs to be expanded to include 'social forces beyond the control of south Indian untouchables, and beyond their comprehension in their present state of consciousness' (1979: 303). Fourth (and implicitly), though Moffatt's detailed analysis is confined to the internal analysis of the caste structure of Endavur and more specifically to its untouchables, he accepts and utilises the three-fold division of the southern Indian castes into Brahmans, non-brahmans and adi-dravidas. By further implications, the continuities discerns between brahmans and adi-dravidas apply also to the non-brahmans, that is 'across the board'. Further, to take a pan-Indian leap, Moffatt's conclusion that 'in common with Dumont and with the ethno-Sociologists... at the deeper levels of Indian village culture so conceptualised, untouchables and higher-caste actors hold virtually identical cultural constructs, they are in nearly total conceptual and evaluative consensus with one another' (ibid.: 290–91) would apply also – if at this stage only as a hypothesis-to the parallel tripartite holistic formula of *dwija, shudra* and *achhut* of *harijan* castes of north India.

While Moffatt's position on the continuities and consensus of hierarchical values and ideologies pervading the caste hierarchy is well taken and, as we shall see below, does not mull over emerging discontinuities even in south India, in the north Indian case the nature of the 'consensus' cannot but be explicated in a political universe of discourse. In this task, the Gramscian concept of 'hegemony' needs to be applied with precision. The reason why from the point of view of the lower castes, Dumont's notion of hierarchy and more particularly Moffatt's rendition of it among untouchables, is capable of being read as hegemony is because Gramsci relates the supremacy of a social group or class as manifesting itself into two different ways: 'domination' ('dominio'), or coercion, and 'intellectual and moral leadership' ('direzione intellectuelle e morale'), and it is the latter type of supremacy which constitutes hegemony. Social control, in other words, takes two basic forms: besides influencing behaviour and choice externally, through rewards and punishments, it also affects them internally, by moulding personal convictions into a replica of prevailing norms. 'Such internal control', writes Femia, 'is based on hegemony which refers to an order in which a common social-norm language is spoken, in which one concept of reality is dominant, informing with its spirit all modes of thought and behaviour. It follows that hegemony is the predominance obtained by consent rather than force of one class or group over other classes' (1987: 24). Hence, the first characteristic of hegemony is the consensual nature of ideological domination in the system of groups or classes. The second important feature of the hegemonic domain is its firm locus in 'civil society' which Gramsci distinguishes sharply from political society. Therefore, again in conformity with the view of hierarchy in the Indian caste system, power or coercion is located at the secondary level also in the Gramscian concept of hegemony. As Femia puts it, 'Gramsci's division of the superstructure into two realms (civil and political society) and his concomitant distinction between hegemony and domination, signal an attempt to construct a theory of the superstructure, which, before Gramsci, constituted a glaring lacuna in Marxist thought' (ibid.). Note, however, that the political implications, including the potential for 'primitive rebellion' are not lacking in the hegemonic regime, for the distinction between civil society and political society is essentially analytical, a convenient device to aid understanding. In reality, Gramsci recognised interpenetration between the two spheres. 'The Proletariat, in other words, wear their chains willingly. Condemned to perceive reality through the conceptual spectacles of the ruling class, they are unable to recognise the nature or extent of their own servitude' (ibid.: 31). Compare this with Moffatt's statement:

The fact that south Indian rural untouchables replicate a system that makes them fundamentally inferior, that they participate willingly in what be called their own oppression, does not mean that they, therefore 'deserve', their position. For this replication, this ideological and social conformity is the result of social forces beyond the control of south Indian untouchables, and beyond their comprehension in their present state of consciousness (1979: 303).

Notwithstanding possible historical-cum-ideological objections to our use of Gramsci's thought in the Indian context, let us carry forward another aspect of his refinement of the concept of hegemony. It ought to be pointed out that hegemony is beset by contradictions and sustained by deception. It is, thus, characterised by equivocal consent – at least as far as the majority is concerned. Seething underneath the substratum of agreement are division and disruptive forces arising from conflicting interests. But in a stable social order the agreement or consensus is so powerful that it counteracts the division and disruptive forces. This agreement must be in relation to specific objects-persons, beliefs, values, institutions, or whatever. In focusing upon what Femia calls 'the superficiality of consent' (1987: 43) within the capitalist system, Gramsci speaks of 'contradictory consciousness' characterising mass consent in advanced capitalist society. As Femia explains: 'The thinking of the common man {in such a society} is neither coherent nor consistent over time; it is instead 'disguised and episodic'; elements of intellectual and moral approbation coexist in unsteady equilibrium with elements of apathy, resignation, and even hostility' (ibid.: 45). It follows that Gramsci speaks of three different levels or types of hegemony; integral harmony, decadent hegemony and minimal hegemony (ibid.: 46–49).

In trying imaginatively to apply the Gramscian scheme to contemporary socio-political developments in India we should be aware not only of the kind of possible objections referred to above, but also of the fact that Gramsci's locus for hegemony is the state and civil society contained in it, whereas our own discussion so far has been confined to civil society – more specifically to the domain of the caste order. However, in keeping with Gramsci's insight about the interpenetration between civic and political society, and commensurately building on the reality of the present day interface between the caste order and political processes in India, generated and monitored by the state, we may distinguish between a broadly south Indian and north Indian pattern of hegemony. Common to both these patterns are an uneasy coexistence with broad agreement and approbation, the phenomena of passivity, 'even hostility', of the subaltern groups vis-à-vis the ruling groups and their ideology.

Imitations of hegemony in the caste system of northern India are numerous in the ethnographic literature. Writing about the untouchable balahi of Madhya Pradesh, Fuchs (1950: 434) observes that their culture is consistent with the culture of the higher caste, but is entirely imitative.

> The Balahis' social customs and conventions are not their own inventions, but are copied after the pattern of other castes. Their moral laws

> and the regulations of public life are not based on high moral ideas, but mainly on fear of public opinion.... The rites and ceremonies... are each and all imitations of the rich ceremonial of their Hindu environment.

The Balahi culture may thus be in agreement with higher-caste culture, but this represents a weak, copied consensus. To be an untouchable is not to be excluded from the culture of caste, but it is to possess this culture in a thinner and less convincing form. Implicit in Berreman's characterisation of rural untouchables in a Himalayan village in north India is also the 'contradictory consciousness' of hegemony. In a short critique of Dumont's structural theory of caste, Berreman claims that when he presented his version of the Dumontian model to the rural untouchables, 'they laughed, and one of them said, you have been talking with Brahmins' (Berreman 1971: 16–23). It is obvious that the untouchables in the village studied by Berreman are fully aware of the high-caste model, and to the extent that they act according to it, share it too. However, Berreman interprets this sharing to be a product not of consensus but of coercion. Kolenda's studies among the untouchable's *chuhras* (sweepers) of Khalapur village in western Uttar Pradesh are even more revealing. She conducted fieldwork among the *chuhras* in 1955 and again in 1984. The untouchable sweepers of Khalapur refuse to apply Karma doctrine to their own low status. As one would expect, while the higher caste accept status, ranking naturally, (e.g., the guna theory) and as divinely ordained (the operation of *karma, dharma* and transmigration), the sweepers – though understanding these doctrines in abstract form – refers their present low status to collective myths which state that they were once of much higher caste, and felldue to a terrible accident motivated by the best of intentions (Kolenda 1964: 74–76). Again, the same author, basing her findings on fieldwork in Khalapur in 1984, provides detailed case studies of the sweepers humour whereby they equalise hypergamously unequal marital kin through teasing, pretence and farce (Kolenda 1990: 116–53). Her ethnography is an excellent example of hegemonic cognition of the lower castes vis-à-vis the hierarchical world view of the dwija castes: while on a general and abstract plane agreeing with the overall framework of the ruling ideology of the system on the situational level, the lower castes (read 'the proletariat') articulate their protest through irrelevant joking. Thus, we may add to Gramsci's list, 'apathy, resignation, and even hostility' (Femia 1987: 45) the veiled dissensus of 'humour'.

Finally, we consider the nature of hegemony with reference to the untouchable caste of *chamars* in Uttar Pradesh. Bernand Cohn writes of a 'communication block' between the higher castes and the *chamars* in the village of Senapur, but this block consists not in a culturelessness of the latter but in elements of a historically pre-Aryan little tradition of the higher castes, especially the brahmin. Cohn mentions certain aspects of the religion of this little tradition: propitiation of goddesses of disease and the use of mediums and exorcists (1955: 58). However, the chamars are at the same time involved in attempting to raise their status through 'sanskritisation'. Thus, the disjunctive contrasts between them and the higher castes have to be considerably qualified so much so that, 'it is almost impossible to sort out those traits which are sanskritic and those which are non-sanskritic... and ... what is idiosyncratic to the chamars as a group and what is common body of ritual and belief held by other low castes and high castes as well' (Cohn 1954: 175). Hence, once again we have intimations of a hegemonic consensus in a hierarchical universe, a situation well summed up by Femia: 'In Aristotle metaphor, all men either sound the same note or else different notes in the same key' (1987: 39). Indeed, if space permitted, we could analyse in the framework of hegemony the ample evidence of sanskritisation not only among the harijans but a number of shudra castes of north India. Such an analyses would reveal not only the 'what' and 'how' of this so-called process of social mobility but, more fundamentally, its 'why', viz, the nature of consensus in the system which motivates positional change, yet at the same time stops short of structural change in the caste system. On the other hand, participation in the modern political process definitely introduces a potential for counter-hegemony. Thus, to return to the chamars:

> Sanskritisation in the form of the Siva Narayan sect, the neo-Hinduism learned from contact with urban temples and religious activity, directs the *chamars* to a traditional form of caste mobility of taking on the style of life and symbols of the upper castes. The Rai Das stories and the speeches accompanying the celebration of Rai Das's birthday point to a turning away from traditional mobility to a use of modern political methods. The ambivalence is a reflection of the situation the chamars and other low castes are in as they strive to improve their social lot (Cohn 1959: 215).

For south India even so staunch an advocate of continuity between upper caste and untouchable social and ideological structures as Moffatt's points to such contemporary disjunctions as: 'blocked communication between the untouchables and others where the latter possess complex skills whose esoteric knowledge can be protected' (1979: 292); personal (rather than social) cynicism among *harijans* about the political dominance of non-brahmin caste of reddiyars (ibid.); presence of ideas among untouchables presaging ideological revision though 'at present thin and inconsistent' (ibid.: 293); belief in transmigration and karma doctrine among the Brahmins and their political allies contrasted with disbelieving untouchables and others (politically neutral non-brahmins); existence of leaders among harijans perceived as agents of the higher castes, co-opted by them to keep their *harijan* caste in check (ibid.: 295); evidence that 'Adi-dravidian radicals have begun to revise, often by inerting, the meaning of such key symbols of untouchability as beef-eating (ibid.: 298); '... Untouchables in the cities are in different environment from those of untouchables in the villages, and are often the carriers of new and clearly disjunctive ideologies' (ibid.: 303); finally, 'those persons who are, in egalitarian terms, among the most oppressed members of Indian society are also among the truest believers in the system that so oppresses them' (ibid.: 304). This characterisation of hegemony in the caste system of south India with its characteristic 'contradictory consciousness' among the untouchables ranges from Gramsci's integral type of what Femia calls 'minimal hegemony'. Obviously, the instability of the system, hastened by its location in wider political processes, may lead to conditions supporting counter-hegemony; however, as our following analysis shows, given the salience of the 'integral' pole in south India, such possibility even in the changed political ambience is not very probable. An early transformation (1880–1925) of horizontal caste solidarities in south India into (social heredity base) ethnic groups under the influence of wider political processes has effectively forestalled such development (Washbrook 1975: 150–203). In somewhat different context that of the eroding legitimacy of caste as the only basis of political power Rajni Kothari writes, about the increase in caste calculations as the sine qua non of caste identifications in the electoral system (1970: 25). Interestingly, he cites in his support an observation from Faizabad district, Uttar Pradesh, where caste is shown to have come down from being a 'determinant' of politics to an 'ethnic variable' (Gould 1967). We have spoken earlier of the contrast in hegemonic patterns between south and north India; before embarking on that comparison, with a detailed study of current northern Indian interface between castes, ethnicity and politics, let us examine the concept of ethnicity in Weber (1978: 385–95; 933–35).

The conceptual framework of Weber's discussion of ethnicity comprises notions of race, status-group, caste, tribe and nation. Although he begins his chapter on ethnic groups by alluding to racial factors, there is an immediate rider about the existence of several million mulattoes in the US disapproving the assumption of a 'natural' racial antipathy even among quiet different races. If abhorrence exists among the whites, this is socially determined by the tendency toward the monopolisation of social power and honour, 'a tendency which in this case (the US) happens to be linked to race' (ibid.: 396). Even endogamy, the practice of confining connubium within a certain group (as contrasted with mere sexual relations), is a function not of race 'anthropological difference' but of status differences, meaning differences due to socialisation and upbringing. It is the social qualification of accepting only endogamous children as full members that characterises the closure of status groups. In the Indian case 'pure' or anthropological type is a secondary consequence of such closure resulting in 'sects' (read castes). Further these 'closed' status-groups or castes coexist with socially despised groups of pariah peoples 'because they have monopolised indispensable skills' (ibid.: 386). It is this conjunction of occupational and racial theories of caste-voluntaristic and western views of hierarchy – which Louis Dumont finds unacceptable.

However remarkable the conjunction here achieved between hierarchy, ethnic difference and division of labour may be, one may wonder whether Weber's failure is not due to the fact that to a hierarchical view he added 'ethnic' considerations through which he wanted to link up widespread ideas on the racial origin of the caste system within the exceptional situation of certain minority communities like Jews or gypsies in western societies (Dumont 1970: 242).

Without prejudice to his dislike of western impositions on Indian reality, Dumont's critique on Weber's view of ethnicity as stressing the racial origin of the caste system is certainly exaggerated for, as already explained, Weber considered as primary the closure of ethnic groups on status criteria and, only in extreme cases, a secondary concurrence between race and status-groups. However, as we shall see presently, there is a ring of social evolutionalism rather than the characteristically Weberian ideal typical elective affinity in this view of ethnically closed status and Indian caste.

But what is ethnicity for Weber? His detailed definition is remarkable for delineating the flexibility of the phenomenon. The universe of discourse, let us reiterate, is that of status-groups tending towards closure.

Any closure trait, no matter how superficial can serve as a starting point for the familiar tendency to monopolistic closure .... Almost any kind of similarity or contrast of physical type and of habits can induce the belief that affinity or disaffinity exists between groups that attract or repel each other (Weber 1978: 388).

Let us also note that Weber regards ethnicity as hiding behind it a number of features all converging on what we have earlier called 'social heredity', and also that he resists the idea of defining 'ethnic groups' rather than considering ethnicity as an omnibus 'category'. Finally, in Weber there is salience of this category for political community.

The belief in group affinity, regardless of whether it has any objective foundation, can have important consequences especially for the formation of a political community. We shall call 'ethnic groups' those human groups that entertain a subjective belief in their common descent because of similarities of physical type or of customs or both, or because of memories of colonisation and migration; this belief must be important for the propagation of group formation; conversely, it does not matter whether or not an objective blood relationship exists. Ethnic membership (Gaminsamkeit) differs from the kinship group precisely by being a presumed identity, not a group with concrete social action, like the latter. In our sense, ethnic membership does not constitute a group; it only facilitates group formation of any kind, particularly in the political sphere (ibid.: 389).

For purposes of a sociological analysis of the contemporary interface between politics and ethnicity in India, Weber's discussion of the political community is a double-edged sword. Weber's insistence on the close nexus between ethnicity and the political process is insightful and strikingly modern. In a recent discussion of ethnicity, for example, 'the term ethnicity refers to the degree of conformity of members of (a) collectivity to shared norms in the course of social interaction' (Cohn 1974: ix-x). In order to tighten this wide definition and to make it useful for purposes of analysis, let us add that 'though the cultures of ethnic groups are universes of formally non-political formations and activities they are *politicised in the course of social action*' (Jain 1985: 180; italics provided). On the other hand, when Weber says, '...it is primarily the political community, no matter how artificially organised, that inspires the belief in common ethnicity' (1978: 389), he has in mind an evolutionary succession of ethnically based 'political community' from tribe to nation linked by the notion of 'people' ('volk') (ibid.: 393–98). In Weber, the historical basis for this evolutionary development lay in the rise of the German nation-state and in its ethnocentric preoccupation with a national sentiment which culminated in the eventual rise of Nazi-fascist nationalism. It seems a pity that almost all discussions of the relationship between ethnicity and politics in India are vitiated by the generalisation and universalisation of this particularistic west European paradigm. Ethnicised political processes, as we shall explore in the case at hand, need not follow the logic of an evolutionary succession from tribe to nation. In this respect the analytical distinction made by Gramsci between civil society and political society in relation to hegemony is salutary. Apropos Marxism, Gramsci made the general methodological point explicitly, as for example in the creative tension contained in the following two statements of Gramsci cited by Femia (1987: 1): 'Marx has not written a catechism, he is not a messiah who left a string of parables laden with categorical imperatives, of absolute, indisputable norms outside the categories of time and space. The only categorical imperative, the only norm is: 'Workers of the world unite'.

Certainly the philosophy of praxis is realised in the concrete study of past history and in the contemporary activity of creating new history. But a theory of history and politics can be made, for even if the facts are always singular and changeable in the flux of historical movement, the concepts can (and must) be theorized ... (ibid.: 23).

Without, then, getting caught in the Weberian paradigm of evolutionary progression-ethnic group-tribe-volk-nation-let us explore with Weber's help the theorisation of ethnicised political processes in contemporary India. Let us go back to Weber's writing on ethnic segregation and caste (1978: 933–35). First, he speaks of religious sanctions guaranteeing status distinctions; in the case of the caste system, every physical contact with a member of any caste that is considered to be lower by the members of a higher caste is considered as making for ritualistic impurity. In addition, individual castes develop quite distinct cults and gods. Second:

A status segregation grown into a caste differs in its structure from a mere ethnic segregation: the caste structure transforms the horizontal and unconnected coexistences of ethnically segregated groups into a vertical social system of super- and sub-ordination. Correctly formulated: a comprehensive association integrates the ethnically divided communities into one political unit (ibid.: 934).

As regards the transformation of ethnically segregated status-groups into a closed vertical social system of castes, Weber arrives at a structurally meaningful location of this 'system' in ritualistic impurity. However, Weber's appeal to a 'comprehensive association' resulting in 'one political uni' of ethnically divided communities is nothing short of a pseudo-historical evolutionary and voluntaristic explanation of the origin of the caste system, so successfully demolished by Dumont (1970). Yet we submit that for analytical purposes not everything is lost in the Weberian thesis on ethnicity. If one interprets his implicity evolutionary formulations into ideal-typical terms and turns on his head the imputations of the closure of status groups into castes, we obtain: (a) the process of the transformation of closed castes into relatively open ethnically segregated status-groups, and (b) the above process being located in the realm of politics, or jockeying for power, viz, not in the procrustean matrix of 'political communities' (e.g, tribe and nation) but in the dynamism of factionalism, party-political formations, deformations and reformations; horizontal solidarities and vertical alliances, etc. In other words, taking a leaf from Weber's (1978) own stated preference for studying the close nexus between politics and ethnicity but convincing ethnicity as a process rather than as a sociology of ethnic groups, we shall, at the same time, commensurate with a move away from ritually-regulated caste distinctions and interdependences and be looking at the dimension of power and conflict in the politically charged arena of relatively open status-groups. Note, however, that these status-groups are relatively open because, like castes at the extreme end of the pole of closure, these groups are also based on a presumption of social heredity or 'descent' which Weber regards as the cornerstone of ethnicity.

It is, thus, in keeping with the spirit of Weberian formulation that the opening up of closed caste groups leads simultaneously to the salience of power dimension in the status-group and to the horizontal solidarity of castes tending to become status categories at the expense of their vertical integration. Seen in conjunction with the distinction between hierarchy and hegemony and (coercive) dominance as theorised by Gramsci, we are in position to interpret the contemporary power dynamics characterised by the groundswell of politics initiated by the shudras ('other backward classes' or OBCs) and the dalits (schedule castes or 'achhuts') in Uttar Pradesh. Although for political reasons, as we shall see presently, a rift has come about between the OBCs and the dalits as evidenced in the state power in UP having been wrested by the BSP through an ouster of the SP, the alliance between the BSP and the BJP which has baffled many an analyst of the Indian political scene can be understood as following an emerging and fast institutionalising pattern of post-mandalisation and post-dalitisation of politics in the Hindi heartland.

Contemporary Politics in Uttar Pradesh

Although we do not here propose to go into the history and details of the processes of mandalisation and dalitisation in northern India, it is our premise that just as sanskritisation was the hierarchy-based hegemonic model of social mobility in the caste system, so the latter two processes (mandalisation and dalitisation) may become the mainsprings of a counter-hegemony-based model of socio-political mobility in the emergent system of ethnicide status-groups. Let us focus on the nature of dominance in the regional social systems of Uttar Pradesh in the erstwhile caste regime and in the present day regime of ethnicised status-groups. In the former regime Srinivas concept of dominant caste fits very well. In UP, the dominant caste in the village was often rajput, brahman, or even jat; it was either a 'dwija' caste or one of the clean sudra castes. The modality of conflict was typically governed by the dominant caste as the fulcrum. This caste was horizontally divided through the formation of vertical factions, consisting of leading members of the dominant caste as leaders and members of sub-ordinate castes as followers. Vertical alliances between caste factions were inversely related to horizontal caste solidarities. One can immediately discern in this arrangement a pattern of consensual hegemony between castes; the super-subordination calculus of the hierarchy was tacitly accepted and activated in village level conflict to the extent that, as Bailey pointed out for the village of Bisipara in Orissa, in 'Doladoli' or dominant caste-based factionalism the recreational quality of 'encounters' (more numerous vis-à-vis 'confrontations' in which resources were destroyed) was paramount. This is very much a description of Gramsci's integral hegemony where the conflictive potential between horizontal caste groups is effectively diffused, (defused) and neutralised by the consensual alliance, vertically, between caste-section. This is our interpretation in the context of the political arena (rather than a diffusionistic and imitation-oriented pseudo-explanation of the process of social mobility in the caste system) of Srinivas' own observation: '... The concept of the dominant caste supplements in some way the concept of sanskritization' (1966: 8).

In a regime of ethnicised status-groups defining the political arenas in Uttar Pradesh today, the situation of dominance assumes a quite different configuration. Here, the numerically dominant *shudra* castes in the villages – the *kachi, kurmi, kori, kahar, yadav, lodha*, so on, under special dispensation obtained through OBC status have assumed 'dominance', using the instrument of 'coercion' in Gramsci's sense of contrast with consensual hegemony. The Srinivasian specification of dominance in the dominant caste concept is at its weakest, as has been noted by many analysts, in its imputed characteristic of being numerically dominant (Kothari 1970: 24). In coercive 'dominance' on the other hand, the fact of numerical predominance and recently acquired material-power clout is of crucial importance. In the political arena, thus, constituted the following significant developments are noticed: the erosion of hierarchy-based hegemony; the strengthening of horizontal solidarity of castes assuming the character of trans-village and regional ethnicised status-groups (this is what the list of 'dominant' shudra castes given above in the political arena); and the demand for representation in village (panchayat); regional (district level party committees and municipalities), and state-level offices (legislative assembly and ministerial) on the basis of ethnicised status-group membership. It follows logically from this changed configuration of the political arena that the erstwhile wielders of power – the *dwija* caste politicians – are among the most strident critics of the 'hooliganism', 'mafia operations', and 'atrocities' of the newly-risen numerically dominant shudra groups of the OBC vintage. This is a clear case of the traumas of transition from hegemony to 'dominance'. The charge of unadulterated coercion in the new regime made by the old guard of dominant caste leaders is surely because the ideological cushion of hierarchy has been removed with the erosion of hegemony. Here, then, in contrast to the integral hegemony pattern of south India, we have in Uttar Pradesh a situation of 'minimal hegemony' as defined by Femia after Gramsci.

If our analysis is correct, then the installation of a dalit (BSP) government in the state of Uttar Pradesh leads by itself to a scenario in which a counter-hegemonic regime becomes a theoretical possibility.

However, we must note immediately that an instant and popular interpretation of the BSP in wielding power with the outside support of an ostensibly dwija-based party (BJP) takes the standard form of the latter having effectively divided the BSP and the SP-the dalits from the *shudras* and muslims – and hence come to rule Uttar Pradesh. Therefore, in most of the media coverage the scenario is one of the neo-hegemony of the reactionary forces rather than of counter-hegemony by the groundswell of dalit and *shudra* voters. The former scenario is so well delineated and publicised that it remains for us to enumerate the salient features for a realisation of the scenario for counter-hegemony.

Here we may provide a schematic picture of the strength of the BSP in UP politics. Our starting point is the advice given by V.P. Singh of the left oriented National Front to Mayawati and the BSP supremo Kanshi Ram soon after Mayawati's assumption of office as chief minister of Uttar Pradesh. He is reported to have told Mayawati to either give up the 'gaddi' (chief ministership) or the popular support among the shudras, dalits and muslims. It is a measure of the self confidence of the BSP that its leaders have taken VP Singh's advice as a challenge, a bid to have both the *'gaddi'* and the popular base. In this context the following strategies of the BSP are relevant:

(1) Various manoeuvrers to keep at bay, if not elbow out, the BJP. Evidence the BJP's lack of support to the VHP and the RSS sponsored idea of holding 'mahayajna' near the mosque site at Janmashtami in Mathura and the eventual change of site by the Hindutva forces. The BSP has been cashing in on and continuously harping upon the fact of non-ideological outside support by the BJP.

(2) Induction of the BSP cabinet in UP of four MLAs of the SP who had rebelled and supported Mayawati in the vote of confidence in the assembly.

(3) Targeting Mulayam Singh Yadav, the erstwhile chief minister belonging to the SP, personally as the perpetrator of 'goonda raj' and thus fomenting disaffection among his followers to defect to the BSP. In this way, the ideological unity of the other backward classes and the dalits is sought to be insulated.

(4) On his part, Mulayam Singh Yadav was forced to criticise not the BSP but the BJP, and he offered to let Mayawati remain the chief minister if the BSP divorced its compact with the BJP.

(5) Ordinary grass-root supporters of the BSP realise that the alliance with BJP is only temporary and motivated by *realpolitik (*i.e, in opposition to the Congress (I) ruling at the centre) (ref. *The Times of India*, 1 August 1995).

(6) BSP leaders' ploy to address the *kori, kurmi, yadav*, and so on through direct mass contact, to win them over to the 'backward' cause rather

than through appeal to formally organised caste associations as in the 1960s (Kothari 1970). This mode of propaganda potential is an outcome of the horizontal solidarities of middle and lower castes transformed as ethnicised status-groups. The mass-contact tactic of the BSP is tailor-made to harness the groundswell of dalit and shudra support for oppositional politics. The politicisation of the backward castes in 1995 is, therefore, no mirror-image of the earlier dwija wooing of backward support. As Amulya Ganguly pointed out, the crucial difference now is that the backwards are no longer content to be camp followers of the higher castes but want to be leaders (*The Indian Express*, 14 June 1995).

The above optimistic reading of the BSP's prospects in Uttar Pradesh could fund its culmination if by the time of the next general election, the political parties with 'backward' leadership and following consolidate themselves with other grass roots parties as the 'third force' in Indian politics. For this scenario the signals from the neighbouring state of Bihar are particularly favourable. The Janata Dal party of Laloo Prasad Yadav has twice come to power in this notoriously backward and politically unstable state of the Hindu heartland. Uttar Pradesh too has an extremely poor record in social development (Seminarist 1995: 51–54). Indeed, it is precisely in the so-called 'BIMARU' states (Bihar, Madhya Pradesh, Rajasthan and Uttar Pradesh) of the Hindi heartland that the groundswell of shudra and dalit politics and politicians is most manifest. The trend suggests an inverse relationship between radical, lower strata ethnic upsurge, and regional socio-economic development. The BBC was quick to point out that the BJP-Shiv Sena were successful in the recent assembly elections in western Indian (Maharashtra and Gujarat) precisely because this is the region which has benefited most from the policies of liberal-isation and structural adjustment in the Indian economy. Viewed in the perspective of what we have said about hierarchical hegemony and the tight caste-oriented arena of the erstwhile ethnicised politics on the one hand, and on the other, the emergence of looser status-groups configura-tions of 'dominance' regimes, the structural contrast between the western Indian states and the Hindi heartland is especially noteworthy. The regional correlation between socio-economic development and the kind of politics also gives a lie to the hegemonic common sense contained in conventional analyses, in which the rise of radical politics are correlated with relatively better initial economic conditions of the underclass (Singh 1995: 111). In this respect the positive correlation between Kerala's higher socio-economic development and radical politics in the immediate post-independence period must be contrasted with the present negative correlation in states like UP and Bihar; the explanation surely lies in the changed nature of hegemony from the earlier 'integral' to the present-day 'minimal' pole. This also bears out the paradoxical nature of Kerala's socio-political 'revolution' – an early Leftist government based on entrenched caste politics! Ironically, a similar paradox cannot be ruled out even in the contemporary developments in the Hindi heartland because, through progressive, the politics still remain ethnicised. Until fortified by a revolutionary ideology and leadership, the fate of current developments in Uttar Pradesh hangs uneasily between neo-hegemony and counter-hegemony. What one may say definitely about the emerging socio-economic and politico-cultural processes in the Hindi heartland, and about comparable mainstream movements in India generally, is that these are not ethnic movements *per se* but ethnicity-based political movements.

Conclusion

(a) Politics is the art of the possible, and the 'possible' is constrained by cultural factors.

(b) Seen in the context of ethnicisation of politics (sample BSP) it is not merely the caste composition in different areas, but structural factors like uneven economic development in the country which provide the macro-setting.

(c) Ethnicity has been dubbed a vague and sliding-scale concept, always responding and adjusting to *realpolik.* This is exactly what is happening in the form of BSP-BJP alliance in UP.

(d) To return to the sociological perspective, here is a case to show that the conceptualisation of caste transforming into ethnicised status-groups is not merely a substantive reality but also analytically insightful.

Notes

1. The word 'pauni' which Baranasi uses as a synonym for shudra is derived from the Hindi word 'pavana', which means something received as due. Paunis, as their list reveals, consisted of specific communities performing certain services or following certain crafts; the reason they were called 'pauni' was because they customarily received a fixed share of agriculture produce in exchange for goods supplied or services rendered over the year. The phrase 'thirty-six paunis' had become a cliché during Baranasi's age. Poets speaking of paunis, spoke of them as 'thirty-six'. The expression occurs in the works of many poets of the period (Lath 1981: 136).
2. Let us state at this stage the two possible objections to this particular rendering of hierarchy as hegemony. First, the notion of a civil society that Gramsci had in mind is 'an ensemble of educational, religious and

associational institutions' in which hegemonic ideological superiority must eventually have solid economic roots. 'It must also have its foundation in the decisive function that the leading group exercises in the decisive nucleus of economic activity' (Femia 1987: 24). The second objection is set historically in the circumstances of late capitalism in Italy.

In our adoption of the concept of hegemony for the caste and extra-caste sociology of contemporary India, we are aware of the historical discussions about feudalism and early capitalism in North India, as also the parameters of violence and the extra-civil phenomenon in the social processes (Chakrabarty 1989), but it is beyond the scope of the present exercise to go into these issues. Moreover, the opposite views of 'communitarianism' which motivate these Marxist interpretations (Mishra 1995a) deserve critical scrutiny which cannot be attempted here.

References

Banks, Marcus. 1992. *Organising Jainism in India and England*. Oxford: Clarendon Press.

Berreman, Gerald. 1971. 'The Brahmanical View of Caste', *Contributions to Indian Sociology (NS)*, 5: 16–23.

Beteille, Andre. 1965. *Caste, Class and Power*. Berkeley: University of California Press.

Bose, N.K. 1953. *Cultural Anthropology and Other Essays*. Calcutta: India Associated Publishing Company.

——. 1975. *The Structure of Hindu Society*. New Delhi: Orient Longman.

Carrithers, Michael. 1991. 'The Foundations of Community among Southern Digambar Jain', in M. Carrithers and C. Humphrey (eds), *The Assembly of Listeners: Jains in Society*, Cambridge: Cambridge University Press, pp. 268–79.

Chakrabarty, Dipesh. 1989. *Rethinking Working Class History: Bengal, 1890–1940*. Delhi: Oxford University Press.

Cohn, Bernard. 1954. 'The Chamars of Senapur: A Study of the Changing Status of a Depressed Caste', PhD Dissertation, Cornell University, Ithaca, New York.

——. 1955. 'The Changing Status of a Depressed Caste', in McKim Marriott (ed.), *Village India*, Chicago: The University of Chicago Press.

——. 1959. 'Changing Tradition of a Low Caste', in Milton Singer (ed.), *Traditional India: Structure and Change*, Philadelphia: The American Folklore Society.

Cort, John E. 1990. 'Models of and for the Study of the Jains', *Method and Theory in the Study of Religion*, 2 (1): 42–71.

Dumont, Louis. 1957. 'For a Sociology of India', *Contributions to Indian Sociology*, 1: 1–22.

——. 1970. *Homo Hierarchicus: The Caste System and its Implications.* London: Weidenfeld and Nicolson.

——. 1982. 'On Value', *Radcliffe-Brown Lecture 1980*, London: British Academy.

Femia, J.V. 1987. *Gramsci's Political Thought: Hegemony, Consciousness and the Revolutionary Process.* Oxford: Clarendon Press.

Fuchs, Stephen. 1950. *The Children of Hari: A Study of the Nimar Balahis in the Central Provinces of India*. Vienna: Verlag Herold.

Gould, Harold. 1967. 'Changing Political Behaviour in Rural Indian Society', *Economic and Political Weekly*, 11 (33–35).

Gupta, Dipankar. 1992. 'Continuous Hierarchies and Discrete Castes', in D. Gupta (ed.), *Social Stratification*, Delhi: Oxford University Press.

Jain, Ravindra K. 1975. 'Bulenda Genealogy and Legends: The Past of an Indigenous Ruling Group of Central India', in J.H.M. Beattie and R.G. Lienhardt (eds), *Studies in Social Anthropology*, Oxford: Clarendon Press.

——. 1985. 'Multi-Ethnicity and Overseas Migration: The Case of Tamils in Malaysia', in A.D. Pant and S. Gupta (eds), *Multi-Ethnicity and National Integration*, Allahabad: Vohra Publishers.

Kolenda, Pauline. 1964. 'Religious Anxiety and Hindu Fate', in E.B. Harper (ed.), *Religion in South Asia*, Berkeley: University of California Press.

——. 1990. 'Untouchable Chuhras through their Humour: 'Equalising' Marital Kin through Teasing, Pretence, and Farce', in Owen M. Lynch (ed.), *Divine Passions*, Delhi: Oxford University Press.

Lath, Mukund (ed.) 1981. *Half a Tale: A Study of the Interrelationship between Autobiography and History.* Jaipur: Rajasthan Prakrit Bharati Sansthan.

Lohia, Ram Manohar. 1964. *Jati Pratha* (Hindi). Hyderabad: Navhind Prakashan.

Marcus, George E. and M.M.J. Fischer. 1986. *Anthropology as Cultural Critique.* Chicago: University of Chicago Press.

Marriott, McKim and Ronald B. Inden. 1973. 'Caste Systems', *Encyclopedia Britannica*, 3: 982–91.

Marriott, McKim. 1976. 'Hindu Transactions: Diversities without Dualism', in B. Kapferer (ed.), *Transaction and Meaning*, Philadelphia: Institute for Studies of Human Issues, pp. 64–83.

Mayer, A.C. 1960. *Caste and Kinship in Central India*. London: Routledge and Kegan Paul.

Mencher, Joan. 1974. 'The Caste System Upside Down, or the Not-so-Mysterious East', *Current Anthropology*, 15: 469–93.

Mishra, Amaresh. 1995a. '1857: The Unfinished War', *Seminar*, 432: 14–18.

——. 1995b. 'BJP's Moves under Cover of BSP Government', *Economic and Political Weekly*, 30 (27): 1643–44.

Moffatt, Michael. 1979. *An Untouchable Community in South India: Structure and Consensus*. Princeton, NJ: Princeton University Press.

Seminarist. 1995. 'An Area of Darkness', *Seminar*, 432.

Singh, Yogendra. 1973. *Modernization of Indian Tradition*. Faridabad: Thomas Press (India).

——. 1995. 'Integration of Marginalised Groups into Indian Society: The Case of the Scheduled Castes, Scheduled Tribes and Other Backward Classes', in M. Dubey (ed.), *Indian Society Today*, New Delhi: Har-Anand Publications.

Srinivas, M.N. 1966. *Social Change in Modern India*. Berkeley: University of California Press.

Washbrook, D.A. 1975. 'The Development of Caste Organisation in South India, 1880 to 1925', in C.J. Baker and D.A. Washbrook (eds), *South India: Political Institutions and Political Change, 1880–1940*, Delhi: Macmillan.

Weber, Max. 1978. *Economy and Society: An Outline of Interpretative Sociology*, 2 Volumes. Guenther Roth and Claus Wittich (eds), Berkeley: University of California Press.

Zelliot, Eleanor. 1992. *From Untouchable to Dalit*. New Delhi: Manohar.

4

Feasibility of Another Modernity

AVIJIT PATHAK

Enough has already been said and written about sociology – its critical engagement with modernity: the modernity that emerged in the West at a crucial juncture of its history. It was often said that Enlightenment philosophers were laying the foundation of a liberal/rational/secular order. And sociology as it evolved – from Comte's law of three stages to Marx's historical materialism – taught us diverse ways of looking at the post-Enlightenment era. Durkheim saw growing differentiation, specialisation, division of labour and resultant organic solidarity in modern industrial societies. Weber saw the process of rationalisation, or the emergence of a bureaucratic form of authority in the new age. And Marx saw capitalism, its market economy, and its inherent contradictions. Not solely that. With the passage of time, sociologists – particularly the adherents of post-modernity – began to critique the very foundation of Enlightenment modernity. In a way, as I see, my growing up with sociology is like engaging myself with modernity (Pathak 2004).

It is also important to look at my own location in history. Yes, the colonial state – with its economic policies, its administrative and legal network, its English education, and its improved modes of transportation and communication – did give us the structure of modernity. But then, the experience of colonial modernity – because of its innate violence, asymmetry and exploitativeness, and its arrogance and skepticism towards our own cultural practices – was often traumatic. What is, however, interesting to note is that after a prolonged struggle for decolonisation the agenda for nation-making that we initiated was filled with the same ethos of optimism which was derived from the principles of modernity. It was like believing in the doctrine of techno-industrial progress, and in a 'nation' that brings political centrality and order amidst cultural diversity. Yet, with the passage of time we witnessed innumerable anomalies and contradictions, the crisis in the secular foundation of the state, the growing identity politics, the political articulation of differences, the environmental movements and multiple voices emanating from the marginalised communities began to cause a severe challenge to the grand agenda of modernity: its centrality and its language of science, development and progress. Not solely that. We also became aware of the specificity of our modernity: something that is different from mere Westernisation and is rooted in our own cultural history.

The project of modernity, needless to add, has become a site of intellectual/academic debate. We see the proliferation of books and literature produced by hardcore modernists, postcolonial theorists, postmodernists, environmentalists, Gandhians and feminists. But what I wish to emphasise is that my interest in modernity is not merely academic and cognitive. It is also experiential, and to a great extent, self-reflexive. Modernity, as I would substantiate, is about contradictory and conflicting experiences. Yes, there are positive experiences relating to the spirit of freedom, criticality and agency. And there are also painful experiences relating to existential and cultural anguish. These experiences arouse my interest in modernity. In other words, my engagement with modernity is sociological, historical and experiential. And possibly, out of these complex experiences emerges my urge to think of an alternative/life-affirming modernity.

I
Core Values of Modernity

There are many definitions of modernity. And there are many culture-specific articulations of modernity. These diverse projects of modernity notwithstanding, there is a set of core values which, I believe, every adherent of modernity seeks to privilege. And possibly even the most adamant critics of modernity would find it difficult to negate the liberating potential of these values. To begin with, I wish to speak of these positive experiences of modernity. Modernity, its adherents argue, is invariably related to the spirit of freedom. This freedom is rooted in *critical consciousness* that it generates. It means: 'Don't take things for granted. Question it, verify it, and subject everything to crucial scrutiny'. There is nothing which is beyond critical examination. Instead, everything – including the most sacred – has to be observed, verified and interrogated. No wonder, this fundamental enlightenment spirit which was evolved through the historic Renaissance and Reformation, broke the static/taken for granted world: a world often legitimated by social customs, religious sanctions and an institutionalised divine order. This breakdown led to the over-expanding discoveries, innovations and experimentations in every field of social life. In a way, modernity gave one the confidence to question the most cherished/established beliefs, and propose new ideas. This freedom from orthodoxy – or the freedom to question, and explore new ideas – is indeed a great achievement of modernity. In the modern age, as Eisenstadt would have argued, 'the sanctity and status quo of the past – of any past – as a major symbolic regulator of social, political and cultural change and innovation, has given way to the acceptance of innovation and orientation to the future as a basic dimension of cultural orientation' (Eisenstadt 1987: 6). It is in this sense that we see modernity in Galileo when he questioned the religious belief regarding the centrality of the earth in the universe. We see modernity in Luther and Calvin. And we see modernity in Rammohun Roy when he fought against orthodox pandits, and he pleaded for a ban on the practice of *sati*. We see modernity in B.R. Ambedkar when he burnt a copy of the *Manusmriti* and raised his dissenting voice against the age-old caste system. And we see modernity in young Gandhi when he disobeyed the verdict of the caste associations and chose to visit abroad. In other words, modernity, because of this critical or Kantian thrust, is experienced as an *emancipatory* quest which, it is argued, is qualitatively different from the taboos of traditionalism. Indeed, in everyday life modernity is often celebrated as freedom: when, to use analogies from our own society, a young girl from rural India commits herself to a cross-religious marriage, or a young boy from Bihar overcomes the parental pressure, refuses to accept dowry and chooses his life-partner from an altogether different community. Possibly it is the new aspiration that Daniel Lerner too talked about while celebrating 'the passing of traditional society'. A traditional man, as Lerner argued, tends to reject innovation by saying: 'It has never been thus', whereas one who is more modern is more likely to ask 'Does it work?' and try the new way without much ado (Lerner 2000: 122). Even though Lerner's dichotomy of tradition vs. modernity is simplistic, it is difficult to deny the spirit of freedom that man cherishes – and cherishes more frequently – in the new age.

Another associated gain of modernity is that it opens up the world. It brings immense dynamism, arouses tremendous vertical/horizontal mobility, and gives us a wide-ranging exposure. The reason is that its inherent criticality leads to diverse experimentations and life-projects. Nothing remains static and stable. Change/innovation tends to characterise the spirit of modernity. No wonder, with modernisation it becomes exceedingly difficult to retain a small, closed, homogeneous and well-insulated community. Instead, as sociologists and cultural anthropologists have repeatedly pointed out, we witness a shift from a small, kinship-oriented, tradition-centric community to a vast heterogeneous/

innovative society. True, this shift could not be easy, smooth and linear. There would be pathos, tensions and resistance. We know that Comte did not appreciate the growing individualism in his time. He sought to restore 'moral communities'. Durkheim was equally concerned with the growing *anomic* disorder in modern societies. In other words, as Robert Nisbet has suggested, the concern for stable/cohesive communities did not escape the attention of sociologists who were otherwise modern (Nisbet 1967). But then, the point I am trying to put forward is that modernity does essentially open up the world, and make us encounter what Peter L. Berger would regard as the 'plurality of life-worlds':

> Compared with modern societies, most earlier ones evinced a high degree of integration. Whatever the difference between the various sectors of social life, these would hang together in an order of integrating meaning that included them all. The integrating order was typically religious. For the individual this meant quite simply that the *same* integrative symbols permeated the various sectors of his everyday life. Whether with his family or at work or engaged in political processes or participating in festivity and ceremonial, the individual was always in the same 'world'. The typical situation on individuals in a modern society is very different. Different sectors of their everyday life relate them to vastly different and often severely discrepant world of meaning and experience. Modern life is typically segmented to a very high degree, and it is important to understand that this segmentation (or, as we prefer to call it, pluralisation) is not only manifest on the level of observable social conduct but also has important manifestations on the level of consciousness. (Berger et al. 1979: 62–63)

It can also be said that modernity gives us the choice: the freedom to select from diverse possibilities. It is in this context that I wish to look at my own process of growing up. I see this 'modern' experience while shifting from a small town to a big city. In a city I see an entirely new world filled with immense possibilities. I see a Satyajit Ray film, a painting exhibition in the art gallery, I listen to an experimental singer, known about innumerable professions and vocations, and the fine diverse groups working in the field of environment, gender, health and education. In other words, the city as a modern site makes things happen, allows me to come out of a small, protected, closed network, and cultivate what Lerner would have regarded as the 'empathy of the mobile personality': the capacity to incorporate new demands upon oneself, or to see oneself in the other fellow's situation (Lerner 2000: 121–23). It is in this sense that modernity expands one's horizon, and perpetually transforms the world around us. This heightened 'psychic mobility' is something I know I would miss if I am asked to live in, say, an insulated village where, as it would be argued, nothing happens except the recurrence of routinised everyday life-practices.

The inherent dynamism of modernity implies the process of *individuation*: individuals can rediscover themselves, unfold their potential, and evolve their own life-projects. Nothing can be imposed on them simply because of their birth in a caste, clan or community. One is not born with one's destiny; one makes it. In other words, modernity means a radical shift: from fatalism to active agency, from ascription to achievement, from passivity to meaningful choice. No wonder, Alex Inkels – a high priest of modernity – would regard the abandonment of passivity and fatalism, and 'the assertion of increasing independence from the authority of traditional figure like parents and priests as the major characteristic of a modern man (Inkels 2000: 134–43). This means that as individuals endowed with agency, we can now choose. My father may be a Brahmin scholar, but I can choose to join a management school, and start my own business. Or, I may be born in a lower caste family in Uttar Pradesh, but I can become the chief minister of the state. The arousal of this active agency, it has to be realised, is, indeed, a great strength of modernity. It gives confidence, particularly to the victims of traditional social order, to rediscover their own possibilities, and create a new world free form burden of *karma*, fatalism and ascriptive status. It is, however, true that the individual cannot be seen in isolation. We know that the liberal ethos of modernity asserts the agency of the individual. As Max Weber would have said, man is a conscious agent capable of attaching his own meaning to the world. But then, there were sociologists who thought somewhat differently. Individualism, for Emile Durkheim, should not be equated with the utilitarian notion of man as a discrete individual concerned only with the maximisation of his own pleasure. Durkheim's individual could not be altogether free from the overwhelming power of the collective. And Karl Marx took class, not bourgeois individualism as the unit of analysis. Yet, neither Durkheim nor Marx – because of their affinity with the core spirit of modernity – could deny the liberating role of human agency. Durkheim saw and celebrated differentiation and specialisation in modern societies. And Marx would have felt happy had he seen that many socio-political movements in our times – from the lower caste movements to the feminist assertion – have been inspired by this modernist belief that we are not puppets, and we can create our own histories. Not solely that. This freedom to choose in a pluralistic universe, it is said, is truly rational. Because the new form of division of labour, it is believed, allows individuals to opt for appropriate vocations that suit their specific aptitudes. Even if my father is a Brahmin priest, I have no particular obligation to choose my father's vocation, if am not inclined to it. I may join a film institute, and become a film maker. The argument is that this division of labour which is rooted in the process of individuation taps the best in each of us. The modern age, therefore, becomes more rational, efficient and productive.

The process of individuation – or the arousal of agency – means that modernity leads to the *democratisation* of society. It intends to free the individual from the tyranny of caste, clan and religion. Not solely that. As an individual one becomes important – a being to be respected in one's own right. In fact, many major movements in modern (particularly Western) thought and culture contributed to the emergence of this new conception. The reformation and Protestantism set the individual conscience free from the religious institutions of the Church and exposed it directly to the eye of God; Renaissance humanism placed man at the centre of the universe; the scientific revolutions endowed man with the capacity to enquire into the mysteries of nature, and the Enlightenment, centred on the image of rational, scientific man, created a social milieu free from dogma and intolerance. Indeed, the birth of the individual as a political subject is a distinctive feature of modernity. He has *rights* as an individual, and these rights cannot be abolished in the name of some communitarian identity, even if communities have their relative autonomy. Democracy must rest on the individual, his autonomy and rights. The various Declarations and Bills of Rights of the American Revolution, the *Declaration des Droits de L'Homme* of the French Revolution, and similar statements in country after country, until the eventual adoption of supranational declarations by the United Nations (1948) became an almost inevitable ingredient of the modern political discourse. Yes, modernity – its primary importance to the individual and his/her rights – makes democracy an integral component of political culture. Political democracy, it would not be wrong to say, is often seen as a hallmark of modernity. And we do experience tremendous gains of this political culture. Democracy means freedom, transparency, openness, the ability to dissent, and the willingness to listen to others. Democracy means that everyone, black or white, rich or poor, has his space, and it has to be respected. As a matter of fact, modernity, because of its democratic spirit, creates a culture of debate, dissent and refutation. Then ban on this intellectual and artistic/aesthetic freedom is seen as sort of pre-modern/medieval orthodoxy.

Yes, modernity gives birth to the 'autonomous' individual. His/her 'private' domain is protected and respected. In other words, modernity, because of its rational/liberal ethos, is likely to abhor the idea of undue interference in one's private life. Yet, this affirmation of an autonomous individual does by no means suggest that there is no shared public space in which private individuals can come, meet, communicate and work together. Instead, modernity, it is asserted by its adherents, promotes an entire matrix of *civil society* – media, educational/cultural institutions and voluntary associations – in which people communicate, articulate their voices, and tend to create a shared inter-subjective world. Between an autonomous individual and the state lies all sort of intermediate institutions. And the vibrancy of modern society depends on this entire network of civil society. In fact, there are proponents of modernity who would argue that it is important to preserve and strengthen this shared public space. Because if the individual becomes isolated, the state adopts manipulative strategies, modernity would degenerate into an 'iron cage', it would lose its humanness, and its open/dialogic character. A vibrant public sphere in which individuals are engaged in free communication would distinguish a truly modern society from an orthodox/closed system. I guess Habermas was hinting precisely at this possibility when he celebrated the ideal of the *public sphere*:

> By the public sphere we mean first of all a realm of our social life in which something approaching public opinion can be formed. Citizens behave as a public body when they confer in an unrestricted fashion – that is, with the guarantee of freedom of assembly and association and the freedom to express and publish their opinions – about matters of general interests ... the expression 'public opinion' refers to the task of criticism and control which a public body of citizens informally practises ... vis-à-vis a ruling class. (quoted in Pusey 1987: 89)

In other words, the vibrant public sphere can well be a site of what Habermas would regard as 'communicative rationality' and leading to social milieu filled with reciprocity, symmetry and the ethos of understanding. Well, Habermas is deeply aware of the fact that late capitalism often distorts the possibility of free communication, because it manipulates the public opinion through the mass media, or the forced articulation of social needs through large organisations. But then, the answer, for Habermas lies not in the escape from modernity. The answer is to unfold the very potential of modernity. He reminds us of his potential, and pleads for a reconstructed rationality in which reason becomes active in politics and history through the free interpretation, in an unrestricted social interaction, of the issues, events and interests that govern our destiny. In other words, modernity does not mean well fed/well-clothed individuals – politically indifferent and culturally insensitive – living in their own little worlds. As Habermas reminds us, it should mean a vibrant public sphere in which people participate and reflect the world.

Even the most enthusiastic adherents of modernity admit that these ideals – critical consciousness, respect to the autonomy of the individual, and open/democratic public culture – are not always easy to practise. Instead, as we have seen, many societies which are otherwise modern (industrial, technologically-developed and urbanised) have betrayed the spirit of democracy; gains of modernity have been monopolised by the select few, not necessarily distributed amongst all. In other words, oppression, inequality and authoritarianism have not altogether disappeared from the modern world. Who can, for instance, forget that in the twentieth century the 'modern' West experienced the worst form of authoritarianism, and brutality of war and violence? This despair could, indeed, be seen in Max Weber's anguish over the 'disenchantment' of the world, in Sigmund Freud's powerful articulations of the 'discontents' of civilisation, in the 'dialectic' of Enlightenment Adorno and Horkheimer talked about, in the existentialist preoccupation with 'death' and 'nothingness', and possibly in the mood of 'deconstruction' in which contemporary postmodernists indulge themselves. But then, what is distinctive about modernity, as its proponents argue, is that it can evolve its own critique; it is self-reflexive; it is capable of finding a solution within the discourse of modernity itself. Modernity, it is argued, is essentially optimistic in nature. Take, for instance, what is broadly known as Marxism. Yes, Marx was modern: a child of enlightenment, a rational thinker who believed in science, and its ability to overcome ideological distortions, and illuminate us with the light of 'true consciousnesses'. He cherished the dynamism in history: the way it evolves itself, assumes a linear path, and moves towards 'progress'. But then, Marx's modernity was not in tune with what he was experiencing in his own time: the capitalist social order filled with commodity fetishism, private property, exploitation of working class, and alienated labour. Yes, capitalism, Marx argued, was a breakthrough; it was a product of industrial revolution, an assertion of the emergent bourgeoisie, and a necessary stage towards historical progress.

> The bourgeoisie, by the rapid improvement of all instruments of production, by the immensely facilitated means of communication, draws all, even the most barbarian nations into civilisations. It has created enormous cities, has increased the urban population as compared with the rural, and has thus rescued a considerable part of the population from the idiocy of rural life. It has made barbarian and semi-barbarian countries dependent on the civilized ones, nations of peasants on nations of bourgeoisie, the East on the West. (Marx and Engels 1975: 47–48)

Yet, the progressive/modernist role the bourgeoisie played, for Marx, was incomplete and contradictory. Because this modernity, he thought, values only callous 'cash payment'.

> It has resolved personal worth into exchange value, and in place of the numberless indefeasible chartered freedoms, has set up that single, unconscionable freedom – Free Trade. In other words, for exploitation, veiled by religious and political illusions, it has substituted naked, shameless, direct, brutal exploitation. (ibid.: 44–45)

No wonder, for the Marxists, capitalism cannot become people's modernity or emancipatory modernity. Yet, this critique does by no means suggest that Marx was cherishing a nostalgia for a 'non-modern' world. Instead, as we have already said, he was a passionate believer in modernity, its rationality and scientificity. He was, therefore, suggesting what his followers would regard as a more mature, fulfilling, affirmative modernity: a socialist/communist society free from the fragmented/exploited character of capitalism.

What we are noticing is, therefore, interesting. For the Marxists, the answer to capitalism – even when 'it has drowned the most heavenly ecstasies of religious fervour, of chivalrous enthusiasm, of philistine sentimentalism, in the icy water of egotistical calculation' (ibid.: 44) – lies in modernity itself, not a regressive journey to the 'golden' past. And for Habermas, unlike his predecessors Adrono and Marcuse, even when late capitalism leads to 'the colonisation of the life-world', the answer is not to grow cynical about modernity, but to accomplish its unfinished agenda. As a matter of fact, what we are seeing is some kind of balanced optimism in modernity. Modernity has its problems, but it is capable of finding a reasonable solution. I wish to recall an example from Anthony Giddens. Giddens is careful enough to reveal the crisis of modernity – its possible 'risks' (Giddens 1990). For instance, in modern times the surveillance capabilities of the state and capitalist enterprise have increased dramatically; there is, indeed, the increased risk of the growth of totalitarian power. Likewise, the second risk is associated with the 'industrialisation of war'. And the third risk is about the potential collapse of economic growth systems. Finally, there is yet another risk that involves the potential for ecological disaster. But then, what is interesting is that Giddens does not succumb to pessimism. He sees immense possibilities in various social movements. The labour movement seeks to address the risk tendencies of capitalism, whereas democratic movements challenge authoritarianism, peace movements challenge militarisation, and ecological movements seek to remedy threats to the global environment. In other words, the proponents of modernity want to convince us that it is capable of innovating itself, and it is in a perpetual process of exploration and experimentation. I feel that Giddens is talking about the same thing when he asserts that 'the reflexivity of modern social life consists in the fact that social practices are constantly examined and reformed in the light of incoming information about these very practices, thus constitutively altering their character' (ibid.: 38).

These values – freedom, criticality, democratisation, openness and optimism for the future – seem to have become desirable ideas/guidelines for the entire human kind. Irrespective of cultural differences, it is difficult to legitimate a civilisation that does not adore these values. It is in this sense that one can argue that modernity is irreversible, and even if you and I have our distinctive projects of modernity, we cannot deny this critical minimum. Take, for instance, our own specific Indian modernity. It is possible to argue that here caste – not liberal individualism – is the governing principle. Yet, as our Constitution acknowledges, the rights of the individual are no less important. Likewise, even if the 'personal' laws of a religious community have their space, it is becoming increasingly difficult to support patriarchal hierarchy and oppression. In other words, no society that seeks to call itself modern can escape the moral pressure of these core values.

But then, there is a complex dialectic that needs to be acknowledged. It is not necessarily right to say that modernity was something that happened only at a specific juncture of history (eighteenth-century Enlightenment) in a specific geographical locality (Europe). True the Enlightenment agenda with its Kant, Voltaire and Montesquie, and subsequent politico-economic changes in the world ranging from the Industrial Revolution to the French Revolution helped consolidating the roots of modernity. But then, even in the past, in tradition, or in 'non-modern' periods one can notice the traces of the core values of modernity which we are talking about. It is in this sense that the dichotomy of modernity and tradition, or modern and non-modern becomes problematic. Look at our own tradition. Even for a vehement critic, it is not difficult to see that our tradition has a space for the culture of criticality and dissent. Each time I read the *Upanishads*, I get inspired by the critical/dialogic spirit that these discourses create. For example, the great philosophic argument and contestation that characterise the conversation between Yajnavalkya and Gargi in the *Brhadaranayak-Upanishad* is immensely illuminating (B.U.III8.1– III 8.12). Likewise, the dissenting voices can be seen in Buddhism and Jainism, or in bhakti/sufi traditions. The question, therefore arises: was Yajnavalkya or Buddha modern or traditional? As a matter of fact, we often realise the limitations of these categories. Possibly the only thing we can talk about is that the core values of modernity not necessarily always Euro-centric. Modernity can also be experienced as a community with tradition. We see this continuity in many finer Indian minds. Tagore, for instance, could reconcile his inclination to the *Upanishadic* prayer with his openness to modern scientific ideas. And Gandhi, despite being a 'santani Hindu', could lead modern political movements. It is, therefore, important not to see modernity as something necessarily 'alien' coming from the West. It is also important not to see tradition as merely a site of superstitions and prejudices. As a matter of fact, such a rigid dichotomy can have disastrous political implications. Every student of sociology knows that the theory of modernity that emerged in the post-war era often legitimated the American hegemony, and produced stereotypes about 'non-modern' cultures. Yes, as I myself have stated, there are positive insights that we can indeed learn from the modernists like Lerner and Inkels. But then, we must be careful about their political implications. If not used creatively, these discourses would produce stereotypes about other cultures.

Having said this, I must also add that we should not underestimate the historic role of the Enlightenment in the making of modernity. Yes, there was a culture of debate and openness in the *Upanishads*, there was a fairly developed system of logic and reasoning in our philosophies like *Nayaya* and *Mimamsa*, and there was Kabir/Nanak interrogating the culture of orthodoxy. But the larger society as a whole could not necessarily universalise and institutionalise these core values. It was only in modern times (and we have to acknowledge the historic contributions of the European Enlightenment) that these values, far from being limited to select saints, mystics and learned castes, would be a collective aspiration, and get institutionalised through a network of new institutions and structures like liberal democracy and a vibrant civil society. In other words, even though there is a continuity between tradition and modernity, there is a distinctive character of modernity in terms of politico-economic and cultural institutions which have legitimated these core values. And, despite many critics of modernity, I believe that these values, if lived in an immensely delicate and creative fashion, can indeed enrich our life.

II
The Other Side of Modernity: Burden of Arrogance

It is, however important to realise that modernity is a double-edged phenomenon. While its core values have a liberating potential, its concrete practices may cause arrogance and violence. It is like being excessively proud of oneself, and looking at others with a sense of contempt. I am rational, modern and enlightened; you are arrogant, superstitious and barbaric! It is like dividing and hierarchising the world. If we look at history, we notice this arrogance of modernity – particularly, the hyper-modernity of the West.

The fact is that here is a project that is terribly proud of itself. This sense of pride lies in its immense achievements and promises. To be part of the modernising process, one is often led to believe, is like celebrating a new world: something that is radically different from all that happened earlier. It creates a world that seems to resemble the design of a perfect rational order. The Kingdom of Reason, it is hoped, is filled with freedom, prosperity and comfort. Possibly the techno-industrial culture that modernity brings with it makes it possible. The modern age, unlike all other periods, knows the science of controlling and tapping natural resources, and utilises these resources for the material well-being of the human species. Not solely that. It knows the technology of mass production. As a result, it is only in the modern period that everyone – at least potentially – is capable of enjoying the fruits of the ever-expanding comfort industry. And, for the first time in human history, it is possible for man to be free from the necessities and enter the domain of freedom. Indeed, Marx could imagine his *whole man* – a man cultivating all the faculties of his being – only in the modern age. Because science is power, and technology promises to rescue man from routinised and time-consuming manual labour. It does things with efficiency and speed, and gives comfort to man. Each new technological discovery speaks of its promise, its almost miraculous power and seduces man. Technologies become more and more sophisticated, efficient and user friendly. From computer to mobile phone, from video camera to washing machine, from MRI scan to latest medical gadget, everywhere one hears the same story: the way technologies make life smooth, easy and comfortable. The more modern we are, the more surrounded we are with technologies. The more modern we are, the more rational/smooth/efficient we are. It is this difference – the ability to do things much faster and more efficiently – that strikes one immediately when one migrates to a 'developed' country (say, the US) from a 'developing' country (say India). These technological comforts that modernity provides declare their own success stories. No wonder, self-advertisement becomes an inseparable component of the age of modernity. It is proud of itself, it is certain in its achievements, and it knows that it is capable of seducing people. It is, therefore, not surprising that in this proud/modern world we experience the all-pervasive culture of ads. Everything around us is filled with ads: narratives, beliefs, hopes and images of success – success of divergent brands of detergent, car, school, hospital. In such a world, Vance Packard is not entirely wrong when he says that 'we no longer buy oranges, we buy vitality; we do not buy just an auto, we buy prestige' (Packard 1982: 15). Yes, modernity makes us believe that nothing is impossible. It exaggerates its achievements, and mythologises its success. Its proud discourse of development attaches a stigmatised identity to 'underdeveloped' nations.

There is yet another reason why so much pride is associated with this brand of modernity. Look at its self-awareness. It assumes that it is capable of generating the foundation of objective, rational and universal knowledge. In other words, the ability to decipher such a foundation, it was hoped, would distinguish the period of modernity from all other periods when men supposedly lived under diverse irrational/mystical religious beliefs, blind social customs and obscurantist practices. This new knowledge, it was believed, would bring enlightenment, overcome darkness, and enable us to understand, control and shape our destinies. Not surprisingly, modernity became triumphant through its scientific knowledge. All 'non-scientific' knowledges were getting marginalised. Because modernity divided the world into dualistic opposites: Baconian empiricism vs. 'idols' filled with sentiments and prejudices; Cartesian disembodied rationality vs. emotive/bodily sensations and feelings, and science vs. metaphysics. Science with its Newton and Darwin became the most privileged/legitimate knowledge – not just about the physical world, but also about the socio-cultural world. History was distinguished from mythology and sociology from philosophy. This pride in science as objective/foundational knowledge became rather manifest in what is known as *positivism*: the belief that it is only through a 'scientific' way of understanding that we can create a new rational world. This pride manifested itself in all modern institutions: universities must teach modern knowledges, not mythology, theology or cosmology; hospitals must cultivate 'modern' medicine, not traditional forms of healing; and institutions must be governed by 'rational' bureaucracies, not traditional/charismatic forms of authority.

> The assumption of the inherent superiority of science has moved beyond science and has become an article of faith for almost everyone. Human relations are subjected to scientific treatment as is shown by education programmes, proposals for prison reform, army training and so on. The power of medical profession over every stage of our lives already exceeds the power once wielded by the Church. Almost all scientific subjects are compulsory on our schools. While the parents of a six year old can decide to have him instructed in the rudiments of Protestantism, or in the rudiments of Jewish faith, or in other religious instruction altogether, they do not have similar freedom in the case of sciences. Physics, astronomy, history must be learned: they cannot be replaced by magic, astrology, or by a study of legends. (Feyerabend 1978: 74)

Indeed, to be modern, it is felt, is to be superior, because one is blessed with scientific knowledge. And because of this pride, Paul Feyerabend is bold enough to reveal that 'the apostles of science acted like 'determined conquerors; they materially suppressed the bearers of all alternative traditions' (ibid.: 102). I can understand Feyerabend's anguish. The modern age defined itself as the age of Reason, and it led to a series of binary oppositions: science against religion and magic, truth against prejudice, and rationality against the rule of custom. No wonder, from the vantage point of modernity, all other forms of life were seen as pathological, a residue of the past – something to be overcome. Feyerabend, who pleaded for the plurality of methods, needless to add, could not give his consent to the hegemony of modern scientism.

Furthermore, scientific rationalism tends to generate the fetish of 'objectivity' that deviates man from himself and turns the act of scientific knowledge into an act of alienation. This possibly explains the capacity of human beings to turn on their environment and their fellows with 'the cool and meticulously calculated rapacity of industrial society' (Roszak 1972: 168). Environmental disaster, it has to be realised, in an inevitable outcome of this sort of scientism which has no sense of humility, wonder and enchantment, and reduces nature into a resource – something to be measured and quantified in terms of the principles of positivistic economics. In fact, it is not just violence against nature out there, it is violence itself: a doctrine of war. I think that it is this criticality that has also led J.P.S. Uberoi to see the devastating Manhattan Project as an expression of the 'science of vivisection' (Uberoi 2002: 82–101).

> Everything is alive in dualistic parts and nothing is whole in this civilization any longer: truth and reality, the good and the bad, life and death, knowledge or contemplation and action, the sprit and the form. God is dead to the world of course, but the human species and the science of nature do not look so good either – at any rate to the non-expert and the non-elite: God is dead, and I am not feeling too well either! (ibid.: 90).

It is at this juncture that I must remind the readers that I am not jumping into the cult of irrationality. I do not belong to a camp that calls itself 'anti-science'. But then, I must say that the arrogance of science must be resisted. Science and science alone can make us to the domain of truth – this cognitive power of science also becomes its political power. Not surprisingly, science often becomes an ideology of the modern nation-state. From scientific management to scientific socialism to scientific development, the dominant ideologies seek to marginalise all alternative voices. If the state manufactures nuclear weapons, it is seen as a development of science. Or, for that matter, if Medha Patkar protests against big dams, it is seen as anti-development and hence anti-science. And the irony is that even some of the alternative voices, in order to prove their legitimacy, begin to appropriate the language of science. Modern godmen quote quantum mechanics, and prove the 'science' of the Vedanta, and traditional healing practices like yoga and ayurveda become 'modern', and appeal to the 'scientific' community. This does not mean that science has to be eradicated, and relativism established. Instead, what is important is to realise that there is a huge domain of uncertainty, and objective/deterministic science alone is inadequate to make sense of the world. It is important to create a world in which a scientist and a mystic, an engineer and a poet, a modern physician and a traditional healer co-exist, and enrich one another. Because, as Uberoi would argue, 'truth emerges from the dialectics of what is the case (present) and what is not the case (absent), the world of reality and the still wider world of possibility' (ibid.: 91). What is sad is that, despite radical changes in the philosophy of science, many of us continue to think in the positivistic mode. As a result, science becomes arrogant; science legitimates the practice of social engineering done by the techno-managerial elite.

As a matter of fact, this certainty implicit in modernity – its self-pride, its assertion that it leads to prosperity and happiness, and its belief that it is based on foundational knowledge – has made it into a terribly arrogant endeavour. Its self-awareness as a superior project has indeed hierarchised cultures and civilisations. Historically we have seen how the modern West – the centre of modernity – distinguished itself from other 'non-modern' (or non-Western) civilisations: how it constructed the notion of the Orient, its backwardness, and its striking isolation from the mainstream of European progresses in science, arts and commerce (Said 1973). Even an emancipatory thinker like Karl Marx, as we are realising with pain and astonishment, could not escape this modernist/Euro-centric pride. For Marx, England, despite the crimes she made in India, played a 'regenerating' role; she abolished the foundation of 'Oriental despotism', she was the unconscious tool of history, and brought India to the 'mainstream' civilisation (quoted in ibid.: 153). Yes, Edward Said's path-breaking work, I would agree, has sensitised us. We can now see the arrogance of the modernist project and how Orientalism sustains itself by making authorising statements about the Orient: 'its eccentricity, its backwardness, its silent indifference, its feminine penetrability, its supine malleability' (ibid.: 206). Orientalism, for Said, exists as 'a Western style for dominating, restructuring, and having authority over the orient' (ibid.: 3). The hierarchy of cultures and the superiority of Western modernity became obvious because the Orient was seen as 'a locale requiring Western attention, reconstruction, and even redemption' (ibid.: 206).

The self-awareness of Western modernity as a 'superior' project, as we are realising, made it inseparable from the history of colonialism. Because what was distinctive about colonialism was that it often legitimised itself through its 'civilising' mission. It asserted that it had introduced reason, science, industry and school; in other words, it illuminated and rescued the colonised from the domain of darkness. A society like ours did experience the arrogance of this sort of colonial modernity. Recall the discourse of modern/English education that Thomas Babington Macaulay introduced in India. He refused to acknowledge anything worth preserving in the Indic civilisation. For him, 'a single shelf of a good European library was worth the whole native literature if India and Arabia' (quoted in Pathak 2002: 79). With his characteristic arrogance (and this arrogance emanated from a belief that the West has already reached the ultimate stage of secular salvation) and the resultant feeling of charity, he argued that only through new modern education could the British save this 'decadent' civilisation.

> ... What is power worth if it is founded on vice, on ignorance, and on misery, if we can hold it only by violating the most sacred duties which as governors, we owe to the governed, and which, as people blessed with far more than ordinary measure of political liberty and the intellectual light, we owe to a race debased by three thousand years of despotism and priest craft? We are free, we are civilized to little purpose if we grudge to any portion of the human race an equal measure of freedom and civilization (ibid.: 79).

What we notice in this colonial modernity is that it demoralises the colonised; it assumes that the colonised have yet to become rational, adult, masculine and civilised, and they need to be taught the lesson of modernity by the colonial masters. It is, therefore, no wonder that colonialism, as Ashis Nandy has argued with a remarkable insight, sanctifies a worldview that privileges 'the absolute superiority of the human over the nonhuman and subhuman, the masculine over the feminine, the adult over the child, the historical over the ahistorical, and the modern or progressive over the traditional or the savage' (Nandy 1983: X). In this process, Nandy adds, 'it helps generalize the concept of modern West from a geographical and temporal entity to a psychological category (ibid.: XI). As a result, the colonised tend to lose faith in themselves. They seek to redefine themselves through colonial categories.

> In the colonial culture, identification with the aggressor bound the rulers and the ruled in an unbreakable dyadic relationship. The Raj saw Indians as crypto barbarians who needed to further civilize themselves. It saw British rule as an agent of progress and as a mission. Many Indians in turn saw their salvation in becoming more like British, in friendship or in enemy (ibid.: 7).

We are now realising that a significant section of the new elite that was born of colonial modernity in India sought to reaffirm the same worldview. Even a Marxist historian like Sumit Sarkar who, unlike recent theorists of postmodernism, believed in the virtues of Enlightenment, could not fail to problematise the early modernist in India. For example, as he argued, it is important to be aware of the fact that Rammohun and his generation ardently welcomed 'the negative, alienating aspects of the English education' (Sarkar 1985: 8). This Renaissance culture, Sarkar believes, entertained an illusion: a long continued faith in basic British good intentions (ibid.: 68). That was indeed the tragedy. Modern colonialism, as Nandy would argue, won its great victories not so much through its military and technological power as through the agenda of modernity: the ideologies of progress, normality and hyper-masculinity, and in theories of cumulative growth of science and technology. That was why, even some of the finest critical minds in India felt that colonialism, by introducing modern structures into the barbaric world, would open up the non-West to the modern critical – analytic spirit' (Nandy 1983: ix).

This arrogance, let it be stated, does by no means suggest that there are no gains of modernity. Modernity, I have already stated, has immense gains and achievements. Furthermore, it is equally important to become humble on our part, acknowledge our shortcomings and see modernity also as a positive reference point. As I feel, it is desirable to think of a truly cross-cultural dialogue, and a spirit of humility and openness, rather than a closed/arrogant mind-set. It is like asserting the need for a two-way process: (a) modern West willing to learn from non-Western traditions in order to correct itself, and (b) we begin to appreciate the core values of modernity in order to create a better world. Let the modern West become humble, and learn that India, despite innumerable problems, didn't live in a dark age as Macaulay imagined. Here is an old/vibrant civilisation sustained by rich philosophic traditions, splendid diversity in cultural practices, and a spirit of syncreticism. Let its Max Webers learn that our religions are not necessarily 'other-worldly'; instead, the ideal of the unity of the material and the spiritual, the sacred and the profane sought to give a distinctively positive meaning to life which, as Sudhir Kakar showed with a remarkably brilliant insight, produces 'not the Oedipuses and the Hamlets but the Nachiketas and the Meeras' (Kakar 1981: 29). But then, it is equally important on our part to acknowledge that we have to overcome many of our fatalistic beliefs and oppressive social practices, and we do not belittle ourselves if we learn from Voltaire and Kant, and if we see something positive that has taken place in the post-Enlightenment West. This mutual learning, or the 'fusion of horizons', I believe, ought to characterise an open world we are striving for. It is, therefore, debatable whether the theorists of postmodernity – the way they relativise cultures, suspect the Enlightenment belief in progress, and delegitimise science as 'foundational knowledge' – necessarily offer a meaningful/sustainable alternative to modernity. However, I wish to argue, it is nevertheless desirable to grow humble; it is better to learn from those who are 'non-modern', who are like 'us'. Modernity can humanise itself if it is engaged in 'the art of civilized conversation'. I give my consent to Zygmunt Bauman when he pleads for humble 'interpreters' of multiple cultural traditions, and the need 'to talk to people rather than fight them; to understand them rather than dismiss or annihilate them as mutants; to enhance one's own tradition by drawing freely on experience from other pools, rather than shutting it off from the traffic of ideas' (Bauman 1987: 143).

III
Existential Anguish and Unhappy Consciousness

Modernity has also its history of pain, anguish and suffering. The promise of modernity, we have been repeatedly told, is its spirit of freedom. Modernity, it should not be forgotten, needs massive structures – techno-industrial enterprises, legal systems and educational machineries which, because of their very nature, are complex, and require expertised knowledge and, therefore, get increasingly mystified. No wonder, these very institutions which are expected to preserve our modern rights tend to become alienating. The spirit of freedom is lost amidst the huge machinery and its technicality. Indeed, it is not at all impossible to experience the constraints of bureaucratic/technocratic rules and disciplinary regimes all around. We begin to realise that we are not as free as we are asked to believe. As a matter of fact, there is often a pressure to submit to what 'experts' and 'specialists' regard as 'normal' and 'desirable'. We realise the politics of knowledge: how knowledge and power are integrally linked, how 'experts', 'specialists', or to use Foucault's words, 'normalising judges' are perpetually observing, disciplining and hierarchising us. Take, for instance, the assertion of Reason: rational/objective/scientific knowledge. All modern institutions – hospitals, schools and courts – seek to protect this discourse, and exercise a power over those they supervise, train and correct, 'over madmen, children at home and at school, the colonised, over those who are stuck at a machine and supervised for the rest of their lives' (Foucault 1982: 29). Because the individual in the disciplinary regime has to be 'described, judged, measured and compared with others; he has to be 'trained or corrected, classified, normalised, excluded etc' (ibid.: 191). If I do not follow 'reason', I am mad, and it is the task of a psychiatrist to control my 'irrationality' so that I can assume 'normality'. If I do not go to school, and do not learn its 'expertised' knowledge and curriculum, I am not 'educated'. In other words, I need to be 'rational', 'educated', 'healthy' and 'normal' – everything as defined by experts, institutions and knowledge-systems. I, therefore, get thoroughly 'disciplined'. My body, my education, my morals and even my death, everything is defined, measured, recorded and decided by 'experts' in this 'disciplinary regime' or the 'administered totality'.

It is in this context that I wish to recall the death of a dear one in our family. One morning she passed away. It was a peaceful death. Her face revealed the beauty of her last journey. But then, I could not really contemplate and make sense of this death because I was reminded by a friend of mine that a doctor had to be called immediately. A doctor – and a doctor alone – with his 'expertised' knowledge could 'declare' her dead. And this death certificate, I was told, I must carry with me while taking her to the cremation ground. I must 'register' her death. In other words, I realise that there was no escape from the 'expertised gaze' even at the ultimate moment of death. Yes, that day I realised why Michel Foucault did talk about 'surveillance' in our times, the way the disciplinary regime situates individuals in 'a network of writing', and 'engages them in a whole mass of documents that capture and fix them' (ibid.: 189). The point that I am trying to state is that the age of modernity, despite its grand promise of freedom has its own story of surveillance. Possibly, this control mechanism has become more subtle, more refined, or more 'scientific'. That is why, I recall Foucault's *Discipline and Punish*, and appreciate the point he made. For example, if we think of penalty or punishment in the new age, the physical torture of the body 'as a public spectacle' is no longer important. Instead, the 'experts' with new knowledges emerge, and begin to 'discipline' us. And this process, needless to add, is now more sophisticated and technically designed.

> A whole army of technicians took over from the executioner, the immediate antagonist of pain: wardens, doctors, chaplains, psychiatrists, psychologist, educationalist; by their very presence near the prisoner, they sing the praises that the law needs; they reassure it that the body and pain are not the ultimate objects of its punitive action. Today a doctor must watch over those condemned to death, right up to the last moment – thus juxtaposing himself as the agent of welfare, as the alleviator of pain, with the official whose task it is to end life. This is worth thinking about. When the moment of execution approaches, the patients are injected with tranquilizers. A utopia of judicial reticence: take away life, but prevent the patient from feeling it; deprive the prisoner of all rights, but do not inflict pain; impose penalties free of all pain ... (ibid.: 11).

Doubtless, in the modern age I am 'free' in the sense that I can vote, choose my representative, and buy any commodity I like from the shopping mall. But then, there is another aspect of my being that is being perpetually observed, measured, compared, documented, and controlled. This disciplinary power, Foucault reminded us, is 'calculated, organised and technically thought out' (ibid.: 26). Time and again we hear the recurrence of this warning: modernity brings with it heavy structures which, because of their very nature, are alienating. Weber saw it as an 'iron cage'. Kafka's novels revealed man's utter helplessness before a huge bureaucratic machinery, critical theorist saw the all-pervasive domination in the techno-scientific apparatus, Illich saw the denial of human freedom in schools and hospitals, and Foucault spoke of the 'revolts against model prison, tranquilizers, isolation, the medical or educational services' (ibid.: 30). It is important to be aware of this darker aspect of modernity. But then, it would be naive to romanticise a 'non-modern' world which, everyone knows, had its own principle of oppression. As we look at our own culture, we could notice these oppressive practices: how, say, the tyranny of caste structures denied man's creativity and agency which possibly led a dissenter Jyotiba Phule to express his anguish over institutionalised Hinduism by arguing that in his ideal family there would be no scope for a Hindu, whereas the father would be a Buddhist, the mother a Christian, the daughter a Muslim and the son a *satya dharmist*. It is, therefore, important to be cautious. The critique of modernity should not be allowed to be hijacked by the revivalists trying to sanctify the 'golden' past. I am suggesting something far deeper. I am arguing that we must rescue modernity from being degenerated into an oppressive/disciplinary regime. We do not want just the scientific efficiency of the machine, or the instrumental rationality of the market. We also need the poetry of life. We need to soften modernity. It is in this context that I wish to recall a great lesson that I have learned from *romanticism*. It defined the worship of Reason, pleaded for the intensity of imagination and creativity, and man's right to deviate from the 'normal' and 'everyday'. It sought to open our eyes, and make us experience the world like enchanted seers, and feel its magic, wonder and beauty that transcend the cold logic of science.

> Sweet is the lore which Nature brings,
> Our meddling intellect
> Mis-shapes the beauteous forms of things:
> *We murder to dissect*
>
> (quoted in Bloom and Trilling 1973: 129)

The poetry of William Wordsworth is indeed a reminder. Not everyone can remain contented with modernity: its reason, its scientificity, and its technicality. Well, it is possible to argue that the anguish/pain/suffering we are talking about has been exaggerated; it is just a small price one has to pay for achieving the enormous gains of modernity. The adherents of modernity might ask: isn't it true that modernity, precisely because of its science and disciplinary devices has enabled us to experience increased longevity, better health awareness, improved literacy and tremendous comfort? Yes, it is indeed true. But then, there is yet another aspect of our being which neither a rationalist nor a technologist understands. Possibly it requires a poet, a mystic, a mad man who make us strive for the heightened imagination – the ecstasy of the transcendental dance, or the willingness to lead a life which, even if not 'rational', is immensely fullfilling and meaningful. I think there is much to learn – even today – from the way Shelley defended poetry way back in the early nineteenth century:

> We want the creative faculty to imagine that which we know; we want the generous impulse to act that which we imagine; we want the poetry

> of life; our calculations have outrun conception; we have eaten more that we can digest. The cultivation of those sciences which have enlarged the limits of the empire of man over the external world, has, for want of poetical faculty, proportionately circumscribed those of the internal world; and man, having enslaved the elements, remains himself a slave. To what but a cultivation of the mechanical arts in a degree disproportionate to the presence of the creative faculty, which is the basis of all knowledge, is to be attributed for abridging and combining labour, to the exasperation of the inequality of mankind? From what other cause has it arisen that these inventions which should have lightened, have added a weight to the curse imposed on Adam? The poetry, and the principle of self, of which money is the visible incarnation, are the God and Mammon of the world. (ibid.: 757).

Here is yet another story of suffering – not physical suffering, but the deeper suffering of the soul. See the immense mobility that modernity generates. Its railway stations, its airports and its express highways to indicate the dynamism of modernity: people are moving and moving for better prospects: for jobs, health, commerce and education. There is restlessness all around: a continual search for something more, something better. Yes, this has its own narratives of achievement – say, a girl from a remote village in Bihar coming to Delhi to get education and livelihood, and thereby altering her life-project, or a boy from Kerala leaving the ancestral village for finding a better prospect in Dubai. Needless to add, these new opportunities elevate the economy, and the mode of living. Yet, beneath these opportunities lies the experience of heightened loneliness. With increasing mobility and migration one tends to lose the living contact with one's parents, siblings, one's community, and the cultural/physical landscape in which one is born. This often leads to the existential anguish called 'homelessness'. There are many who cannot escape this sadness: the sadness born out of the ambiguity inherent in the modernising process. It gives you comfort, carrier and opportunities; yet, it deprives you of unconditional intimacy. Because of the 'migratory character' of his experience, Berger has shown with remarkable sensitivity, modern man has suffered from a 'deepening condition of homelessness' (Berger et al. 1979: 77). It is not at all surprising. Here is a world in which an increasing number of individuals is uprooted from their original social milieu. Not solely that. As Berger adds, 'no succeeding milieu succeeds in becoming truly home either' (ibid.: 165). Yes, a world in which everything is in constant motion is a world in which, to borrow Berger's words, 'certaintanties of any kind are hard to come by' (ibid.: 165).

Yes, this homelessness, it would not be wrong to say, manifests itself rather strikingly in modern cities. True, as we have already stated, cities are fascinating sites of modernity. In cities things happen: technologies flourish, experimentations take place, market economy grows. But then, cities are also terribly lonely places. In everyday life one encounters innumerable strangers. The anonymity/alienation in this mode of living causes some kind of indifference and hardness. Life tends to lose its warmth, intimacy and spontaneity. Indeed, what George Simmel wrote about the metropolis and mental life seems immensely relevant even today. For Simmel, the very act of living in a metropolis causes the 'intensification of nervous stimulation' because of the 'rapid crowding of changing images', or the 'unexpectedness of onrushing impressions'. Furthermore, the predominance of money economy in the metropolis, adds Simmel, has led to a terribly pragmatic orientation to life.

> Money is concerned only with what is common to all: it asks for the exchange value, it reduces all quality and individuality to the question: How much? All intimate emotional relations between persons are founded in their individuality, whereas in rational relations man is reckoned with like a number, like an element which is in itself indifferent. (quoted in Bolock and Thompson 1992: 467)

And this, Simmel would argue, is responsible for the growth of the 'blasé attitude'. The mind becomes incapable of discriminating diverse objects. They appear to the blasé person in an evenly flat and grey tone, no one object deserves preference over any other. This invariably implies what Simmel regarded as 'reserve' – cold/heartless indifference.

> We frequently do not even know by sight those who have been our neighbours for years. And it is this reserve which in the eyes of the small town people makes us appear to be cold and heartless. (ibid.: 468–69)

But then, the search for a new 'home' – a land filled with warmth, intimacy, and informality – continues. And we do notice that modernity seeks to evolve new communities: housing societies, literary associations, book clubs, drama groups. And modernity also evolves institutional solutions to the new crisis emanating from the breakdown of the family support system, or the loneliness/suffering of old people. We see growth of 'old age ashrams', or 'boarding schools'. Yet, despite these modern solutions, there remains a deep-rooted feeling of an absence: absence of a real, living, intimate community. At times, this search leads to a mythical construction of 'lost homes' – the ideal village! Many great Indian minds – from Gandhi to Tagore – often thought of this village, and contrasted its beauty and naturalness from the artificial/contractual relationships prevalent in modern cities. And even today during the festivals – *Holi, Eid,* or *Diwali* – one notices the search for this home: people working in cities go back to their ancestral villages: their 'real' homes to celebrate the festive moments. Or, as we are seeing in our times, Hindi films try to reconstruct the 'homeland' for the rootless NRIs! The point we are trying to state is that there is suffering and anguish of the soul – the search for something which has been lost (or something which possibly never existed). Possibly it is this anguish that is often exploited by the fundamentalist politics that wants to go back to the 'roots', and seeks to overcome the 'corrupting' influences of modernity!

Technology, it is said, liberates us. It frees us from the hardship of manual labour, brings comforts and makes life easy, smooth and efficient. But then, if we think deeply we feel that it also oppresses us. It oppresses us in the sense that it causes excessive indulgence, makes us terribly dependent on the ever-changing needs it creates, and hence paralyses many important human faculties. Take, for instance, the entry of the ever-expanding technological devices in our everyday life. Instead of evolving a creative relationship with these devices, we tend to become terribly dependent on them. Technology, in fact, evolves its own logic to which we are almost compelled to submit. Progress means getting adjusted to the technological rationale rather than allowing it to listen to our inner voices. No wonder, irrespective of the socio-political system in which we live, we accept the relative autonomy of technology, and begin to equate, say, 'communication' with internet, television and mobile phone, 'seeing' with video camera, 'movement' with cars, and 'standard of living' with technological comforts. This dependence (and this dependence is legitimated in the name of Science and Progress) tends to make us incapable of evolving an alternative mode of living – say, the ability to derive joy in writing a long/hand-written/intimate letter to a friend, the urge to see the sun-set, the changing colour of the sky while walking in silence, or as what Schumacher would have regarded as the willingness to do 'the kind of work that man enjoys most: creative, useful work with hands and brains' (Schumacher 1983: 126). Indeed, I understand why Theodore Roszack equated the technological society with the world's fair in its last days, 'indefinably sad and shady despite the veneer of orthodox optimism' and exhibiting a 'vale thickness' (Roszack 1972: 64).

In other words, life loses its naturalness; it becomes incapable of seeing beyond a paradigm of technology. Indeed, 'a comfortable, smooth, reasonable, democratic unfreedom', as Herbert Marcuse wrote in his prophetic style, 'prevails in advanced, industrial civilisation, a token of technical progress' (Marcuse 1966: 1). It is the irony of the modern age that man is advised to rediscover this 'naturalness' by experts, councillors, psychiatrist and modern physicians. That is why, we witness the frequent warning: do manual work, go in for yoga, jogging and regular exercise, don't watch too much of television, or otherwise be ready for a high blood pressure, heart disease, diabetes and mental stress. Technology has caused so much indulgence that we now need yet another industry:

'medico-spiritual art of living industry' to teach us the lesson of naturalness! See the suffering. Technology is also making it difficult to live in silence. Man needs silence – contemplative moments to listen to his own inner music. But then, pathos of modernity is that the 'speed, efficiency and technological smartness' seem to kill this silence. How often I have felt terribly sad looking at my young students. With mobile phones they are talking and talking (nobody knows what they are saying). Meanwhile, they miss the poetry all around: a butterfly roaming around, a bird singing, and perpetual hide and seek of the sun in a clouded sky. Or, how tragic it is when I see my colleagues driving their cars to the department, while missing a pleasant 20-minute walk! Or, isn't it sad to see young children using only internet to 'download' the learning material, while missing the opportunity to see and explore the world with their own eyes? Had William Wordsworth been alive today he would have shared his poetry with us to make us awake:

> The world is too much with us; late and soon,
> Getting and spending, we lay waste our powers:
> Little we see in Nature that is ours;
> We have given our hearts away, a sordid boon!
> This sea that bears her bosom to the moon;
> The winds that will be howling at all hours,
> And are up-gathered now like sleeping flowers;
> For this, for everything, we are out of tune;
> *It moves us not ...*
>
> (quoted in Bloom and Trilling 1973: 174)

This seems to be the reason why, despite so many gains of technology, sensitive minds have always warned us of the danger implicit in our excessive dependence on it. Modernity makes us see and adore technological power. Amidst its visibility, bigness and concreteness, seldom do we notice what Schumacher realised with such great sensitivity:

> Strange to say, technology, although of course the product of man, tends to develop by its own laws and principles, and these are very different from those of human nature or living nature in general. Nature always, so to speak knows where and when to stop. There is measure in all natural things – in their size, speed, or violence. As a result, the system of nature of which man is a part, tends to be self-balancing, self-adjusting, self-cleansing. Not so with technology. Technology recognises no self-limiting principle – in terms, for instance, of size, speed, or violence. It therefore does not possess the virtues of being self-balancing, self-adjusting, self-cleansing. In the subtle system of nature, technology, and in particular the super technology of the modern world, acts like a foreign body ... (Schumacher 1983: 122)

Or, as Herbert Marcuse would have argued, technological rationality creates, a totalitarian universe in which there is really no alternative left, because life itself is equated with the gratification of the ever-expanding needs that technology creates. In such an environment 'the people recognise themselves in their commodities; they find their soul in their automobiles, hi-fi set, split level home, kitchen equipment, and social control is anchored in the new needs which it produced' (Marcuse 1966: 91). Yes, these experiences of suffering, some might argue, touch only the intellectual elite, or the poetic tribe; otherwise, people in general seem to be quite happy with modernity – its technological comforts, the opportunities it provides, and its dynamism, speed and efficiency. Furthermore, it is possible to argue that in a country like ours that has yet to receive all the gains of modernity, speaking of its discontents does not make us sense. That is precisely the problem. If modernity becomes too arrogant to listen to its shortcomings, how can it grow, evolve and become truly self-reflexive?

IV
Complex Trajectory of Indian Modernity

When we look at India we see divergent and complex responses to modernity. It is obvious. Modernity seeks to universalise itself, and no society can remain insulated from it: its core ideals and achievements, and its pain and agony. No wonder, there are adherents as well as critics of modernity. Before we reflect on this spectrum of responses, one thing becomes clear to all of us. Ours is a society that has definitely sought to accomplish the modernist agenda. As historians would argue, the intellectual roots of this agenda could be seen in the making of new India itself: the way we encountered colonialism, coped with the West, critiqued some of the oppressive/traditional practices, engaged in the struggle for de-colonisation, marginalised revivalist trends, and evolved a broadly secular/progressive agenda of the freedom struggle which, despite internal differences, celebrated equality, freedom, justice and human dignity (Chandra 1988). The legacy of this historic struggle that caused grand nationalist consciousness could also be seen in the *Constitution* that the new nation chose as its guiding principle. Indeed, the Constitution as the embodiment of our collective aspirations reveals our willingness to embrace the spirit of modernity: say, the republican spirit in political democracy, acknowledgement of the individual and his/her fundamental rights, an independent judiciary to check the abuse of power, directive principles for social welfare and justice, and moreover, a secular ethos that seeks to resist the tyranny of majoritarianism. This modernity was further intensified by divergent 'nation-making' endeavours. The result was the consolidation of huge modern structures in India: the speedy growth of techno-industrial infrastructure which Nehru was fond of regarding as 'temples' of new India, proliferation of scientific/professional institutions and universities, massive network of transportation and communication, expansive army structure, and above all, emergence of a new social class trained in modern knowledge systems, having a 'progressive' orientation to the world. Indeed, the emergent bourgeoisie, the professional middle class and the powerful state celebrating science as the language of development further legitimated modernity as a cherished ideal.

Yes, there was grand expectation from modernity. It was seen as a promise, an emancipator quest for a new world free from traditional/hierarchical structures and stagnant/ritualistic modes of life. Modernity meant reason, science and development – something that we must incorporate in order to embrace the new age. Not surprisingly, Nehru – the architect of new India – pleaded strongly for a modernist project. He seemed to be a strong believer in modernity – its rationality, its scientific spirit, and its development ethos. He saw the devastating consequences of 'the heavy burden of the past'. The condition of 'mental stupor and physical weariness', he didn't hesitate to argue, caused India's degeneration (Nehru 1983: 54). No wonder, he welcomed the new age, the ethos of reason and scientific method, or, as he put it, 'the adventurous and yet critical temper of science, the search for truth and new knowledge, the refusal to accept anything without testing and trial, the capacity to change previous conclusions in the face of new evidence' (ibid.: 512). Science, for Nehru, ought to be seen as the 'temper of a free man' that we must cultivate in the new age. It was, therefore, quite natural that Nehru could not always agree with the man he otherwise adored most. Yes, Gandhi's moral/spiritual approach, and his critique of some of the principles and practices of modernity, Nehru wrote in his autobiography, did not appeal to him (Nehru 1984: 504–14). Nehru saw our future in modernity. It may have many problems, but then, it has the capacity to rid itself of those evils. 'We cannot stop the river of change or cut ourselves adrift from it, and psychologically we who have eaten the apple of Eden cannot forget that taste and go back to primitiveness' (ibid.: 511).

Yet, Nehru was immensely romantic. He was willing to 'discover' India: not always as a modern 'modern critic', but as someone eager to understand the mystery of a five thousand year-old civilisation. This negotiation with Indian culture and its enduring civilisational structures somewhat softened his modernity. It made him humble. He could appreciate the philosophic depth of the *Upanishads*, the eternal significance of the *Bhagvadgita,* the wisdom of Buddha, or Gandhi's engagement with the masses. The quest for modernity, he realised, should not make us blind to the depth of our civilisation.

> Behind and within her battered body one could still glimpse a majesty of soul. Despite the woeful accumulations of superstition and degrading custom that had clung to her and borne her down, she had never wholly forgotten the inspiration that some of the wisest of her children, at the dawn of history, had given her in the *Upanishads.* Their keen minds, ever restless and ever striving and exploring, had not sought refuge in blind dogma or grown complacent in the routine observance of dead forms of ritual and creed. They had demanded not a personal relief from suffering in the present or a place in paradise to come, but light and understanding: 'Lead me from the unreal to the real, lead me from darkness to light, lead me from death to immortality'. (ibid.: 429–30)

At this juncture, I wish to make yet another significant point. Nehru's romanticism – or his enthusiasm over the philosophic significance of our great/classical tradition – was not necessarily shared by the victims of history: the marginalised casted and communities. They experienced the hierarchy of caste structure, its trauma and oppression. Any softness, or nostalgic attitude towards our civilisation, they might have feared, would reproduce the hegemony of upper caste Hindu ideology. Possibly this led them to strive for modernity, and modernity alone. Its rational/universal ethos, its egalitarianism, and its doctrine of human rights, it was believed, would pose a meaningful challenge to the age-old religious ideology. Look at, for instance, B.R. Ambedkar's uncompromising modernity, his deep-rooted faith in the Enlightenment doctrine of equality, liberty and fraternity, and hence his vehement critique of the philosophy of Hinduism (Ambedkar 1987). Hinduism, as he argued, upholds privilege and inequality: it means that each man has his vocation preordained; it has, therefore, no relation to capacity nor to innovation. Hinduism, far from spreading knowledge, is a 'gospel of darkness', it refuses to large section of the population of the light of education; moreover, its textual/scriptural form of learning is old-fashioned; it cannot cope with the new age. In other words, Ambedkar posed a rational/modernist critique of the philosophy of Hinduism. Never did Ambedkar feel comfortable with Gandhi. Gandhi, for him, was old-fashioned, a proponent of the *varna* system, and an enemy of modernity. In machinery and technology Ambedkar saw a new hope for the common man. Gandhi's philosophic critique of modernity made no sense to him.

> Gandhism may well be suited to a society which does not accept democracy as its ideal. A society which does not believe in democracy may be indifferent to machinery, and the civilisation based upon it. But a democratic society cannot. The former may well content itself with a life of leisure and culture for the few and a life of toil and drudgery for the many. But a democratic society must assure a life of leisure and culture to each one of its citizens. If the above analysis is correct then the slogan

> of a democratic society must be machinery, and more machinery, civilisation and more civilisation. Under Gandhism the common man must keep on toiling ceaselessly for a pittance and remain a brute. In short, Gandhism with its call of back to nature means, back to nakedness, back to squalor, back to poverty and back to ignorance for the vast mass of people. (Ambedkar 1998: 148)

In other words, modernity, for Ambedkar and his disciples, must play a historic role in India. It must fight casteism and hierarchy, abolish Hinduism, introduce machinery, technology and science for liberating the toiling masses, and create a just society.

Yes, modernity in India, as I have already indicated, is a fact to reckon with. But then, what kind of modernity is it? Does it fulfil all its promises? Is it like what is broadly known as 'Western modernity' with its technical efficiency, universality and orderly institutional structures? Or, is it chaotic, inefficient, something lagging far behind the developed Euro-American world? True, modernity in India has its own problems and contradictions. We often experience the absence of technical efficiency that a modern society is otherwise proud of. Our banks, hospitals, public institutions and transportation system demonstrate this failure time and again. Institutions collapse; the chaos is all around: when one stands in a long queue in a bank to withdraw money, and discovers with utter dismay that the computer is not working, when doctors fail to entertain patients in a dirty, over-crowded hospital; and when we demonstrate our irresponsibility to public space by reducing it into a sort of garbage. If 'order', 'rational planning' and 'meticulous calculation' characterise the efficiency of modernity, we fail time and again. This failure, every 'modern' Indian feels, is a matter of shame, and a cause of embarrassment, particularly before the foreigner. What would they think of us: our chaotic urban centres, our dirty railway stations, our bad roads? – we often ask with a sense of shame and anxiety. Furthermore, we also notice the absence of what is known as professionalism. A universal scale of achievement based on professional aptitude and merit, it is believed, is often sacrificed, and particularistic criteria based on family/kinship ties acquire undue importance in the selection of teachers, doctors and engineers. Possibly this explains the anguish of a sociologist/historian like Satish Saberwal when he laments that we Indians, because of our confinement to a 'small-scale segmented universe', have proved to be incapable of coping with the requirements of a modern 'mega-society' (Saberwal 1996). Likewise, it is alleged that because of the heavy weight of traditionalism modernity fails to assert itself. If newness and innovation characterise modernity, we are lagging behind. Because India continues to look 'old' and 'traditional'. Even when the 'youthfulness' of new India is seen in select sites in New Delhi,

Bangalore and Chandigarh, you cannot escape the 'old' India – in the streets of Haridwar and Varanasi, in innumerable traditional rituals and customs, in dowry death, female infanticide and caste violence. India has not yet been able to overcome its past. This inertia, it is argued, has done severe damage to our modernity.

In other words, modernity in India has not yet succeeded in presenting itself as 'praise worthy', something that can be compared with 'Western modernity'. This has possibly led a sociologist like Dipankar Gupta to lament, and regard our modernity as 'mistaken modernity' (Gupta 2000). Modernity, for Gupta, is not just about technology and contemporary artefacts. Modernity, he asserts, means 'dignity of the individual, adherence to universalistic norms, elevation of individual achievement over privileges or dis-privileges of birth, and accountability in public life' (ibid.: 2). As far as these deeper meanings of modernity are concerned, we seemed to have failed. Well, there is a move from tradition; but, as Gupta reminds us, we are not yet modern. 'If the clock were to stop here, the final diagnosis would, or rather should, declare India as still un-modern' (ibid.: 3). He sees no hope in the Indian middle class. It may try to project itself as modern or Western, but it is not truly modern or Western. It is just 'Westoxicated'. 'Unlike westernization, which implies the establishment of universalistic norms and the privileges of achievement over birth, westoxication is about superficial consumerist display of commodities and fads produced in the West' (ibid.: 11). Even though he is not romanticising the existing Western society, he does not hesitate to conclude that 'in balance, these societies are preferable because they do not discriminate against individuals the way pre-modern societies and still do' (ibid.: 16). Gupta wants India to overcome this 'mistaken modernity'. He entertains no ambiguity, and argues that 'there is no alternative but to resolutely press on with the modernist agenda' (ibid.: 13–14).

There is, however, another way of seeing our destiny. It does not necessarily condemn our modernity as 'mistaken'. Instead, it sees the possibility of differences, and reminds us of the specificity of our modernity. For example, modernity in India need not necessarily be seen as an antithesis of tradition. As a matter of fact, traditional symbols, values and structures have been modernised; and modernity itself has reinforced traditions. For instance, caste, far from withering away, has acquired a new political meaning because of modern democracy. Or, to take yet another illuminating example, Gandhi's life demonstrated how the traditional ideal of a renouncer could be experienced in a modern mass movement. Likewise, modern modes of transportation and communication have intensified religious festivals and pilgrimage. In other words, we see the continual interplay of tradition and modernity (Rudolph and

Rudolph 1967). This distinctiveness of our modernity, it is argued, needs to be appreciated. We need not to feel apologetic if our society does not resemble what the West regards as modernity. In fact, Yogendra Singh has argued, the 'historicity of modernisation' is a fact to reckon with (Singh 1996: 213–15). It should not be forgotten that between tradition and modernity 'a selective process of assimilation and syncretism' occurs. For example, a person who is well trained in modern role structure with high instrumental value – say, a surgeon or an engineer or a scientist, may be deeply committed to traditional categorical values. Because, as Singh says, 'categorical values enjoy autonomy over the instrumental values' (ibid.: 214). There is, therefore, no escape from 'the diversity in the pattern of modernisation in different societies'.

Yes, modernity in India has its specificity and uniqueness. But then, we should also be careful enough: we need not feel excessively proud of it. In fact, our modernity also has immense problems. How often we have seen that mobilisation of caste for a supposedly radical purpose like 'empowerment' has caused tension-ridden, violent and exclusivist identity politics. We also have seen how at times the doctrine of nationalism and the tyranny of majoritarianism have become almost inseparable. And even though our modernity, as the matrimonial columns suggest, has not destroyed the practice of arranged marriages, we are also witnessing the resurgence of dowry, and an unholy alliance of patriarchy and consumerism. True, we need not find solutions in what is being loosely regarded as a standardised/universal Western modernity. But we have to acknowledge the problems with our own modernity, and think of more innovative and sensitive solutions.

But before we explore these possibilities, it is important to understand that there is also a critical voice amongst us that dislikes the idea of modernity itself, and critiques it relentlessly. They are not-old fashioned traditionalists who regard modernity as an immoral/materialistic/hedonistic life-practice. As a matter of fact, these critics include sophisticated social scientists and refined thinkers. They see the principle of colonial aggression in modernity: the way it annihilates alternative traditions through the ideology of nationalism, scientific planning and mythology of progress (Madan 1983; Nandy 1987). They see the essential dualism in modernity, and resultant violence (Uberoi 2002). Modernity is being alleged as elitist and anti people. This sort of 'post-colonial' critique of modernity is also being supported by those who speak subaltern movements: the movements that seek to recover local traditions, indigenous knowledge and subdued/forgotten memories and histories. While modernity is centralising, these critics plead for fragments and differences (Chatterjee 1994). Not surprisingly, nationalism, state, science, development – all grand ideals, of modernity are suspected. Indeed, we see an assertion of an intellectual milieu characterised by post-colonialism, postmodernism and some sort of reinterpreted Gandhism (Pathak 1998).

It is not difficult to understand this critique. Because modernity, as we have analysed, is a complex phenomenon. It has its achievements, promises and possibilities. And it has its own history of pain, agony and suffering. Modernity is bound to have its adherents as well as its critics. We have to live with this complexity. We have to learn perpetually from the tension and ambiguity, and create a more humane world. One thing is, however, clear. There is no way we can negate modernity completely; the logic of history would not allow it to happen. Furthermore, we are at a stage of evolution when it is no longer possible to live without some of the gains of modernity – its core values, its democratic ethos, or some of its technological achievements. Yet, self-reflexivity demands that we keep our eyes open, explore better possibilities and retain the courage to innovate. We need not become prisoners of modernity. It is in this context that, I believe, we can learn a couple of lessons from what is being loosely regarded as 'Indian thinking' emanating from visionaries like Sri Aurobindo and Gandhi. This does not mean that we succeed in arriving at immediate and instant alternatives. Possibly we continue to live with our ambiguities. Yet, we must keep this reflexivity alive. Only then it is possible to innovate, and make our contribution to the making of a more humble, dialogic and life-affirming modernity.

First, I wish to recall the lesson we can learn from Sri Aurobindo's profound analysis of the 'curve of the rational age' (Aurobindo 1977: 180–207). Yes, it was the 'revolt of reason' in a modern society that caused one of its remarkable achievements: the creation of individualistic democratic ideal. It was believed that the autonomous individual could question, interrogate and choose his/her own destiny. But then, reason alone could not create an ideal order. We saw the conflict between the powerful and the powerless; in real terms, individualistic democracy meant, as Sri Aurobindo felt, 'the role of a dominant class over the ignorant, numerous and less fortunate mass' (ibid.: 185). Possibly this discontent led to yet another manifestation of reason: the ideal of democratic socialism. It was, however, no less problematic. It too degenerated onto a 'collective mystique'. We saw 'a rapid crystallization of the social, economic, political life of the people into a rigid organisation' leading to 'a complete unanimity of mind, speech, feel, life' (ibid.: 193). The massage, for Sri Aurobindo, was clear enough. Even though the age of reason as an advance upon the comparative immobility of 'infrarational' societies, it could not arrive at perfection by its own methods, because 'reason is neither the first principle of life, nor can be its last, supreme and sufficient principle' (ibid.: 202). It is high time we realise that no machinery invented by reason could perfect either the individual or the collective man. Neither the market nor the state – the twin symbols of modern/rational age – can replace what is urgently needed: man's inner transformation. Each of us ought to realise the source/inspiration behind an ideal/harmonious society: 'the spiritual comradeship of oneness'. Only then it is possible to transcend the conflict between the individual and the collective, and realise the shared divinity that arouses love, brotherhood and solidarity.

> The solution lies not in reason but in the soul of man, in its spiritual tendencies. It is a spiritual, an inner freedom that alone creates a perfect human order. It is a spiritual, a greater than the rational enlightenment that can illuminate the vital nature of man and impose harmony on its self-seekings, antagonisms and discords. (ibid.: 206)

It is, indeed, true that the central thrust of modernity is towards the mastery of the outer world. It knows how to tap natural resources, create technologies, and evolve mechanical structures to fit the world into its cognitive map. It overemphasised the role of its scientific/bureaucratic machinery, its market and technology. This excessive inclination to the outer world is like over-emphasising the vital/physical aspect of the human being. It is filled with terrible *rajasic* energy. But in the process it seems to have forgotten the higher ideal of calmness, inner transformation and spiritual evolution. That is the crisis of modernity. And, for Sri Aurobindo, it is high time we realise the need of 'the inward view of the East which bids man seek the secret of his destiny and salvation within' (ibid.: 250–51). This spiritual evolution, or this new journey beyond the age of reason does by no means negate the achievements of Western modernity. Because, as Sri Aurobindo repeatedly emphasised, for the pioneers of the new age, nothing would be alien to them, nothing would be outside their scope.

> For every part of human life has to be taken up by the spiritual – not only the intellectual, the aesthetic, the ethical, but the dynamic, the vital, the physical; therefore for none of these things or activities that spring for them will they have contempt or aversion, however they may insist on a change of the spirit and a transmutation of the form. (ibid.: 251)

Essentially, this meant a new way of seeing, living and experiencing – a radical shift from the age of reason to the spiritual age. Indeed, amidst the noise of the triumphant modernity, it is important to retain a zone of silence, undertake a journey to the inner world, see beyond the stumbling intellectual reason, and experience the light of what the saint regarded as the 'luminous intuitive super-mind'.

Perhaps this discussion would remain incomplete unless you and I recall Gandhi. Yes, it is quite easy to come to an instant conclusion that

Gandhi, despite the historic role he played in our freedom struggle, was old-fashioned: someone who could not fit well into the ethos of the new age. Indeed, his insistence on ascetic principles, his inclination to the centrality of the village in our socio-economic life, and his discomfort with modern machine, railways and the legal system might give the impression that Gandhi is irrelevant. As I have already indicated, even Nehru – the disciple and admirer of Gandhi – could not resist expressing his disagreement. He did not seem to feel comfortable with Gandhi's blueprint, his 'glorification of poverty and suffering'. But then, my point of departure is different. What I wish to argue is that it is important to learn from his spirit, not to get obsessed with external forms and symbols. It is desirable to learn from this sprit, use it creatively and alter the trajectory of the prevalent form of modernity. It is in this context that I would make two points.

First, Gandhi's notion of *swaraj* is immensely illuminating. He wanted us to regain the power of 'soul-force', and become independent of the huge techno-economic enterprise of modernity. We have seen how modernity elevates the power of the techno-scientific structure and the nation-state. It is our contention to deny that these modern structures have made our life easier. But then, these very structures, as we have indicated, have also led to an 'iron cage' or an 'administered totality' that tends to paralyse our own agency and reflexivity. In other words, we become increasingly dependent on the 'expertised' solutions emanating from the techno-bureaucratic elite. This, as Gandhi worried, had belittled man. If I have a problem with my neighbour, I am now incapable of negotiating and arriving at a solution. Instead, I become more and more dependent on an anonymous/impersonal legal structure: its lawyers and courts.

> If people were to settle their own quarrels, a third party would not be able to exercise any authority over them. Truly, men were less unmanly when they settled their disputes either by fighting or by asking their relatives to decide for them. They became more unmanly and cowardly when they resorted to the courts of law. It was certainly a sign of savagery when they settled their disputes by fighting. Is it any the less so, if I ask a third party to decide between you and me? Surely, the decision of a third party is not always right. The parties alone know who is right. We, in our simplicity and ignorance, imagine that a stranger, by taking our money, gives us justice. (Gandhi 1989: 51)

Likewise, if I fall sick, I am incapable of looking after myself, and altering my life-project. Instead, I begin to rely more and more on the medical expert. Indeed, 'the doctors induce us to indulge, and the result is that we have become deprived of self-control, and have become effeminate' (ibid.: 53–54). Gandhi sought to alter it. He thought that we must cultivate our 'soul force' – our moral/spiritual power – to revitalise ourselves, our villages, and our communities. In a way, Gandhi's notion of swaraj was far deeper, not just the replacement of one kind of authority by the other.

Second, Gandhi felt that the modern civilisation was based on the centrality of *desire*. It cultivates and stimulates man's desire for the ever-expanding needs and never-ending comforts. This causes perpetual restlessness for more and more.

> We notice that the mind is restless bird; the more it gets the more it wants, and still remains unsatisfied. The more we indulge our passions the more unbridled they become. Our ancestors, therefore, set a limit to our indulgences. They saw that happiness was largely a mental condition. A man is not necessarily happy because he is rich, or unhappy because he is poor. Observing all this, our ancestors discarded us from luxuries and pleasures. (ibid.: 55).

Even though it is naive to imagine that we can go back to the world in which our ancestors lived, the essence of what he was saying needs to be understood. This excessive desire, we should not forget, has two disastrous consequences: *(a)* it deprives one of evolving a zone of peace, and *(b)* it violates the ecological principle: a harmonic engagement between man and nature. Gandhi critiqued this 'immoral' or 'satanic' force which contemporary critics often regarded as the seduction of consumer culture. He was thinking of a life: truly independent in the sense that it is not a slave of desire. This is possibly the other meaning of *ahimsa*. Yes, modernity has indeed done a lot of good things; but it has also caused severe damage to our life and environment. We moderns would lose nothing except our arrogance if we learn a couple of lesions from Gandhi's visionary insight.

V
Realm of Possibilities

Am I expecting the impossible? It may be alleged that while I wish to get all good things of modernity, I seek to avoid its negative consequences. It may be argued that if I adopt the spirit of freedom, individuation and critical consciousness, I must be willing to pay a price – an experience of homelessness, or alienation from the community. Or, if I wish to be benefitted by science and technology, I must be ready to accept the inevitability of power – the power emanating from the specialised discourse of scientists and technocrats. Yes, I am aware of the complexity of living; nothing is possible to achieve without bearing some of its unintended consequences. Yet, I would argue that with sufficient self-reflexivity it is possible to have a more creative mode of living and a network of social institutions.

It is in this context that I wish to speak of the possibility of transcending the duality of freedom and relatedness, rebellion and love, and individual and community. As I have already stated, a major achievement of modernity is that it inspires us to privilege the spirit of freedom: the criticality to question and interrogate. But then, this quest need not necessarily be seen as an expression of duality: my science vs. their religion, my rationality vs. their communitarianism, my progressiveness vs. their conservatism. I critique and resist, but my criticality is not necessarily hostility; it can be an urge to involve even those I am revolting against, and to try – as collective subjects – to alter the world. In other words, criticality can also be experienced as a dialogic engagement; freedom can be seen as higher form of relatedness, and individuality as an articulation of an enriched community. Kabir, for instance, critiqued orthodoxy; he did not become an alien outsider; he became everybody's Kabir. Gandhi's 'experiments' did not prevent him from remaining a Hindu. And even young Marx saw communism as a transcendence of all dualities.

> It is the genuine resolution of the conflict between man and nature and between man and man – the true resolution of the strife between existence and essence, between objectification and self-conformation, between freedom and necessity, between individual and the species. (Marx 1977: 97)

This is what I regard as an urge to *spiritualise* modernity. We should not negate it as merely utopian. Instead, we must try to live, and experience it. I believe that a new sensitivity is evolving, and it is nice to see Roy Bhaskar – the proponent of critical realism – striving for the same experience:

> Now if you take the ideal from Mahayana Buddhism of the Bodhisattva, he may be the most realised human being but he will postpone his enlightenment, his own bliss, his own *nirvana* until the realisation of every other being in the world. That is very similar to the standpoint of Marx – and Marx was an atheist – when he said that in a communist society the free development of each would be the condition of the free development of all. In other words, your well being, your flourishing was the condition of mine. That is also precisely the standpoint of Buddhism. And if you go into it deeply enough, at some level, this is the standpoint of all great religions and also even political inspirations and aspirations. There is no contradiction between spirituality and radical social change. (Bhaskar 2002: 301)

Likewise, it is important to see beyond scientism and relativism. And I would argue that is possible. Yes, I have already spoken of the danger of scientism. I am also aware that contemporary postmodernism delegitimises science and celebrates multiplicity of narratives without privileging any of these as the master truth. Possibly there is an element of relativism in the postmodern doctrine of heterogeneity. But then, the point I am trying to put forward is that it is possible as well as desirable to affirm science in its appropriate context without being indifferent to other possibilities in different domains. Let me give an example. Once I met with an accident, and my right elbow was displaced and severely fractured. I chose to consult a modern orthopaedic surgeon. I legitimated his scientific knowledge of complex surgery, because I did not believe that the other traditions like *unani* or *ayurveda* could have helped me. But then, I am aware that there are contexts in which alternative medicines work, and work brilliantly. So, while I can safely go to an orthopaedic surgeon for a complex elbow surgery, I can listen to immensely devotional *bhajan* songs to relax my mental stress, and take *tulsi* and *neem* to save myself from common cold and fever. In other words, it is possible to live while creating multiple sites for diverse traditions. Modernity then becomes humble, open and inclusive – not something characterised by the certainty/dogma/hegemony/of modern science.

All this implies that I am speaking of the ability to distinguish *enabling* technology from a ruthlessly technologised culture. I would give an example from my own experiential domain. I have not yet bought a car. I do not undermine the significance of cars. I, however, insist that the idea that every middle-class professional must have his own car reflects a culture in which technology tries to salvage the atomised individual. Possibly we need more and more improved modes of transportation and roads that, far from being just car-friendly, are accommodative and allow a dignified space for those who love to walk, or who are fond of bicycles. I would imagine a radical form of urban designing that would not compel one to buy a car. What I wish to suggest is that technologies can be used meaningfully and creatively, and not in a way that non-technical solutions become redundant. It is really sad to see that technological indulgence has acquired such intensity that we now need yet another form of bureaucratic/legal control – say, the ban on use of mobile phones at schools. Why should we allow ourselves to reach such a stage? Mobile phones can be used by a doctor, by a police official, or sometimes even by ordinary people like us for absolutely emergency needs. But when a school kid cannot imagine his existence without it, when television channels receive nothing but SMS messages from the viewers, and when in application forms one is asked to give one's mobile number, one realises that technology, far from liberating us, has killed our imagination. Life is essentially a delicate art, not a technological spectacle. And our modernity must learn it.

Let me give yet another example relating to our engagement with nature. Nature is extraordinarily complex – full of ambiguities. Nature is abundantly beautiful. Nature nurtures and sustains us. Nature arouses poetry and adoration – a sense of humility, and an urge to pray. I often recall the *Vedic* hymns, and experience the beauty of this enchantment.

> Upward, O Agni, rise thy flames, pure and resplendent, blazing high. *Thy lustres, fair effulgences.* (RV.VIII: 44.17)
>
> Bless us with shine, bless us with perfect day light, bless us with cold, with fervent heat and lustre.
>
> *Bestow on us, O Surya, varied riches, to bestow us in our home and when we travel* (RV.X: 37.10)

I am, however, aware that nature is not just beautiful; it is no less violent, unpredictable and destructive. Possibly the very logic of survival has led man to discover the science of conquering nature. It is rather strikingly in the Beconian understanding of nature, in the Cartesian duality of body and mind, and in ruthless technological development. But then, as history suggest, this techno-scientific enterprise often become a monster. It loses control over itself. It seeks to conquer everything. Big dams displace people, industries pollute the environment, and malls colonise the urban space. I am not suggesting that science is unimportant, and we should surrender before nature. But it is definitely possible to have a sense of humility, and relate to nature in a more complex and creative fashion. It is like recognising 'core ecological values' like (a) live in harmony with nature, (b) overcome anthropocentric prejudice, and (c) recognise intrinsic value in beings other than humans (Hayward 1994).

And finally, I wish to speak of participatory institutions. I have already indicated that it is important to acknowledge the crisis emanating from the dynamics of power in modern institutions. Take, for instance, the overwhelming power of schools in modern societies. Schools seek to monopolise the domain of knowledge, and one is almost led to believe that without schools there is no learning. Schools process knowledge and people, school measures one's morality, emotion and cognition; and schools – with their characteristic rituals of examination and time table – have almost absolute control over the child's body and mind. Likewise, modern medicine is yet another discourse of power. Big hospitals with their characteristic anonymity, doctors with their super-specialisation, and sophisticated medical gadgets which perpetually fragment and objectify the human body have made it almost impossible for a patient to have a meaningful engagement with the medical establishment. From the birth of a baby to one's death at the ICU in a mega hospital – everything is now monitored and recorded.

I am not suggesting that these discourses of power are only negative and repressive. There is indeed a positive and productive dimension of power. After all, we know something at schools, and doctors do cure us. But then, it is possible to restructure these institutions. One way of doing it is to introduce a great deal of freedom and choice. And then, as Leo Tolstoy imagined, 'the school will, perhaps, not be a school as we understand it – with benches, blackboards, a teacher's or professor's platform – it may be a panorama, a theatre, a library, a museum, a conversation' (Tolstoy 1967: 15). Likewise, doctors would begin to combine the technicality of medicine and the art of human conversation to evolve a more integral practice of healing, and patients would overcome their stigmatised identities and acquire a meaningful voice in deciding the way they wish to live and die. This is to strive for more participatory, humane and dialogic institutions.

This journey to a decentralised, ecological, humane, reflexive and humble modernity need not be seen as utopian. Yes, it is exceedingly challenging task. But it is not impossible, provided we want it with absolute zeal and sincerity. What else is modern, if not the enthusiasm to experiment and innovate?

References

Ambedkar, B.R. 1987. *Philosophy of Hinduism* (Dr. Ambedkar's Writings and Speeches, Vol. III). Government of Maharashtra: Education Department.

——. 1998. 'Gandhism: The Doom of the Untouchables', in Fred Dallmayr and G.N. Devy (eds), *Between Tradition and Modernity: India's Search for Identity: A Twentieth Century Anthology*, New Delhi: Sage Publications.

Aurobindo, Sri. 1977. *The Human Cycle: The Ideal of Human Unity, War and Self-Determination*. Pondicherry: Sri Aurobindo Ashram.

Bauman, Z. 1987. *Legislators and Interpreters: On Modernity, Post-Modernity and Intellectuals*. Cambridge: Polity Press.

Berger, Peter L., Brigitte Beger and Hansfried Kellner. 1979. *The Homeless Mind*. New York: Penguin Books.

Bhaskar, R. 2002. *From Science to Emancipation: Alienation and the Actuality of Enlightenment*. New Delhi: Sage Publications.

Bloom, H. and L. Trilling (eds) 1973. *Romantic Poetry and Prose*. New York: Oxford University Press.

Bolock, R. and K. Thompson (eds) 1992. *Social and Cultural Forms of Modernity*. Cambridge: Polity Press.

Chandra, B. 1988. *Indian National Movement: The Long-Term Dynamics*. New Delhi: Vikas Publishing House.

Eisenstadt, S.N. (ed.) 1987. *Patterns of Modernity*, Vol. 1. London: Frances Printer.

Feyerabend, P. 1978. *Science in a Free Society*. London: Verso.

Foucault, M. 1982. *Discipline and Punish: The Birth of the Prison*. Middlesex: Penguin Books.

Gandhi, M.K. 1989. *Hind Swaraj or Indian Home Rule*. Ahmedabad: Navajivan Publishing House.

Giddens, A. 1990. *The Consequences of Modernity*. Cambridge: Polity Press.

Gupta, D. 2000. *Mistaken Modernity: India between Worlds*. New Delhi: Harper Collins.

Hayward, Tim. 1994. *Ecological Thought: An Introduction*. Cambridge: Polity Press.

Inkels, A. 2000. 'Making Men Modern: On the Causes and Consequences of Individual Change in Six Developing Countries', in J.T. Roberts and A. Hite (eds), *From Modernization to Globalization: Perspectives on Development and Social Change*, Oxford: Blackwell.

Kakar, S. 1981. *The Inner World: A Psycho-analytic Study of Childhood and Society in India*. New Delhi: Oxford University Press.

Lerner, D. 2000. 'The Passing of Traditional Society', in J.T. Roberts and A. Hite (eds), *From Modernization to Globalization: Perspectives on Development and Social Change*, Oxford: Blackwell.

Madan, T.N. 1983. *Culture and Development*. New Delhi: Oxford University Press.

Marcuse, H. 1966. *One Dimensional Man: Studies in the Ideology of Advanced Industrial Society*. Boston: Beacon Press.

Marx, Karl and Frederick Engels. 1975. *Manifesto of the Communist Party*. Moscow: Progress Publishers.

Marx, K. 1977. *Economic and Philosophic Manuscripts of 1844*. Moscow: Progress Publishers.

Nandy, A. 1983. *The Intimate Enemy: Loss and Recovery of Self under Colonialism*. Delhi: Oxford University Press.

—. 1987. *Traditions, Tyranny and Utopias: Essays in the Politics of Awareness*. New Delhi: Oxford University Press.

Nehru, J. 1983. *The Discovery of India*. New Delhi: Jawaharlal Nehru Memorial Fund.

—. 1984. *An Autobiography*. New Delhi: Jawaharlal Nehru Memorial Fund.

Nisbet, R. 1967. *The Sociological Tradition*. London: Heinemann.

Packard, V. 1982. *The Hidden Persuaders*. New York: Penguin Books.

Pathak, A. 1998. *Indian Modernity: Contradictions, Paradoxes and Possibilities*. New Delhi: Gyan Books.

——. 2002. *Social Implications of Schooling: Knowledge, Pedagogy and Consciousness*. New Delhi: Rainbow.

——. 2004. 'Teaching/Learning Sociology: A Critical Engagement with Modernity', *Sociological Bulletin*, 59 (1): 31–48.

Pusey, M. 1987. *Jurgen Habermas*. Chichester: Ellis Horwood Ltd.

Roszak, T. 1972. *Where the Wasteland Ends: Politics of Transcendence in Postindustrial Society*. New York: Doubleday and Company.

Rudolph, L.L. and S.H. Rudolph. 1967. *The Modernity of Tradition: Political Development in India*. Chicago: The University of Chicago Press.

Saberwal, S. 1996. *Roots of Crisis: Contemporary Indian Society*. New Delhi: Sage Publications.

Said, E. 1973. *Orientalism*. London: Routledge and Kegan Paul.

Sarkar, S. 1985. *A Critique of Colonial India*. Calcutta: Papyrus.

Schumacher, E.F. 1983. *Small is Beautiful: A Study of Economics as if People Mattered*. London: Abacus.

Singh, Y. 1996. *Modernisation of Indian Tradition*. Jaipur: Rawat Publications.

Tolstoy, L. 1967. *On Education*. Chicago: The University of Chicago Press.

Uberoi, J.P.S. 2002. *The European Modernity: Science, Truth and Method*. New Delhi: Oxford University Press.

5

Transmodernity, Postnational and Post-ethnic Transformations

ANANTA KUMAR GIRI

To our dialogue on modernity and ethnic processes in India, I wish to bring in this essay such wider and inter-linked issues of theory and practice such as transmodernity, postnational and postethnic transformations. Ethnic mobilisation in India, especially in the North-East, has followed the modernist logic of nation-state and has struggled for carving out sovereign nation-states as in the case of ULFA in Assam and various groups in Manipur and Nagaland (cf. Prabhakara 2012). There is not only anti-foreigner agitation in Assam but anti-nontribal agitation in many areas of the North-East. As Gurudas Das writes: 'The fear of being swept over by non-tribal, ala Tripura, has led the tribal groups in Meghalaya, Nagaland, Mizoram and Arunachal Pradesh to pose a violent anti-nontribal position which keeps inter-ethnic schism to dominate the social space' (2012: 151). Das also tells us: 'Much of the demand for political autonomy by the minority ethnic groups would have withered away had democracy worked at the grass-roots level. Thus, it is a far better option to make democracy work at the grass-roots level so that grievances for minorities could be attended through the foundation of local self-government' (ibid.: 151–52).[1] North-East is the home of the sixth schedule and the Autonomous Council[2] mode of local organisation but these do not have the necessary financial autonomy. Much of the secessionist problem in North-East can be transformed if units of governance had financial power over resources. Instead of revenues from resources first going to the Centre and then the Centre dolling out developmental packages; if the units of governance starting from Panchayats had financial power and then they were paying from bottom up rather than following the centralised financial apparatus, we would not have such violent local and ethnic mobilisations against Indian state over secession and alleged discrimination and step-motherly attitude. This then calls for transforming the working of the State – its financial architecture and the discourse and practice of sovereignty.

There is an integral link between modernity and nation-state and Europe, the dominant home of both, in recent times is painfully part of post-national transformations such as the rise and functioning of European Union (cf. Habermas 2010). To transform the predicament of modernity and entrenched boundaries of both state and ethnicity, we can fruitfully engage ourselves with discourses and practices such as transmodernity (to be presented shortly) and post-national transformations. In our parts of the world, SAARC, ASEAN could have done much towards post-national transformation in South and East Asia with transformation in both India and China. Here in the North-East, along with creative mobilisation of institutions of local democracy, such trans-national and post-national initiatives such as 'Bay of Bengal Initiative for Multi-Sectional Technical and Economic Co-operation,' 'Bangladesh, Bhutan, Dhaka and Nepal Growth Triangle,' 'The Mekong-Ganga Initiative,' and 'The Kunming Initiative' can help us realise peace and prosperity in the region as well as create post-national institutions for sharing of resources.[3] In this context, India's Look East policy has to be much more than a policy facilitating global flow of capital, it has to initiate people-to-movements as well as transformation of nation-state in the countries of the region such as India and China.

In this context of the predicament of the present and the challenges of the future, we should not forget our complex past of interaction and flows. The present-day ethnic mobilisation in North-East is many a time is accentuated by an ideology of by cultural separatism. It is in this context, we should never forget that North-East India, as part of India, *Bharatavarsha*, in her complex journey of pluralisation, was a land of multi-directional cultural exchange and flows. As B.P. Singh writes: 'The Mongoloid cultural values and ways of life greatly contributed towards a liberalization in the orthodoxy of Hinduism. The Tantric form of worship, which originated in North-East India was a reminder of the fusion between Hinduism and tribal animism' (1987: 32). Singh also tells that the people of the hills and the people in the plains were in interaction through marriage networks and markets.

Beyond Modernity and Ethnicity: Transmodernity

Transmodernity is a concept offered by Latin American philosopher Ernique Dussel (2010) which is different from postmodernity.

Transmodernity refers to creative engagement with both tradition and modernity going beyond the limits of both. Postmodernity continues the Eurocentric bias of modernity but transmodernity emerges from those cultures which are outside the Euro-American imperium. They might have been colonised by the Euro-American processes of colonisation but they were not annihilated by it. Transmodernity builds on the 'unsuspected cultural richness, which is slowly revived like the flames of the fire of those fathoms buried under the sea of ashes from hundreds of years of colonialism' (Dussel 2010: 14). Transmodernity refers to 'a process of rebirth, searching for new paths for future development.' In transmodernity, cultures respond from the 'perspective of their own cultural experiences ... and therefore have the capacity to respond with solutions which would be absolutely impossible for an exclusively modern culture' (ibid.). For Dussel, 'A future trans-modern culture - which assumes the positive moments of Modernity ... will have a rich plurivocity' and would be at the front of inter-cultural dialogue.[4]

If ethnicity is linked to modernity and nation-state, then the rise of transmodern has implication for rethinking ethnicity. It can also lead to post-ethnic consciousness where ethnic groups are not just interested in maintaining their boundaries but in boundary-crossing inter-cultural dialogues and communication (cf. Barth 1969).[5] Transmodernity involves creative memory work and here ethnic mobilisation can take the form of creative retrieval and reconstitution of memory such as building local museums and preserving and developing local knowledge which again can cut across ethnic boundaries while presenting uniqueness of groups involved.

Transmodernity and Transformation of State: The Calling of Post-National Transformations

Transmodernity has the potential to transform the existing linkage between ethnicity, modernity and nation-state. It calls for going beyond the logic of sovereignty not only at the level of nation-state but also at the level of self and ethnicity. It pleads for practice of shared sovereignties as well as realise the integral dimension of non-sovereignty to any claim for sovereignty (see Dallmayr 2005; Giri 2009). Post-national transformation thus involves new political organisation and imagination. In the context of India, South Asia and the world, it is facilitated by grass-roots democratisation and genuine decentralisation as well as by cross-state collaborations.

Transmodernity and post-national transformations involve a new art of border-crossing and integration (Giri 2011). In stead of centralised political integration, it calls for a new art of weak and gentle integration

(Giri 2010). It calls for a new organic integration rather than continuing the political project of mechanical integration in modernity. If earlier both ethnic mobilisation and statist mobilisation were based upon models of strong integration, transmodernity and communicative ethnic mobilisations call for a new art of weak and gentle integration involving both weak nationalism and weak ethnicity. Such a new art of border-crossing and integration is now urgent in the context of challenges to both nation-state and statist models of ethnic mobilisation coming from processes such as climate change. Climate change has put pressure on all of us in terms of a new art of survival and transformation which call for new art of sharing of resources and sovereignties. For this, there is need for greater creative collaboration across state and ethnic boundaries.[6] Transmodernity and post-national and post-ethnic transformations can facilitate this.

Notes

1. Das here further writes: 'As the demand for political autonomy by ethnic minorities often results from non-mitigation of a set of grievances, for example, reservation of jobs, recognition of a dialect/language, political representation, and so on, the state can resolve the autonomy issue by negotiating the demands of minorities within the existing framework. Moreover, creation of an upper chamber of the state legislature and accommodation of the representatives of ethnic minorities in it might be another option for the multiethnic states in the NER to promote the politics of inclusion' (2012: 152).
2. As Das tells us: 'Formation of Autonomous Council under the Sixth Schedule of the Indian Constitution has successfully restored peace in Tripura and prevented escalation of violence in Assam and Meghalaya. Use of this tool in Manipur may provide a clue to the resolution of Meitei-Naga conflict in Manipur where Nagas residing in the hills aspire to merge with their brethren in Nagaland and Meities aspire to protect the historically evolved territorial integrity of the state. [..] Devolution and decentralisation of state power is a better option than suppressing the autonomy aspiration of the minorities that may result into long-drawn bloody civil war for secession or separation. [..] However, as the NER is the home of innumerable ethnic categories, Sixth Schedule type federal solution also bears the probable danger of social disintegration' (2012: 151).
3. About Bay of Bengal Initiative for Multi-Sectoral Technical and Economic Cooperation (BIMSTEC), Das writes: 'The launching of the BIMSTEC in 1997, involving Bangladesh, India, Myanmar, Sri Lanka, and Thailand

and subsequently joined by Myanmar, Nepal, and Bhutan, has a profound development and security implications for the NER. BIMSTEC is the first grouping of its kind in which two ASEAN members have come together with five countries from South Asia to form an association for economic cooperation. The forum aims at utilising the untapped resource potential in the subregion for mutual benefits' (2012: 32).

4. What Dussel writes in the following paragraph deserves our careful attention in order to understand his concept of Transmodernity: 'Europe began to function as the 'centre' of the world market (and therefore to extend the 'world system' throughout the world) with the advent of the industrial revolution; on the cultural plane, this produced the phenomenon of the Enlightenment, the origins of which, in the long run, we should look for (according to the hypothesis of Morrocan philosopher Al-Yabri, who we will discuss later) in the Averröist philosophy of the caliphate of Córdoba. Europe's crucial and enlightened hegemony scarcely lasted two centuries (1789–1989). Only two centuries! Too short term to profoundly transform the 'ethico-mythical nucleus' (to use Ricoeur's expression) of ancient and universal cultures like the Chinese and others of the Far East (like the Japanese, Korean, Vietnamese, etc.), the Hindustanic, the Islamic, the Russian-Byzantine, and even the Bantu or the Latin American (though with a different structural composition). These cultures have been partly *colonised* (included through negation in the totality, as aspect A of Diagram 1), but most of the structure of their values have been excluded – *scorned, negated and ignored* – rather than annihilated. The economic and political system has been dominated in order to exert colonial power and to accumulate massive riches, but those cultures were deemed to be unworthy, insignificant, unimportant, and useless. The tendency to disparage those cultures, however, has allowed them to survive in silence, in the shadows, simultaneously scorned by their own modernised and westernised elites. That negated 'exterior', that alterity – always extant and latent – indicates the existence of an unsuspected cultural richness, which is slowly revived like the flames of the fire of those fathoms buried under the sea of ashes from hundreds of years of colonialism. That cultural exteriority is not merely a substantive, uncontaminated and eternal 'identity'. It has been evolving in the face of modernity itself; what is at stake is 'identity' in the sense of process and growth, but always as an exteriority.

   These cultures, asymmetrical in terms of their economic, political, scientific, technological, and military conditions, therefore, maintain an alterity with respect to European Modernity, with which they have coexisted and have learned to respond in their own way to its challenges. They are not dead but alive, and presently in the midst of a process of rebirth, searching for new paths for future development (and inevitably at times taking the wrong paths). Since they are not modern, these cultures cannot be 'post'-modern either. They are simultaneously pre-modern (older than modernity), contemporary to modernity, and soon, to Transmodernity as well. Postmodernism is a final stage in modern European/North American culture, the 'core' of modernity. Chinese or Vedic cultures could never be European post-modern, but rather are something very different as a result of their distinct roots.

Thus, the strict concept of the '*trans*-modern' attempts to indicate the radical novelty of the irruption – as if from nothing – from the transformative exteriority of that which is always distinct, those cultures in the process of development which assume the challenges of modernity, and even European/North American post-modernity, but which respond *from another place, another location.* They respond from the perspective of their own cultural experiences, which are distinct from those of Europeans/North Americans and, therefore, have the capacity to respond with solutions which would be absolutely impossible for an exclusively modern culture. A future *trans*-modern culture – which assumes the positive moments of Modernity (as evaluated through criteria distinct from the perspective of the other ancient cultures) – will have a rich pluriversality and would be the fruit of an authentic intercultural dialogue, that would need to bear clearly in mind existing asymmetries (to be an 'imperial-core' or part of the semi-peripheral 'central chorus' – like Europe today, and even more so since the 2003 Iraq War – is not the same as to be part of the postcolonial and peripheral world). But a post-colonial and peripheral world like that of India, in a position of abysmal asymmetry with respect to the metropolitan core of the colonial era, does not for this reason cease to be a creative nucleus of ancient cultural renewal which is decisively distinct from all of the others, with the capacity to propose novel and necessary answers for the anguishing challenges that the planet throws upon us at the beginning of the twenty-first century' (2010: provide page numbers please).

5. In his introduction to his influential book on the subject, Barth does talk about poly-ethnic societies and models of 'political integration' which are 'poly-centric in character' (1969: 16). My proposed pathway of inter-ethnic and post-ethnic communication and collaborative social organisation builds upon such realities and possibilities. It also resonates with Barth's generative view to the analysis: '[..] rather than working through a typology of forms of ethnic groups and relations, we attempt to explore different processes that seem to be involved in generating and maintaining ethnic groups' (ibid.: 10).

6. We all hear about Bangladesh deeply affected by the ensuing climate change. But when it happens, people may have to come to hills but then they may not be welcomed by the people in the hills such as Chittagong Hill Tracts because the nation-state of Bangladesh has applied the same model of statist and ethnic exclusion to the people of CHT that the freedom fighters were fighting against vis-à-vis the state of Pakistan (cf. Mohsin 2001).

References

Barth, Fredrik (ed.) 1969. *Ethnic Groups and Boundaries*. Oslo: Scandinavian University Press.

Dallmayr, Fred. 2005. *Small Wonder: Global Power and its Discontents*. Lanham, MD: Rowman & Littlefield.

Das, Gurudas. 2012. *Security and Development in India's North-East*. Delhi: Oxford University Press.

Dussel, Enrique. 2010. 'Transmodernity and Interculturality: Philosophy of Liberation'. Paper presented at the International Symposium on 'Learning Across Boundaries', University of Luxembourg, June.

Giri, Ananta Kumar. 2010. 'Towards a New Art of Integration'. Paper presented at the International Symposium on 'Learning Across Boundaries', University of Luxembourg, June.

——.2011. 'Towards a New Art of Border-Crossing', *Journal of Indian Council of Philosophical Research*, 36 (3): 109–30.

——. (ed.) 2009. *The Modern Prince and the Modern Sage: Transforming Power and Freedom*. Delhi: Sage Publications.

Mohsin, Amena. 2001. *Rethinking Social Transformation: Criticism and Creativity at the Turn of the Millennium*. Jaipur: Rawat Publications.

Prabhakara, M.S. 2012. *Looking Back into the Future: Identity and Insurgency in Northeast India*. New Delhi: Routledge.

Singh, B.P. 1987. *The Problem of Change: A Study of North-East India*. Delhi: Oxford University Press.

6

Ethnicity, Nationalism and Modernity

Exploring the Linkages

D.V. KUMAR

Ethnicity and nationalism have become quite salient in the recent past in the context of the deepening process of modernisation (modernity in action). What modernity has done, as we shall see, is that it has changed the *nature* and *character* of inter-ethnic cultural differences and made them assume the shape of ethnicity and nationalism. It is not that inter-cultural differences were absent in the pre-modern times. They were very much present then. Whatever conflicts which occurred in the pre-modern times were not viewed as mainly ethnic conflict between rulers, tribes, pastoral and sedentary people and popular uprisings against tyrannical rule were explained in non-ethnic terms. Although there were revolts by ethnically different slaves, they did not proclaim any sovereign rights based on their ethnic identity: instead, they merely demanded more humane treatment. This has changed now. In our contemporary world system, it has been increasingly observed that ethnic and nationalist conflicts have become a major force. One only had to look around to see the enhanced salience of ethnic and nationalist conflicts. The conflicts between Catholics and Protestants in Northern Ireland, the conflicts among the Croats, Serbs and Muslims in Bosnia, the massive genocide in Rwanda and closer home, the continuing tension manifesting itself in conflicts of different kinds in Kashmir all point to the perpetual salience of ethnicity and nationalism. Nationalism and ethnicity continue to remain key categories with which one makes sense of what is happening around us. One of the ugly ways in which nationalism gained scholarly attention in the early 1990s was the Serbian programme of 'ethnic cleansing'. Serbs who had earlier allied themselves with the vision of a multi-ethnic democratic Bosnia-Hercegovina resorted to invocation of ethnic solidarities in the face of civil war and demanded that the Serbs as whole should be willing both to kill and to die for the nation. The events in Yugoslovia are a sufficient indicator of the continued salience of nationalism and ethnicity. Neither ethnic conflicts, nor the discourse of national identified nor the practical power of nationalist mobilisation has seceded into the premodern past despite the confidence of many earlier social scientists (see Debray 1977; Nairn 1975, 1977; Schwartzmantel 1991). We need to understand why this is so and how modernity has become a major factor in explaining away such conflicts.

What is modernity and how does one engage with it, are the questions that have been dealt with elsewhere (Kumar 2008). I would, therefore, refrain from elaborating on it again. However, briefly recapitulating main arguments here, it may be stated that modernity can be looked at in three important ways which are different but not contradictory to one another (Callinicos 1999: 297). First, modernity can be looked as a philosophical idea. As an idea it represents a radical rupture with the past. It privileges progress, science, optimism and universality. It critiques superstitions, blind faiths and pessimism. It encourages us to adopt alternative ways of looking at world and its possibilities. Secondly, modernity can also be looked at as a form of society which would be characterised by distinctive economic, political and social characteristics. Economically, for example, there would be increasing mechanisation of production (use of inanimate sources of energy), a shift from agriculture to industry, growth of urbanisation as workers need to move from place to place where industries are located (Levy 1966). In the social sphere, a modern society has come to be associated with important shifts in values and institutional devices. In terms of value orientations, as Talcott Parsons (1964: 339–57), there would be a shift from particularism to universalism, ascription to achievement and so on. Thirdly, modernity can also be look at as an experience, an experience which is full of contradictions. On the one hand, it promises many things: progress, advancement, removal of ignorance, power, joy, and so on. On the other hand, it seeks to destroy everything we have and known by. It introduces an element of uncertainty, risk and confusion (Berman 1982: 15). Scholars like Riggs would also like to look at modernity as essentially ambivalent. For him modernity combines both positive and negative consequences. In his own words, 'we view 'melodies' as beautiful and 'maladies' as ugly. Yet both apply with equal force to the consequences of modernity' (1998: 270). They are others who, much before Riggs, tried to problematise modernity by focusing on the destructive and alienating consequences of modernity. Be that as it may, we leave it at that as we are here concerned with exploring the linkages between modernity and ethnicity and nationalism.

Before we proceed further, some conceptual clarification may be in order about the two categorical notions we are concerned with, that is, ethnicity and nationalism (and by implication nation). Ethnicity refers to the consciousness of ethnic identity. De Vos and Rose define it as 'subjective, symbolic or emblematic use by a group of people – of any aspect of culture in order to differentiate themselves from other groups' (1975: 16). As Brass says, ethnicity is to ethnic category what class consciousness is to class. As far as nationalism is concerned, Smith offers us a good starting point in this connection. He defines nationalism as, 'an ideological movement for the attainment and maintenance of self-government and independence on behalf of a group, some of whose members conceive it to constitute an actual or potential 'nation' (1983: 171). It is tempting to explain national identities as a transformation of ethnic or cultural similarities wrought by state-building. But there is a crucial difference between them. Nations are primarily and intrinsically political communities, as sources of sovereignty while this is not central to the definition of ethnicities. Nationalism need not be simply seen as a claim of ethnic similarity, but a claim that certain similarities should count as *the* definition of political community. For this reason, nationalism needs boundaries in a way ethnicity does not. Nationalism demands internal homogeneity throughout a putative nation, rather than gradual continua of cultural variation or pockets of sub-cultural destination. Perhaps, most distinctively, nationalists commonly claim that national identities overpower other personal or group identities (such as gender, family or ethnicity) and link individuals directly to the nation as a whole. This is sharply contrary to the way in which most ethnic identities flow from family membership, kinship and membership in intermediate groups. Nations, in short, involve a distinctive new form of group identity or membership. This depends on new forms of collective imagination and also on communicative capacities and social organisational conditions that encourage a sense of identity with large population of distant and largely anonymous others. It also depends crucially on modern ideas of individual equivalence.

Modernity of Nationalism

The discourse on nationalism is distinctively modern, not before the seventeenth century at the most. In the early modern era, the idea of nation as an aggregate of people linked by co-residence or common socio-cultural characteristics took political and cultural connotation in struggles with and between states and over state-building. This led to the distinctively modern invocation of nationalism as 'a theory of political legitimacy, which requires that ethnic boundaries should not cut across political ones and in particular, that ethnic boundaries with a given state – a contingency already excluded by the principle in its general formulation – should not separate the power-holders from the rest' (Gellner 1983: 1). As Kedourie sums up neatly 'that humanity is naturally divided into nations, that nations are known by certain characteristics which can be ascertained and that the only legitimate type of government is national self-government' (1960: 9). It may also be mentioned here that the modern notion of individualism is embedded in the categories of ethnic group and nation. Earlier, in pre-modern times, people were essentially seen as members of social groups by virtue of their occupation of a variety of ascribed statuses based on descent, kinship, age and the like. The modern role of self as individual changed this. Personal identity can be increasingly seen as the attribute of a self-contained individual, what Taylor (1989) called as the 'punctual self'. As Schwarcz wrote about protagonists in China's largely nationalism New Culture movement, 'the alternative to playing the role of so-and-so's son, so-and-so's mother, etc., is to gain a positive sense of one's own individuality' (1986: 112). Such thinkers made it common to understand that social groups (including nations and ethnic groups) as sets of equivalent person rather than webs of relationships and persons as hierarchies of positions. Let us take ethnic group as an illustration. Ekeh (1990) noted that there has been a tendency to replace tribe with ethnic group in the description of countries in Africa. But this has the effect of imposing a categorical notion as a collection of individuals marked by common ethnicity in place of relational one. Where the notion of tribe pointed to the centrality of kin relations, the notion of ethnic group implies that detailed, serious analysis of kinship is more or less irrelevant. Barth (1969) took this a step further and abandoned even the notion of subjective belief in common descent, replacing it with simply the existence of recognised group boundaries. Here the categorical logic achieves complete supremacy. An ethnic group is simply a bounded set of individuals, not necessarily characterised by any internal pattern of relationships, much less one of kinship order. Once ethnic groups are treated in this purely categorical way – as they are in everyday contemporary discourse as well as in academic studies – similarities, rather than relationship, form the definite connection among members. This opens the doors to new members for conformity.

Apart from this, nations are genuinely seen as logical equivalents and themselves as individuals. In Meinecke's words (1970: 89), 'nations are individualities with particular talents and the possibility of exploiting those talents'. Anderson has seized on this aspect of individuality as central to the modern understanding of nation. In his own words, 'the idea of sociological organism moving calendrically through homogenous, empty time is a precise analogue of the idea of the nation, while it is also conceived as a solid community moving steadily down (or up) history' (1991: 26). As stressed by him, the category of nation unites the living and the dead. This is a crucial explanation for why the nation can demand such extraordinary sacrifices and commitments from its members. It joins the biographies of individual persons and of the nation as a whole in a common historical narrative. Not only does the nation locate individual temporarily in relation to past and future generations and in the global context as members of one among many nations, the nation also locates each individual biography as one among the many comparable biographies of the members of the specific nation.

The rise of imperialism, industrialisation, urbanisation, migration and deepened process of democratisation are all viewed as essentially modern processes which have contributed in their own way to the sharpening up of ethnic and nationalist consciousness. Imperialism is inextricably connected with the project of modernity and its decline has been considered as a positive thing. But it must be remembered that the end of imperialism has left many states in a highly disturbed state of affairs. Sharper hostility between ethnic nation and weak states is one of the most conspicuously negative consequences of modernity. The Industrial Revolution and rise of modern empires have led to massive migration of people looking for job opportunities and/or safer places to live away from oppression in their own 'home' states. As a result, interethnic interaction has increased substantially leading at times to friction among them. The groups whose expectations and hopes have not been fulfilled have sought to structure their language of frustration in ethnic and nationalist terms. In the wake of communism's collapse, nationalism and ethnic conflict became the primary issues in the realignment of Eastern European politics and identity. Appeals to the idea of nation organised movements of ethnic separation from Quebec (Birch 1989; Taylor 1992) to the post-colonial states of Africa (Davidson 1992). New nationalisms have proliferated through the developed west (Smith 1981) and attempts are made to decolonise the discourse of nationalism in the Third world and claim it for indigenous movements and meanings (Blaut 1987; Chatterjee 1986).

There is a strong view which sees not only nationalism but nationhood as basically following from rather than shaping the rise of European modernity. Nations are, in this view, produced by the rise of states and/or the capitalist world system. As Giddens puts it, 'by a 'nation', I refer to a collectivity existing within a clearly demarcated territory, which is subject to a unitary administration, reflexively monitored both by the internal state apparatus and those of other state'. A nation, as I use the term here, only exists when a state has a unified administrative reach over the territory over which its sovereignty is claimed' (1984: 116). In his understanding, the relationship between nationalism and ethnicity is more or less coincidental. It is the modern state that defines nationhood, and preexisting ethnic relations are revised either to coincide more or less with its boundaries to constitute the basis of counter-state movement for the formation of new state. Such movements are rooted in power relations, not ethnic solidarities or distinctive per se.

Nationalisms, it must also be mentioned, vary between claims to have superseded traditional identity such as ethnicity by the founding of a free and modern nation and claim to national identity and sovereignty rooted precisely in ancient ethnicity. The paradigmatic contrast of these two forms in the literature on nationalism is that between France and Germany. In both cases historical narratives are mobilised to underpin the nationalist myth. The French narrative traces the nation to a modern act of founding by its members who were not constituted properly French until the radically novel founding. It emphasises the nation-making political form of the republic and the idea of citizenship (Beet 1988). In Germany, nationalist history writing pushes further back in pursuit of a 'naturalising' account of German ethnicity. Germany must be rooted in an 'always already existing' ethnic identity. German nationalists from Herder and Fichte have emphasised ethnic rather the 'political' or 'civic' criterion for inclusion in nation (see Aler 1989; Kedourie 1960). When Renan (1990) described the nation as a 'daily plebiscite' he was not making a universalising statement or offering a definition. He was distinguishing those nations (such as France) that were the result of the free choices of their member from those (such as Germany) whose identity and cohesion are given to their members independently of any voluntary will. Such differences in nationalist narratives have practical consequences. Since voluntary will is so crucial to the narrative of French nationalism, France makes it easier than Germany does for immigrants to attain citizenship.

Nationalism and the Modern Economic Process

Nationalism has come to be closely identified with the massive modern economic changes that have characterised the West to begin with and which later spread to all parts of the world. It has been argued that one can not look at nationalism in isolation from the modern processes which are currently underway (Kumar 2010). According to Gellner, nationalism is inextricably connected to modernity. Though there was a pre-existing ethnicity, it can not adequately explain the renewed salience of nationalism in the modern period. His understanding of nation and nationalism, their birth and growth, has become so powerful and dominant that one can not remain indifferent to it. The most essential point he makes about nationalism is that it is nationalism which leads to nations rather than the other way around. Nations emerge out of the ideology of nationalism. Nationalism invents nations where they already do not exist. The question comes: How does nationalism emerge? Before that what is nationalism for Gellner? One can not but quote him at length on the definition of nationalism. In his own words, 'nationalism is the general imposition of a high culture on society, where previously low had taken up the lives of the majority and in some cases the totality of the population. It means the general diffusion of a school-mediated, academy-supervised idiom, codified for the requirements of a reasonably precise bureaucratic and technological communication. It is the establishment of an anonymous impersonal society, with mutually substitutable atomised individuals, held together above all by a shared culture of this kind, in place of the previous complex structure of local groups, sustained by folk cultures reproduced locally and idiosyncratically by the micro-groups themselves' (Gellner 1983: 57).

Gellner looks at the birth of nationalism in terms of both positive social foundations and, for want of a better term, what can be called negative social foundations. Positively, nationalism is a product of the process of industrialisation. This process requires the development of highly advanced forms of communication as the work to be done is mostly semantic which in turn requires development of standardised means of communication, that is development of a uniform language. A uniform language generates greater cultural identification. In his own words, 'modern people do not in general become nationalists from sentiments or sentimentality atavistic or not, well-based or myth-founded: they become nationalists, through genuine, objective, practical necessity, however obscurely recognized' (Gellner 1964: 160). It could be represented as follows:

Industrialisation ->nationalism->nation

Such a way of looking at the emergence of nationalism is explicitly functionalist in nature. His theory of nationalism is credited with having almost reified functionalism. In fact, Perry Anderson, grandfather of the Marxist New Left, argues that the 'most arresting feature of Gellnerian theory of nationalism is its single-minded economic functionalism' (1992: 207). One could go directly to Gellner and indicate the functionalist cast of his argument in his own words: 'So the economy needs both the new type of central culture and the central State; the culture needs the State and the State probably needs the homogenous cultural branding of its flock. In brief, the mutual relationship of a modern culture and State is something quite new and springs, inevitably, from the requirement of a modern economy' (1983: 48). If one takes this proposition to its logical conclusion, one would arrive at five important formulations (Elster 1983: 135). First, nationalism is inevitably an effect of modernisation. Secondly, nationalism is beneficial for modernising states, because a highly specialised division of labour requires a unified high culture, which is underpinned by a highly developed and specialised educational system. Thirdly, nationalism (in Gellnerian sense) is unintended by the actors producing modernisation. Fourthly, the causal relationship between nationalism and modernisation is not recognised by the agents operating in modernising societies. Lastly, nationalism functionally maintains modernisation by a feedback loop operating through the action of modernising states.

Negatively, the uneven spread of modernisation has a huge potential in generating nationalist aspirations. Uneven modernisation aggravates the existing inequalities among differently placed groups and the intelligentsia from the deprived groups harp on their separate distinctive identity as a means, a weapon in their hands for overcoming the structures of inequality. The result is the birth of nationalist movements. In Gellner's own words, 'nationalism is not the awakening of nations to self-consciousness: it invents nations where they do not exist but it does need some pre-existing differentiating marks to work on, even if these are purely negative' (1964: 168).

It is now a part of his philosophy of history that looks at three important phases in human societies, viz., pre-agrarian, agrarian and industrial. In the pre-agrarian societies it would be senseless to talk of nationalism as there were essentially stateless societies and speaking in terms of nation-state about them would be meaningless. In the agrarian societies, the elites did not share a common culture with masses and in the absence of a common culture, nationalist ideology would have had no basis. The industrial society, on the other hand, needs to have a proper communication among its people which would mean that there has to be a common language to facilitate such a communication.

A nation is, in Anderson's (1991) evocative phrase, an 'imagined community'. He suggests that we regard nationalism as a distinct mode of understanding and constituting the phenomenon of belonging together, comparable to kinship or religion. A nation, thus, 'is an imagined political community. It is imagined because the members of even the smallest nation will never know most of their fellow-members, meet them or even hear of them, yet in the mind of each lives the image of their communion' (ibid.: 6–7). The nation is imagined as linked because even the largest of them, encompassing perhaps a billion living human beings, has finite, if elastic boundaries, beyond which lie other nations. It is imagined as sovereign because the concept was born in an age in which Enlightenment and Revolution were destroying the legitimacy of the divinely-ordained, hierarchical dynastic realm. Finally, it is imagined as a community because regardless of the actual inequality and exploitation that may prevail in each, the nation is always conceived as a deep horizontal comradeship.

In the context of nationalism he offers three main arguments. First, he looks at language as an essentially cultural condition of nationalism. Nationalist imaginings took place through a language. By looking for ever-larger markets, capitalist cultural production (in the form of books and newspapers, a distinctly modern process) called forth 'unified fields of exchange and communication below Latin and above the spoken vernaculars' (ibid.: 44). That is, in early, modern Europe capitalism sought markets larger than the small number of elite readers of Latin and larger than the number of speakers of nearly all local vernaculars. Thus, they pioneered the creation of the specific linguistic communities associated with eventual national ideologies. Secondly, after talking about the role of language in the creation of ethnic foundations for nationalism, Anderson's formulation of 'print-capitalism' also help to make sense of the new kind of imagining of community more directly. The readers of the same novels and newspapers were joined in imaging communities of other such readers and of imaging commonality with protagonists of the stories they read (ibid.: 24–36). The readers of daily newspapers not only learned the same news as each other, they learned 'wholly new ideas of simultaneity' (ibid.: 37). They learned to situate themselves in terms of the activities of many individuals (and nation) taking place in the same temporal moment, not solely in a linear development. This also allowed for a sense of shared paths, which could arise historically only when substantial groups of people were in a position to think of themselves as living lives parallel to those of other groups of people – if never meeting yet certainly proceeding along with same trajectory. Thirdly, the importance of communication media to nation integration has certainly been noted before (see Deutsch 1953). In most earlier treatments, the categorical identity of the nation is preserved and research is focused on how the development of communication capacities enhances the social and political integration of the nation. Anderson's central contribution is to explain how communicative forms figured in creating the categorical identity or imagined community of the nation itself.

Against this backdrop, however, one also needs to be aware of alternative voices. Anthony Smith (1983, 1986 and 1991) argues that nationalism has stronger roots in pre-modern ethnicity. Nations are rooted in relatively ancient histories, though he admits that nationalism, as ideology and movement, dates only from the eighteenth century. Nevertheless, he says that ethnic origins of nations are much older. He argues that 'myths, symbols, memories and values are 'carried' in and by artifacts and activities which change only very slowly, so ethnic, once formed, tend to be exceptionally durable under 'normal' vicissitudes and to persist over many generations, even centuries forming 'moulds' within which all kinds of social and cultural processes can unfold and upon which all kinds of circumstances and pressures can exert an impact' (1986: 16). Rooted in ethnicity, nations are long-term processes, continually reenacted and reconstructed, they require ethnic cores, homelands, heroes and golden ages if they are to survive. Small, breakaway nations rooted in particularist, quasi-religious visions are the most common new nationalist projects today. In his own words, 'modern nations and nationalism have only extended and deepened the meanings and scope of older ethnic concepts and structures. Nationalism has certainly universalised these structures and ideals, but modern 'civic' nations have not in practice really transcended ethnicity or ethnic sentiment' (ibid.: 216).

Smith does not claim that ethnicity is natural, rather socially constructed. His argument is that ethnicity is very slow to change. He acknowledges also that pre-modern ethnic boundaries were no sharply fixed, though he does claim that they maintained a level of integrity. Above all, he suggests that it is possible to trace 'genealogy of nations' in which both cultural and social structural variables can be introduced to account for which ethnies become nations. The crucial moment in such genealogies, he suggests, is that transformation of the members of an ethnie into citizens. This is a cultural transformation of the character of membership, stressing the lateral ties that link members despite class divisions and that form the basis for potential political mobilisation (ibid.: 166). The important point to be remembered is that he stressed continuity in ethnic groupings and the relation of cultural similarity that defines them.

Conclusion

The relationship between nationalism, ethnicity and modernity is highly complex. Both nationalism and ethnicity are very much part of a modern set of categorical identities invoked by elites and other participants in political and social struggles. These categorical identities also shape everyday life offering both tools for grasping preexisting homogeneity and difference and constructing specific versions of such identity. Numerous dimensions of modern social and cultural change, notably state-building, individualism and the integration of large-scale webs of indirect relationship all serve to make both nationalism and ethnicity salient. Nationalism, in particular, remains the preeminent rhetoric for attempting to demarcate political community's claim right of self-determination and legitimate rule by reference to 'the people' of a country in the modern era. Ethnic solidarities and identities are claimed most often where groups do not seek 'national' autonomy but rather a recognition internal to or cross-cutting national or state boundaries. The essential point that emerges from the above discussion is that nationalism and ethnicity are organically connected to the project of modernity.

References

Anderson, B. 1991. *Imagined Communities: Reflections on the Origin and Spread of Nationalism*. London: Verso.

Anderson, P. 1992. 'Science, Politics and Enchantment', in J.A. Hall and I.C. Jarvie (eds), *Transitions to Modernity: Essays on Power, Wealth and Belief*, Cambridge: Cambridge University Press, pp. 202–32.

Alter, P. 1989. *Nationalism*. London: Edward Arnold.

Barth, F. (ed.) 1969. *Ethnic Groups and Boundaries*. Oslo: Scandinavian University Press.

Beet, G. (ed.) 1988. *The Permanent Revolution: The French Revolution and its Legacy*. Chicago: Chicago University Press.

Berman, M. 1982. *All That is Solid Melts into Air: The Experience of Modernity*. London: Verso.

Birch, A.H. 1989. *Nationalism and National Integration*. London: Unwin Hymen.

Blaut, J. 1987. *The National Question: Decolonising the Theory of Nationalism*. Atlantic Highlands, NJ: Zed Books.

Callinicos, A. 1999. *Social Theory: A Historical Introduction*. Cambridge: Polity Press.

Chatterjee, P. 1986. *Nationalist Thought and the Colonial World: A Derivative Discourse*. Atlantic Highlands, NJ: Zed Books.

Chirot, D. (ed.) 1990. *The Crisis of Leninism and the Decline of the Left: The Revolution of 1989*. Seattle: University of Washington Press.

Debray, R. 1977. 'Marxism and the National Question', *New Left Review*, 105: 20–41.

Deutsch, K.W. 1953. *Nationalism and Social Communication: An Inquiry into the Foundations of Nationality*. Cambridge: MIT Press.

De Vos, George and Lola Romanucci-Ross (eds) 1975. *Ethnic Identity: Cultural Continuity and Change*. California: Mayfield Publishing Co.

——. 1969. *Nationalism and its Alternatives*. New York: Knopf.

Elster, J. 1983. *Explaining Technical Change*. Cambridge: Cambridge University Press.

Ekeh, P.R. 1990. 'Social Anthropology and Two Contrasting Uses of Tribalism in Africa', *Comparative Study of Social History*, 32 (4): 660–700.

Gellner, E. 1964. *Thought and Change*. London: Weidenfeld and Nicolson.

——. 1983. *Nation and Nationalism*. Ithaca: Cornell University Press.

Giddens, A. 1984. *The Nation-State and Violence*. Berkeley: University of California Press.

Kedourie, E. 1960. *Nationalism.* New York: Praeger.

——. 1974. *Nationalism in Asia and Africa*. New York: New American Library.

Kohn, H. 1967. *The Idea of Nationalism*. New York: Collier.

Kumar, D.V. 2006. *Modernisation and Ethnicity*. New Delhi: Mittal Publications.

——. 2008. 'Engaging with Modernity: Need for a Critical Negotiation', *Sociological Bulletin*, 57 (2): 240–54.

——. 2010. 'Gellnerian Theory of Nation and Nationalism: A Critical Appraisal', *Sociological Bulletin*, 59 (3): 392–406.

Levy, Jr M.J. 1966. *Modernisation and the Structure of Society*. Princeton, NJ: Princeton University Press.

Meinecke, F. 1970. *Cosmopolitanism and the National State*. Princeton, NJ: Princeton University Press.

Nairn, T. 1975. 'The Modern Janus', *New Left Review*, 94: 3–30.

Parsons, T. 1964. 'Evolutionary Universals in Society', *American Sociological Review*, 29 (3): 339–57.

Renan, E. 1990. 'What is a Nation?', in H. Bhabha (ed.), *Nation and Narrative*, London: Routledge, pp. 8–22.

Riggs, Fred W. 1998. *The Modernity of Ethnic Identity and Conflict*. London: Sage Publications.

Seton-Watson, H. 1977. *Nations and States*. Boulder: Westview Press.

Schwartzmantel, J. 1991. *Socialism and the Idea of the Nation*. Hemel Hempstead: Harvester Wheatsheaf.

Schwarcz, V. 1986. *The Chinese Enlightenment: Intellectuals and the Legacy of the May Fourth Movement of 1919*. Berkeley: University of California Press.

Smith, A.D. 1981. *The Ethnic Revival in the Modern World*. Cambridge: Cambridge University Press.

——. 1983. *Theories of Nationalism*. London: Duckworth.

——. 1986. *The Ethnic Origin of Nation*. Oxford: Blackwell.

——. 1991. *National Identity*. London: Penguin.

Taylor, C. 1989. *The Sources of Self-Knowledge*. Harvard: Harvard University Press.

——. 1992. *The Politics of Recognition*. Princeton, NJ: Princeton University Press.

Weber, E. 1976. *Peasants into Frenchmen*. Stanford: Stanford University Press.

7

Modernity and Ethnicity

An Intersectionality Analysis

V. BIJUKUMAR

The term intersectionality became prominent in the late 1960s and 1970s in connection with the multiracial movements. It was a part of the critique of radical feminism and the emergence of black feminism. The term gained wider currency in the 1990s when sociologist Patricia Hill Collins, reintroduced the idea as part of her discussion on black feminism. According to her the oppression of women in any society was not influenced by only one category - gender - but intersection of multiple categories such as race, gender, class and ethnicity (Collins 1990). Intersectionality is a feminist sociological theory first developed by Kimberle Crenshaw. It analyses the multiple forms of oppression and discrimination faced by women in a society not only gender but also race, class, sexuality, ageism, disability (Crenshaw 1993: 1241–99). According to this view, the complexities of gender as it intersect with race, sexuality, class and caste (in the Indian case). In other words, intersectionality views that social categories such as race, gender, sexuality, class, not only intersect but overlay one another (Weasel 2004: 184). The rationale for the understanding of intersectionality based on the assumption that 'the potential for both multiple and conflicting experiences of subordination and power required a more wide-ranging and complex terrain of analysis (McCall 2005: 1780).

Feminism claimed to speak universally for all women. However, feminist researchers have been actually aware of the limitations of gender as a single analytical category. Intersectionality emerged as a critique of the limitation of gender as a single analytical category in locating women's position in a society. It was a critique of a universal identity rather favours multiple identities and categories should be taken into account. Intersectionality as an approach focuses on the range of diversity and difference within the groups. Many feminists interested in intersectionality are trying to uncover differences within multiple categories working in discrimination. It is argued that 'the intersection of identities takes place through the articulation of a single dimension of each category' (ibid.: 1781).

During the second wave of feminism questions were raised about the authenticity of sticking on one identity to explain discrimination and oppression faced by women in a patriarchal society. According to McCall, 'one could even say that intersectionality is the most important theoretical contribution that women's studies, in conjunction with related fields, has made so far' (ibid.: 1771). As Shields argues that 'the theoretical foundation for intersectionality grew from study of the production and reproduction of inequalities, dominance and oppression. The evolution of intersectionality as a theoretical framework has been traced to Black feminist responses to the limitation of the accumulated disadvantage model' (Shields 2008: 303). Intersectionality, thus, poses a critique of middle class educated White women and their experiment in equality with other. According to the UN, 'an intersectional approach to analysing the disempowerment of marginalised women attempts to capture the consequences of the interaction between two or more forms of subordination. It addresses the manner in which racism, patriarchy, class oppression and other discriminatory systems create inequalities that structure the relative position of women, races, ethnicities, class and the like ... racially subordinated women are often positioned in the space where racism or xenophobia, class and gender meet. They are consequently subject to injury by the heavy flow of traffic travelling along all these roads' (United Nations 2001). The commitment to ensure equality and social justice in a liberal democracy depends on the understanding of intersectional discrimination in a society.

Approaches to Intersectionality

Intersectionality can be defined as an 'integrated' approach identifying and analysing the simultaneous operation of multiple forms of inequality and privilege (Bishwakarma, Hunt and Zajicek 2007: 28). It is believed that 'instead of focusing on the characteristics of individuals, intersectionality provides a relational and contextual approach to social inequalities' (ibid.: 28). Intersectionality approach consists of three approaches: anticategorical complexity, intercategorical complexity and intracategorical complexity. It is argued that 'the three approaches, in brief, are defined principally in terms of their stance towards categories, that is how they understand and use analytical categories to explore the complexity of intersectionality in social life' (McCall 2005: 1773). In anticategorical complexity, 'social life is considered too irreducibly complex – overflowing with multiple and fluid determinations of both subjects and structures – to make fixed categories, anything that simplifying social fictions that produce inequalities in the process of producing differences' (ibid.). It stands for deconstruction of categorical divisions as they are arbitrary construction of history and language. The manifestation of oppression and inequality in a given society is due to the existence of categories such as race, class, sexuality and gender and to eliminate discrimination and oppression depends on the removal of these categories. In intercategorical complexity, 'scholars provisionally adopt existing analytical categories to document relationships of inequality among social groups and changing configurations of inequality along multiple and conflicting dimensions' (ibid.). It is more concerned with the nature of relationship among various social groups. The intracategorical complexity interrogates the boundary-making and boundary-defining process itself, though that is not its reason d'etre. It stands between the earlier to approaches – anti-categorical and intercategorical. It recognises the importance of social categories to the understanding of society and crosses the boundary created by different groups and categories in the understanding of the society.

Walby, on the other hand, proposed five approaches to intersectionality. They are: criticism of false overgeneralisations; reductionism to a single primacy axis of social inequality; micro-reductionism of intracategorical interesectionality; rejection of categories or anti-categorical approach; and segregationary reductionist – which identifies a single and separate base for each inequality strand (Walby 2007: 451–52). Though, intersectionality primarily concentrates on feminist theory, it has its impact on the study of social movements, international human rights, public policy and electoral behaviour research (Hancock 2007: 63).

Intersectional approach contends that no social group is homogenous and different categorisation exists within the groups. Intersectionality, thus, provides an alternative to the homogenising identity politics. As Simien argues that 'intersectionality is an analytical tool that rejects the separability of identity categories, as it recognises the heterogeneity of various race-sex groups' (2007: 265). Crenshaw, in fact, viewed that intersectionality as a critical intervention into traditional 'identity politics' (1993: 179). It is against the assimilationist universalistic politics of Enlightenment thinking (Yuval-Davis 2006).

Emergence of Modernity

Modernity is the product of Western Enlightenment which is often described as the 'first wave of modernity' (Strauss 1975). The second wave of modernity is associated with Rousseau and the third wave with Nietzsche. Enlightenment modernity is based on the assumption that human beings are equal and find no differentiation based on any identity. This modernity is associated with capitalist economic system, industrial production, the rise of the democratic nation-state, the emergence of rationality and a growing individualisation of social structures. It is based on disengaged reason – delinking reason from beliefs, norms and traditions ignoring people's identities and cultural traditions. The western modernisation took only particularistic view of rationality which was defined in terms of particular and dominant groups. Hamilton identified ten features of modernity – reason, empiricism, science, universalism, progress, individualism, toleration, freedom, uniformity of human nature and secularism (1992: 21–22).

Modernity and Intersectionality

Modernity often addressed the issues of larger identity and in the process it is ignoring the smaller identities. Some groups are well placed in a society and others are discriminated due to intersectionality. The western modernity and its manifestation like nation-states and other institutional structures instead of accommodating different groups rather discriminated. Intersectionality has, thus, emerged as a compelling critique of group identity. Though enlightenment modernity is based on social justice, reason and emancipation, it perpetuates social exclusion, violence, deprivation of some communities.

The western modernity, while believing in universal identity and rationalism, often ignores different forms of categories and their intersectional relationship leading to social oppression and inequality. The response to this discrimination and oppression is manifested in the form of identity assertion. The anticategorical stand taken by western modernity often met with serious repercussions. Ethnicity is a result of such deliberate sidelining of different categories. According to Hancock, 'multiple marginalisations of race, class, gender, or sexual orientation at the individual and institutional levels create social and political stratification' (2007: 65).

The propagators of western modernity believed that modernity would wean away the traditional beliefs, norms, practices and institutions in the society. For instance, western scholars like Samuel Huntington views that 'modernisation is a progressive process. The traumas of modernisation are many many profound, but in the long run modernisation is not only inevitable, it is also desirable' (1971: 290). The western modernisation is depicted as a progressive force moving away from tradition and dark ages. It other words, it was 'man's emergence of from his 'self-imposed' immaturity' (Kant 1789). Huntington viewed that 'modernisation in the long run enhances human well-being, culturally and materially' (1971: 290). The postmodernists and communitarians raised many criticisms against western modernisation as it is based on grand narratives and ignoring community values, respectively. The particularistic values and norms of communities and social groups are undermined in the process of modernisation.

Retrieving 'Self' in Modernisation

The western modernisation creates a 'self' detached from communal atmosphere has an implication for ethnic consciousness and ethnic mobilisation. Ethnicity in this context can be seen as a counter effect of 'self' created by modernity fearing the detached self. In order to realise their self, every community and social groups visualise their own modernity, not a universal modernity or monolithic modernity. Modernity creates individualistic values and takes away the social self of individual. It is argued that 'stronger, exclusive identity increases the chances for an in-group to defame, and justify discrimination against, an out group with the development of stereotypes' (Jeong 2008: 55).

The imposition of universal identity led to the distortion of the self. As Giddens (1991) argues that the self is not a reflexive agent that is actively involved in the practice of self-construction. Modernity redefines one's self from situated self to individual self. It has to be remembered that during feudalism, it was situated self which gave birth to individual self in capitalism. It was conceived that self is a social construct and in modernisation process, it is taking 'self' away from social context.

Modernisation and Nation-States

The emergence of modern nation-state is related to the modernisation process. State is adopting repressive measures in the course of modernisation. State, instead of correcting the pitfalls of modernisation, suppressing various groups and communities who voiced their concern against exclusionary practice of the capitalist modernity. The state, in many instances, pressurised smaller identities to assimilate into the national identities. The nation-states redraw the social boundaries of different groups and communities. Giddens, for instance, sees modernity as multidimensional; as it cannot be explained in single term only. According to him, the four main institutional aspects of modernity are capitalism, industrialism, administrative power and military power (Giddens 1985). As Deutsch argues that 'the state failed to play its role in shaping communicative spaces, assimilating minorities and enforcing legal discrimination against smaller communities' (1953: 32) The modern nation-state is witnessing different forms of domination and exclusion and also witnessing the interplay between national inclusion and exclusion along ethnic lines.

Modernity brought drastic changes not only in polity, economic and society but also in the individual human life in the form of decline of community life and alienation of individual from individuals. Ethnicity as a collective identity based on shared culture, beliefs and practices, such as languages, history descent, and religion. It is a matter of subjective belief in common ancestry. It is argued that 'modernity not only disrupted existing form of community and civic life, but also sharpened the distinction between the work and home, between the public and private sphere, and between the state and civil society' (Puri 2004: 46).

Modernisation and Identity Formation

The intersectional discrimination brought out by the process of modernisation generated identity consciousness among number of social groups. Modernisation touches upon all kinds of identity but more easily ethnic identity. In other words, modernity shook ethnic identity rather than any other kind of identity. It is argued that 'ethnicity acquires enormous power to mobilise people when it becomes a predominant identity and means more than just a particular ethnic origin; it comes to define people as speakers of a certain language, belonging to a particular religion, being able to pursue some careers but not others ...' (Wolf 2006: 31). It was widely believed that ethnic bonds will decline as industrialisation and urbanisation take root in the context of modernisation. However, when modernisation progresses various ethnic groups demand 'equal access to resources and equality of opportunity for members of ethnic-minorities' (ibid.: 41). It is argued that 'intensive industrialisation and urbanisation often uproot individuals from different ethnic backgrounds and brings them to new urban and industrial areas to compete over scarce jobs, housing, education and other resources' (Malesevic 2004: 55).

Modernisation often suggests homogenised development ignoring the specificies of community, social forces and regional dimensions. In many cases, ethnic conflict generate in modernising societies than already modernised society. In modernising societies, the discontent and relative deprivation is more visible. According to Brass, the ethnic identity formation is viewed as a process that involves three sets of struggle. First, 'within the ethnic group itself for control over its material and symbolic resources', secondly, 'between ethnic groups as a competition for rights, privileges, and available resources' and thirdly, 'between the state and the groups that dominate it, on the one hand, and the populations that inhabit its territory on the other' (Brass 1991: 247).

Ethnicity as an Intersectional Category

The emergence of ethnicity or ethnic consciousness is not merely because of one factor but number of other factors – language, tribe, culture, gender, religion, caste, and so on. For instance, ethnic movements in India are the result of intersectionality of tribal identity in North-East India, religious identity in Punjab and cultural and linguistic identity in Tamil Nadu. The discriminatory nature of the western modernity manifested in political, economic and socio-cultural realms. All these realms failed to accommodate the interests of all sections of the community. As Noyoo (2000), in this context, argues that ethnicity has two components – instrumental ethnicity, which eminates from material deprivation and symbolic ethnicity which is based on the anxiety to preserve one's cultural identity.

The ultimate goal of modernity is to do away with ascriptive and primordial identities. Ethnicity is the 'phenomenon of an ethnic group coming to self-awareness that enables it to reaffirm its identity and pursue its interests' (Heredia 1997: 1011). When modernisation progresses the alienation of some groups take place leading to identity mobilisation in the forms of ethnicity. For instance, the emergence of United Liberation Front of Assam (ULFA) is the product of the total alienation of Assamese youth from the Indian state (Gohain 1996).

The interesectionality created by modernisation has an impact on the emergence of ethnic nationalism. Most case of ethnic nationalism is related to the intersectionality created by civic nationalism and due to uneven and exclusivist modernisation. As Wolf argues that 'although not always a conflict prone as ethnic nationalism, civic nationalism may be discriminatory as well, if only in the sense that it does not acknowledge ethnic differences and thus potentially deprives members of ethnic communities other than a country's dominant group opportunities to preserve, express, and develop their distinct identities' (2006: 32).

Ethnicity is often considered as the outward expression of discrimination – discrimination in accessing resources and opportunities. Ethnic group as a minority group faces racial, linguistic, religious discrimination. Institutional discrimination based on intersectionality too often contributes to the emergence of ethnic identity. In this case 'discrimination is built into the normal operating procedures of institutions' (Yinger 1997: 169). The primordialist view of ethnicity as an identity related to human history and related to human identity. According to them ethnicity is based on descent, race, kinship, territory, language, history, and so on. Accordingly, ethnicity can be found long before the emergence of nations and nationalism. On the other hand, instrumentalist view that ethnicity is by no means as indisputable historical fact rather a mobilisation device by the leaders to gain economic gain or political power. As Puri argues that 'ethnicity encodes important questions about identity, belonging, tradition, boundaries, race, and a group's past and future, questions that are especially relevant from the perspective of nationalism' (2004: 176).

Modernity gives both hope and despair among communities. In India, for instance, the dawn of postcolonial modernity brought hope for the middle class and despair for the marginalised tribal communities of the North-East India. The state led modernisation and the emergence of ethnic movements can be traced to a number of factors. It is argued that 'the gradual erosion of the traditional normative frameworks and an increasing impetus to the ideologies of democracy, equality and distributive justice, with the perception and projection of the ruling regimes as being discriminatory and oppressive in ethnic terms. Such a linkage of ethnic consciousness occurs in the wider process of socio-economic changes in the polity' (Phadnis 1990: 256). Beck (1992), a German sociologist, believed that modernity leads to the emergence of risk society. The intersectional discrimination perpetuated by modernity leading towards such a risk society.

Language, Intersectionality and Ethnicity

Often, language policies in multi-linguistic societies would create ethnicity. This is obvious in the case of ethnic movements in Tamil Nadu in the 1960s and Sri Lanka. Language is heart to any ethnic community either as a medium of education or as a medium of deliberative process. The minority ethnic communities assert their language in a multi-linguistic society because they find education and deliberation difficult. The modern democratic constitutions made clear provision for accommodating linguistic minorities. As Yinger argues that 'the language policies of a society are part of the larger political process. They reflect the comparative powers of linguistic groups as well as more general political institutions and values. These, most often, reinforce the strength of the dominant groups, but in democratic society there are some built-in restraints that set limits to linguistic dominance. These include minority linguistic communities, laws, a culture of pluralism and international ties' (Yinger 1997: 303).

The domination of one language over other has an adverse effect on the deliberative process in representative institutions. Moreover, the increasing educational gap between different ethnic communities found in the marginalisation of minority languages. As Yinger argues that 'if some ethnic groups face persistent discrimination that blocks integration and acculturation, they may develop an intense, partly reflexive ethnicity within which their distinctive language or dialect is emphasised' (ibid.: 304). As Brass argues that 'the kinds of language policies chosen may be very important in influencing whether or not an ethnic group becomes assimilated or demands recognition as nationality' (1991: 53). Language deprivation would lead to the cognitive deprivation of the minority groups in a multicultural society. The assertion of minority language has an implication in the power structure. It is argued that 'the power structure of the dominant society is revealed and supported by its language, so a counter-language is used by the oppressed to construct a new reality' (Yinger 1997: 310).

Ethnic Consciousness and Ethnic Conflict

In the course of time, ethnic consciousness emerged out of intersectionality leading to conflict between various communities and conflict with the state. In other words, the intersectional discrimination created by the faulty modernisation is considered to be one for the reasons for ethnic conflicts. As Wolf argues that neither ethnicity nor nationalism in itself causes ethnic conflict but when the state ignores the legitimate political, social and economic grievances of the disadvantaged groups leading to ethnic conflicts (2006: 5). Wolf further adds that 'ethnic conflicts are a form of group conflict in which at least one of the parties involved interprets the conflict, its causes, and potential remedies along an actually existing or perceived discriminatory ethnic divide' (2006: 2). Landis and Boucher identified seven factors contributing to interethnic conflicts. They are the perceived differences between groups, stereotypes, and ethnic identity; land tenure and homeland issues and migration versus native status; involvement of outsiders, disparate allocation of power and resources; effect of language and language policy; process of conflict resolution; and religion (1987: 19–23).

The objective reality emerged out of intersectional discrimination influences the subjective consciousness of individuals and groups in a society. The ethnic assertion emerges out of the subjective consciousness which includes factors such as language, race, territory, colour, and so on. Brass, in this context argues that 'ethnicity or ethnic identity also involves, in addition to subjective self-consciousness, a claim to status and recognition, either as a superior group or as a group at least equal to other groups' (1991: 19). As Roy argues that 'formation of a rebel consciousness in the ethnic formation is an obvious corollary of this (the hegemony of state in nation building) hegemonic goal of the Indian state. The 'rebel consciousness' has found articulation in the formation of 'nations from below', which, by nature, contests the state-centric Indian nation' (Roy 2005: 2176).

Postcolonial Modernisation

The 1960s and 1970s witnessed the emergence of many ethnic movements and upraisals in Asia and Africa questioning the modernisation process. One of the offshoots of modernisation process is the ethnic boundary-making based on the specificity of identities. When the modern nation-state tried to build a wider national identity, ethnic communities started breaking away from national identity and asserting their own separate identity leading to autonomy and secessionist movements. When the state with its all powerful authority constructs national identity, many social groups are turning towards different nation. The absence of indigenous modernity, or the adoption of derivative modernity pushing through the instrument of state, identities felt discrimination.

There are lot of distinction can be drawn between western enlightenment modernisation and postcolonial modernisation. The western modernisation developed out of a longer process – Renaissance, Reformation, Enlightenment and industrial capitalism. Further, it is the outgrowth of structural factors – industrialisation, differentiation, secularisation, and so on. But in postcolonial societies modernisation was not preceded by these structural conditions. Moreover, the postcolonial modernisation was the superimposition from the top and the society was not prepared to accept it.

Unlike the western context, in the postcolonial situation, state is engaging in nation-building process. The nation-building process involves building a new idea of national community based on solidarity. In the process of nation-building, the nation-states were often struck by the 'melting post' syndrome. It is argued that 'in many cases, minorities are meant to remain permanently outside of the sphere of national imagination but insider the state's territory' (Wimmer 2006: 339). Since modernisation is a 'homogenising process' (Huntington 1971), it has many repercussions in diverse societies.

In postcolonial societies modernisation shows its 'exclusive' character ignoring some social groups and communities. As Smith views that 'ethnic conflict after independence tended to be seen as a conflict between the primordial values of the tribe and race and modern values of nationalism.' (1996: 81). In the process of modernisation, the state and its bureaucratic apparatus is penetrating the everyday life of the people leading towards the colonisation of life world and cultural impoverishment (Habermas 1987). The postcolonial modernisation instilled the feeling of relative deprivation among various groups and classes (Gurr 1970).

The political modernisation intended to integrate smaller identities into larger identities. The modernisation process adopted liberal democracy at the political level brought exclusion of some social regroups. The intersectional discrimination barring some social group in exercising their citizenship rights and political participation in the democratic process. The postcolonial economic modernisation aimed at bringing capitalist modernisation tinkering with traditional substance based economy. The identity based intersectional discrimination further brings impoverishment for socially marginalised sections. Pathak, in this context, talks about the relationship between economic marginalisation and one's stigmatised identity (2006: 153). The socio-cultural modernisation aimed at bringing changes in values and beliefs.

Indian Case of Modernisation and Ethnicity

India witnessed two kinds of modernisation - first, the modernisation initiated by the colonial powers to benefit their interest. Second, the modernisation initiated in the aftermath of postcolonial India, initiated under the aegis of the modern liberal state. The proponents of state-led modernisation believed that modernisation would decline ethnicity and ethnic identities. State as an instrument of modernisation can assimilate all ethnic identities towards nation-building process. On the contrary, modernisation created ethnicisation as it brought crisis of collective identity.

In the North-East India, the institutional accommodation was guaranteed them to face the challenges of postcolonial modernisation. The Sixth Schedule guarantees special provision for the tribal people to protect their distinct cultural identity. The inauguration of modernisation project in this region raised new hope and aspirations among the people but what happened in reality is different. The state as an instrument for modernisation became more security state for facilitating security for the free play of the market forces. Unlike rest of India, the capitalist modernisation produced social tension as the society is ravaged by ethnic identities. The processes of tribal economy rather than creating stability in society generated social tensions. The imposition of western modernity by the state on the indigenous conception of modernity in tribal modernity created discontent in the society.

In the nation-building process, Nehru tried to accommodate various tribal communities in the path of nation-building process dispelling their fear, anxiety in the majoritarian Hindu state. It has to be remembered that the wide feeling among the tribal communities that religion as a category intersects with ethnic identity leading to discrimination and oppression. Keeping this in view, Nehru along with Verrier Elwin, an ethnographer, initiated the *Panchasheel* (the five principles of tribal development). These five principles reiterated the government's commitment to instill a feeling among the tribal communities that the possible intersection of religion, culture, language and ethnicity would not lead to exclusion in the mainstream. Elwin, for instance, viewed that development should not cause a breakdown of values of tribal societies (1959: 116). However, the state centred development in the form of capitalist development adopted by the Nehruvian Modernisation led to the extraction of resources, displacement and unequal regional development. It is argued that 'the tribal life-world suffered heavily owing to the introduction of the state-sponsored agencies to govern development' (Biswas and Suklabaidya 2008: 124). As Biswas and Suklabaidya argue that 'Nehru's apprehensions about the role of the state in enforcing and imposing a homogenising process of development took into account the historical precedents of annihilation of tribal culture by civilisations to suggest a discourse of sympathy and care for the cultural distinctiveness of the tribals' (ibid.: 116).

Conclusion

The process of modernisation is multidimensional as it involves political, economic and socio-cultural. Though it, in all its dimensions, emerged as a libratory force – liberating people from the clutches of feudalism and the 'self-imposed immaturity' – it is often appearing as a stimulating factor for intersectional oppression and discrimination. While the elite internalise the values of modernisation, the majority feel the process of modernisation as stumbling block to their realisation of life world. This tendency is more manifested in the postcolonial societies rather than in the industrial societies. The outcome of this incongruity leads to the generation of ethnic consciousness, virulent form of ethnic mobilisation and fierce ethnic conflict in postcolonial societies. The growing tendencies of ethnic mobilisation and ethnic conflict in India in general and North-East India in particular can be seen in this wider context.

References

Beck, Ulrich. 1992. *Risk Society: Towards a New Modernity*. London: Sage Publications.

Bishwakarma, Ramu, Valerie H. Hunt and Anna Zajicek. 2007. 'Educating Dalit Women: Beyond a One-dimensional Policy Formulation', *Himalaya*, XXVII (1–2): 27–39.

Biswas, Prasenjit and Chandan Suklabaidya. 2008. *Ethnic Life-Worlds in North-East India*. New Delhi: Sage Publications.

Brass, Paul R. 1991. *Ethnicity and Nationalism: Theory and Comparison*. New Delhi: Sage Publications.

Collins, P.H. 1990. *Black Feminist Thought: Knowledge, Consciousness, and the Politics of Empowerment.* Boston: Unwin Hyman.

Crenshaw, Kimberly. 1993. 'Mapping the Margins: Intersectionality, Identity Politics, and Violence against Women of Color', *Stanford Law Review*, 43: 1241–99.

Deutsch, K.W. 1953. *Nationalism and Social Communication: An Inquiry into the Foundations of Nationality*. Cambridge, MA: MIT Press.

Elwin, Verrier. 1959. *A Philosophy for NEFA*. Shillong: NEFA Research Department.

Giddens, Anthony. 1985. *The Constitution of Society*. Cambridge: Polity Press.

——. 1991. *Modernity and Self-Identity: Self and Society in the Late Modern Age*. Cambridge: Polity Press.

Gohain, Hiren. 1996. 'Extremist Challenge and Indian State: Case of Assam', *Economic and Political Weekly*, 31 (31): 2066–68.

Gurr, Ted Robert. 1970. *Why Men Rebel?* Princeton, NJ: Princeton University Press.

Habermas, Jurgen. 1987. *Life World System: A Critique of Functionalist Reason*, Vol. II of *The Theory of Communicative Action*, English Translation by Thomas McCarthy. Boston: Beacon Press.

Hamilton, P. 1992. 'The Enlightenment and the Birth of Social Science', in S. Hall and B. Gieben (eds), *Formations of Modernity*, Cambridge: Polity Press.

Hancock, Ange-Marie. 2007. 'When Multiplication Doesn't Equal Quick Addition: Examining Intersectionality as a Research Paradigm', *Perspectives on Politics*, 5 (1): 63–79.

Heredia, Rudolf C. 1997. 'Ethnicity, Class and Nation: Interrelationships in a Multicultural State', *Economic and Political Weekly*, 32 (19): 1010–15.

Huntington, Samuel P. 1971. 'The Change to Change: Modernization, Development, and Politics', *Comparative Politics*, 3 (3): 283–322.

Jeong, Ho-Won. 2008. *Understanding Conflict and Conflict Analysis.* London: Sage Publications.

Kant, Immanuel. 1789. 'What is Enlightenment?'. Accessed from: http://www.saylor.org/site/wp-content/uploads/2011/02/What-is-Enlightenment.pdf.

Landis, Dan and Jerry Boucher. 1987. 'Themes and Models of Conflict', in Jerry Boucher, Dan Landis and Karen Arnold Clark (eds), *Ethnic Conflicts: International Perspectives*, London: Sage Publications, pp. 18–32.

Malesevic, Sinisa. 2004. *The Sociology of Ethnicity*. London: Sage Publications.

McCall, Leslie. 2005. 'The Complexity of Intersectionality', *Signs*, 30 (3): 1771–800.

Noyoo, Ndanga. 2000. 'Ethnicity and Development in Sub-Saharan Africa', *Journal of Social Development in Africa*, 15 (2): 234–46.

Pathak, Avijit. 2006. *Modernity, Globalisation and Identity: Towards a Reflective Quest*. New Delhi: Aakar Books.

Phadnis, Urmila. 1990. *Ethnicity and Nation-building in South Asia*. New Delhi: Sage Publications.

Puri, Jyoti. 2004. *Encountering Nationalism*. Oxford: Blackwell Publishing.

Roy, Sanjay K. 2005. 'Conflicting Nations in North-East India', *Economic and Political Weekly*, 40 (21): 2176–82.

Shields, Stephanie A. 2008. 'Gender: An Intersectionality Perspective', *Sex Roles*, 59: 301–11.

Simien, Evely M. 2007. 'Doing Intersectionality Research: From Conceptual Issues to Practical Examples', *Politics and Gender*, 3 (2): 264–71.

Smith, B.C. 1996. *Understanding Third World Politics: Theories of Political Change and Development*. London: Macmillan.

Strauss, Leo. 1975. 'The Three Waves of Modernity', in Hilail Gildin (ed.), *An Introduction to Political Philosophy: Ten Essays by Leo Strauss*, Detroit: Wayne State University Press, pp. 43–56.

United Nations. 2001. 'Background Briefing on Intersectionality', Working Group on Women and Human Rights, 45 Session of the UN CSW. Accessed from: www.cwgl.rutgers.edu/csw01/background.htm>.

Walby, Sylvia. 2007. 'Complexity Theory, Systems Theory and Multiple Intersecting Social Inequalities', *Philosophy of the Social Sciences*, 37 (4): 449–547.

Weasel, Lisa H. 2004. 'Feminist Intersections in Science: Race, Gender and Sexuality through the Microscope', *Hypatia*, 19 (1): 183–93.

Wimmer, Andres. 2006. 'Ethnic Exclusion in Nationalizing States', in Gerard Delanty and Krishan Kumar (eds), *The Sage Handbook of Nations and Nationalism*, London: Sage Publications, pp. 334–44.

Wolf, Stefan. 2006. *Ethnic Conflict: A Global Perspective*. Oxford: Oxford University Press.

Yinger, J. Milton. 1997. *Ethnicity: Source of Strength?* Jaipur and New Delhi: Rawat Publications.

Yuval-Davis, Nira. 2006. 'Human/Women's Rights and Feminist Transversal Politics', in Myra Marx Ferree and Aili Mari Tripp (eds), *Global Feminism: Transnational Women's Activism, Organising, and Human Rights*, New York: NYU Press, pp. 123–35.

8

Everyday Ethnic Engagements

Malayalee Associations in Goa

MANISH THAKUR

Much of the recent sociological literature on migration has accorded disproportionate attention to the formation of diasporic identity in the context of overseas or transnational migration (see, for example, Ghai 2000; Israel and Wagle 1993). The conventional literature too has generally treated migration in terms of the successes, or otherwise, of the processes of cultural adaptation on the part of migrants in the new and alien (largely urban) settings besides the mandatory references to the usual push and pull factors (Mathew et al. 2005). Students of political science have been more engaged with the ways migration leads to nativistic assertions and ethnic conflicts (Katzenstein 1979) not to mention the more specific concerns of geographers and demographers wherein migration turns out be an important variable in the context of rate and growth of urbanisation.

Such studies of ethnicity (mostly in relation to migration and urbanisation) end up being a balance-sheet of nativisation and localisation. They reveal nothing more than the oft-repeated assertions that migrants huddle together be it Pune, Madras or Bombay to maintain and preserve their native identity (see, for example, Gregory 2002; Jain 1987; Kumaran 1992a, 1992b; Lewandowski 1980, 1991; Rowe 1973; Sharma 1984). With the passing of generations, the processes of adaptation and assimilation become easy and non-noticeable. Some of them dig deeper to argue that most of these ethnic/voluntary associations are highly correlated with sociological variables as caste, class or religion (Driver 1982; Driver and Driver 1982; Rao 1981). At times, the general role of ethnic associations in containing/promoting parochialism/cosmopolitanism has also been debated. No doubt, these studies have helped correct many biases of conventional urban sociology. Yet, they take ethnicity as a fixed identity. Thus, *Kerala Migrants in the City of Madras*, by definition, becomes an ethnic group. So is the case with South Indians in Bombay or Pune. Even North Indian migrants in Bombay turn out to be a quintessential ethnic group. In this paper, we attempt to question this uncritical acceptance of ethnicity as a given primordial identity marker thereby questioning the fixity and permanence of ethnic identities (McElreath et al. 2003). Also, we wish to take issue with the equivalence of ethnic identity with urban migrants as even in urban India caste has been found to be a continuing basis of ethnic identity (Dushkin 1980; Punekar and Haribabu 1980; Sabharwal 2006; Sandhu 1984).

Most of these studies also have a tendency to focus on the formation and unfolding of ethnic identities in a conflict situation thereby according undue importance to its mobilisational aspects and neglecting everyday patterns of interaction. The existing literature, more often than not, ends up underlining the potentially explosive or real violent nature of ethnic interactions thereby making ethnicity a buzzword for understanding collective violence in larger part of the world. Ethnicity turns out to be a shorthand term for mapping out multiple identitarian cleavages that criss-cross our social universe. Its uncritical coupling with nationalism makes it such an emotionally charged category that we tend to forget that all ethnic identities do not necessarily lead to potentially subversive and secessionist micro-nationalism (Baruah 1994). After all, polity/state is the binding matrix in relation to which ethnic identities flourish either in co-operation or contestation (Glazer 1987).

There is another silence in most of these studies. Most of the researchers tend to look at ethnic associations as some sort of pressure groups meant for the articulation of sectional/particularistic articulation of interests. Some of them argue that ethnic associations, in fact, protect and nurture minority rights in a pluralist polity (Jenkins 1997; Subramanian 1999). While all these assertions are true, recent advances in the ethnography of the state and anthropology's growing engagement with modern political forms have brought to our attention the multi-layered character of the agency of the state (Edelman and Haugerud 2005). The functioning of the state and its intermeshing with society can only partially be understood at the level of macro discourses on institutions and processes (Fuller and Benei 2000). As hitherto untouched sections of society have come to appreciate the value of the state and appropriate the functioning of the state in their own distinctive ways, a careful account of the everyday encounters between the social and the political has the potential to yield valuable insights. Of necessity, there is a need to turn our critical lens on the state itself which is no longer understood as an undifferentiated monolithic actor but rather one composed of varied and sometimes competing actors and agencies with distinct bureaucratic interests and agenda.

Based on the premise that everyday workings of the state and the way migrants engage with it have implications for the identity and representation of the migrant community, this paper looks into the everyday politics of representation as it criss-crosses identities such as caste, class, religion and gender. Rather than uncritically privileging the given cultural distinctiveness of a migrant community, it seeks to argue that a careful unpacking of the everyday ebb and flow of the negotiation of the migrant identity in relation to the local state and the host community has the potential to rework the dominant conceptualisations where predefined and predetermined socio-cultural groups (migrants) encounter equally predetermined 'natives' either in terms of adaptation or confrontation.

Viewed thus, this paper examines the everyday negotiations between the migrants and the host community through the agency of ethnic associations of the migrants. Substantively, it focuses on the self-conscious involvement of the agencies and actors in representing Malayalee migrants to the host community in the state of Goa. Towards this end, the empirical universe for this paper comprises four major Malayalee organisations/associations currently active in Goa: Kerala Samajam, Kerala Sangham, the Sri Narayana Dharma Paripalana (SNDP) and the Nair Service Society (NSS). In their different ways, all these organisations speak for the migrants and/or for their various segments. Not only do they engage in multifarious 'cultural' activities projecting their distinctive traditions, rituals and values but also attempt to put forward a benign, positive and favourable image for themselves to the local state and community. To look at such attempts as knee-jerk defensive responses to the all-pervasive local stereotypes of the migrants as *bailos* (outsiders) and *ghantis* (from across the Ghats) would amount to ignoring larger processes of representation animating the migrants' search for identity in a setting different from their own.

Quite explicitly, this paper intends to understand ethnicity as a processual mechanism of differentiation as well as integration within and between communities in a migrational context. It focuses on the nature and scope of identity transformations in the context of migration within the boundaries of the nation-state. While assessing the role of ethnicity in enabling the migrants in adapting to the migratory context and/or in resisting the processes of local dominance, it investigates into sociological fault-lines of caste, class, language and religion in the making of the ethnic identity.

For the purpose of this paper, ethnicity emerges as a contextualising frame of reference that is always in the making. Our aim is not to document the aspects of social and cultural detentions and identity within Kerala's diverse religious communities under the all-embracing label of 'Malayalee' ethnicity (Cf. Kurien 1994; 2002). Without denying the possible use of ethnicity as a potent resource facilitating adaptation on the part of migrants in an alien setting, or helping them obtain or maintain crucial sociocultural resources as a collectivity (Nair 1978, 1979), we want to highlight its nature, a carefully crafted and constructed identity form. Generally, this constructedness becomes apparent in times of political mobilisation, and in times of ethnic wars, where competing ethnic resources have to be deployed for dominance and/or survival. An entire tradition of theorists, known as *instrumentalists*, has highlighted the shifting contours of ethnic identity and its embeddedness in multitudinous struggles for securing political power and economic resources. We want to follow them but with a view to extend the analysis in the context of everyday business of life and migrants' encounter to the local state in the course of their living. In general, sociologists get enamoured with the phenomena when they seem to burst out at the seams of everyday and ordinary. No wonder, most of the studies concerning ethnicity in India are around those contexts where ethnic assertions have taken violent forms and have led to somehow sustained mass political mobilisations threatening to unsettle either the legitimacy of the nation-state or jeopardising political distribution of resources in the case of one of its constituent units. Textbooks of political sociology, as a rule, illustrate ethnicity by way of Shiv Sena in Bombay (Gupta 1982; Weiner 1978; Weiner et al. 1981), the Assam Movement (Baruah 1994), and the burning cauldron of the India's North-East, etc.

Discussion

Keralites (Malayalees) constitute the second largest group of migrants in Goa next only to the Kannadigas. We do not consider Maharashtrians in our account given linguistic/cultural overlaps between them and the Goan Hindus. Since the Marathi language has substantial presence in the sociocultural life of Goan Hindus, it is difficult to make a definite sense of Goan/Maharashtrian ethnic divide even though it is often politically charged. The status of Marathi vis-à-vis Konkani has been a festering political issue ever since Goa got liberated in 1961 and subsequently attained statehood in 1987. The declaration of Konkani as the official language of administration of the state in 1987 has added grist to this persisting controversy. Indeed, the popular pejorative term *ghanti* is used by the Goans to refer to the Maharashtrian migrants in Goa who are generally a source of great resentment given the fact that in the popular Goan imagination Maharashtra wanted to gobble up Goa through merger which could only be avoided thanks to the outcome of the Opinion Poll in favour of a separate political entity of Goa in 1967.

So far as the Kannadigas are concerned, one discerns a subterranean resentment against them as by their sheer numbers they appear to be everywhere in Goa right from the state secretariat to the sprawling slums in cities like Wasco-da-Gama and Mapusa. In fact, they straddle a range of occupations from the professional white collar jobs to the most menial ones. Yet, they are equally indispensible for the local economy owing to Goa's tiny population and the high rates of out-migration. The Kannadigas, in particular the ones from the drought-prone areas like Bijapur, supply almost all the manual labour in Goa. There is large presence of Udupi hoteliers as well who mostly cater to the vegetarian segments of the substantial number of domestic tourists. The ones from North Karnataka (mostly Muslims) control the trade in fruits, vegetables, clothes and the sundry items of household necessities. While the manual labourers and petty traders are indifferently tolerated by the locals, the ones in white collar jobs have occasionally been the target of popular attacks. An organisation called *Goa Hitkarini Parishad* has often raised issues concerning the appointment of outsiders (*bhailos*), meaning mostly Kannadigas, to the university and other white collar jobs. Ever since the liberation of Goa their influx has been quite visible as they came to occupy lower level government jobs in this contiguous territory. The introduction of English as the language of officialdom with the departure of the Portuguese went in their favour besides the geographical proximity. The fact that a large number of lower level bureaucrats in the initial years after liberation were from Karnataka has further contributed to the growing indignation at their presence in the white collar jobs.

By contrast, Keralites have hardly ever been the target of local annoyance, explicit or otherwise. To begin with, they have had certain amount of goodwill on the part of the local population as the very first military governor of Goa Colonel Candeth was from Kerala and was held to be an upright and efficient administrator. Secondly, most of the Keralites belong to the service class and the range of occupations they engage in is narrower than that of the Kannadigas. Of course, some of them are in petty trade and retail as well. Few of them run bakeries whereas garages and tyre repair shops are their monopolies. Several of them have also moved to the real estate, and a small number of them are also present in financial sector apart from being scientists, teachers, journalists and administrators. Yet, in popular perception, they are not seen to be the usurpers of white collar jobs that should have ideally belonged to the Goans. The facile explanation that Christianity could have facilitated such a reception to the Keralites in Goa is inadequate to account for the large number of Hindus among the migrants in Goa. Moreover, there are not many Roman

Catholics (they are preponderant in Goa) in Kerala as most of the upwardly mobile migrants belong to the Orthodox Jacobite sects (Syrian Christians in popular parlance). Language could also not have been a facilitator despite the presence of few Konkani speaking pockets in Kerala, something that binds Goa with the coastal Karnataka.

This general bonhomie towards the Keralites (and its absence in relation to some other migrant communities outlined above) brings us to the kernel of the issue of ethnic identity and the role of ethnic associations in its management. For this purpose, I conducted fieldwork in Goa in four brief spells over the past two years: April–May 2009, August–September 2010, April–May 2011, and December–January 2011–12. Besides, I had the initial familiarity with the broad setting as a faculty member at the local university for almost a decade (1997–2007). However, I started looking at the issue only in mid-2006, and I presented some of the preliminary ideas at the All India Sociological Congress held in Chennai in 2006. During my fieldwork, I focussed more on my participation in cultural events held by these associations rather than going for individual interviews with the migrants. Indeed, I interviewed the office-bearers and the active members of these associations after having attended the larger events. As a rule, most of these events coincide with the secular festival of 'Onam' which also sees organisation of community feast along with dance, drama, rangoli, and singing competitions. As part of my field work, I attended two such events on the eve of 'Onam': one in Mapusa and the other in Madgaon. The discussion that follows is based on my field observations of these events as well as the interview data that I subsequently collected.

What is noteworthy is that, for most of these big events, the chief guest would invariably be a minister or some key political functionary from the state. For example, at the Onam function at Rabindra Bhawan, Madgaon in 2011 the Chief Guest was none other than the then Chief Minister of Goa, Shri Digambar Kamat. Likewise, at another function, the chief guest was the Chairperson of the Madgaon Municipal Corporation. For events in smaller places like Porvorim or Ponda, the sitting MLA representing that particular constituency or a Minister from the locality would be the key invitees. In their speeches, these dignitaries would stress the similarities between the two communities in terms of their proximity to sea, fondness for fish and spices, exchange of ecclesiastical persons in the past, the type of houses, climatic conditions like heavy monsoon and the sundry points of convergence that make them 'natural' neighbours and comrades-in-arms in the growth and development of the local economy, society and culture. Another leitmotif of these speeches would be the recollection of one's sustained association with people (as friends/colleagues/neighbours) belonging to the state from where the migrants come to underline the historic ease of interaction between these two communities. Alternatively, these dignitaries would narrate the life story of some inspirational figure from the state (Kerala) who left a deep imprint on the speaker in question. One does not fail to notice that at one level these addresses may just have been immediate responses to a given particularistic audience – an act of playing to the gallery. However, even these superficial accounts and narration of one's disposition to a given community has implications for the latter's dealings with what we have called the everyday state.

Very often, these discourses travel to the larger society including the petty functionaries of the state mostly belonging to the host community. Thus, points of interface with the local state acquire different meanings for different migrant communities. Acts like visiting a local police station to lodge an FIR, or going to Mamlatdar's office to get a residence certificate, or applying for a gas connection, or transferring the title deed of a plot of land recently purchased, or getting a driving license at the RTO, or getting the map of the proposed construction approved by the executive engineer in the municipality would be a different experience for a Malayalee than a Kannadiga or a Maharashtrian.

These subtle and nuanced instrumental payoffs apart, these events also help the Malayalees project for themselves a cosmopolitan image to the host community. As Hindus and Christians from Kerala equally participate in organising these events, the religious divide takes a back seat and their regional-ethnic identity comes to the fore. This gels well with the religious demography of the Goan society where any inclusive political project has to have a Hindu-Catholic constituency to succeed. Impliedly, this mutuality becomes another basis for the resemblance between the Malayalee and the Goan community. There is no denying that there exists a subterranean Hindu-Christian rivalry so far as control of the two organisations is concerned: Christians have more control over Kerala Samajam whereas Hindus appear dominant in Kerala Sangham. Yet, both the organisations are open to all, and have members of both the communities in their key committees.

Till recently, the special invitees for these functions would be some high ranking officials posted in Goa though belonging to Kerala. The Director General of Police or the Director of Fire Brigade or the senior bureaucrat would be the usual guests on such occasions. The presence of these guests in community events would act as morale booster for the migrants by giving them implicit assurance of access to the everyday state. The realisation that some of the crucial jobs in the state are managed by their brethren would remind them of their valuable contributions to the host community and, thus, would potentially mitigate their unwelcome presence amidst the Goans. These would be the occasions to reiterate their usefulness to the host society in myriad ways. Interestingly, there would be no articulation of having equal claims on Goa as Indians despite the presence of few (Keralite) activists who have devoted their lifetime to public issues concerning Goa.

In a way, the language-based reorganisation of states has legitimated a new nativism on the part of both the natives and the migrants. Not surprisingly, the endeavour of these ethnic associations would be to avoid trespassing on what they hold to be the first right of locals in the state, and to continually prove their credentials as an ideal migrant community mindful of their limits. The eagerness to learn Konkani, or not to publicly articulate their opinion on the so-called Goan identity issues (be it Konkani-Marathi debate or Konkani-English debate or the issue of script for Konkani or the sharing of Madhei waters with Karnataka or the demolition of red light areas in Wasco-da-Gama blaming the outsiders or the mining issue) can be read in this light. This definitely narrows down the possibility of a vibrant civil society as large number of inhabitants keeps themselves indifferent to local issues out of the fear of exceeding their brief. In a way, the practice of inviting the political functionary of the state is a sure sign of growing acquiescence to the nativist moral claims of the locals.

By contrast, the other two organisations – the SNDP and the NSS – have largely been the dormant branches of the main entities headquartered in Kerala. Their historically being caste-based organisations somehow ill-dispose them to construct an all-inclusive Malayalee ethnic identity. I have heard people whispering about some members of the Kerala Samajam who were also associated with the NSS. The general impression one gets is that somehow association with these two organisations is seen as detrimental to the larger cause of a unified Malayalee identity. This may have been the reason why those Keralites whose association overlaps these two types of organisations would be less forthcoming about their involvement with the caste-based ones. Moreover, the NSS has often articulated its intense socioeconomic rivalry with the more advanced Syrian Christians in Kerala. That history may not offer a congenial resource for the construction of a common identity through that platform. Likewise, the SNDP has often struggled against the Namboodiri and Nair dominance in Kerala, and the upward mobility of the Izhavas makes common forums like the Kerala Samajam and the Kerala Sangham more suited for their identity needs in contemporary times. Caste-based mobilisation may have been a useful resource for upward mobility in the past; however, it is class that matters in 'areas for public recognition, power and influence' (Lewandowski 1991: 298). Other observers have also noted the process of gradual 'decastification of status' in the urban context (Sabharwal 2006). At a more general level, it alludes to the oft-repeated primordialist-instrumentalist debate that even when ethnicity is instrumentally used certain ascriptive resources are more suited for this purpose than certain others (Brubaker et al. 2004).

Conclusion

The foregoing discussion underlines the need for revisiting the place of caste-based associations in the construction of ethnic identity in urban India. Is it possible to talk of dominance of caste and kinship associations in the city in the same way as we did in the early decades after Independence? Is the privileging of caste and kinship as bases of residence and interaction a continuing phenomenon in our urban milieu? These questions have a bearing on our understanding the political ramifications of the ethnic question in terms of the emergent politico-social integration (Rowe 1973). A peep into the changing forms of association can suggest insights into the potentiality of caste associations to become involved in the politics of the modern state (Chandra 2006).

At another level, ethnicity as an urban political phenomenon can be seen in relation to an emergent 'culture of enterprise' that has held sway in urban India in the wake of liberalisation. This has encouraged some of us to don the mantle of ethnic entrepreneurs in an increasingly competitive economic environment. The events in Madgaon were not merely sponsored by different business groups based in Kerala but there were also neatly clad employees of some firms distributing booklets to one and all. Muthoot Finance, jewellery firms and some of the banks were visibly prominent. This reliance on the commonality of ethnic identity to further one's enterprise is a reality howsoever we talk about the relational and contingent nature of ethnicity. 'Yet the core of ethnic politicization is not instrumental. What we see very generally today is a retreat from social into group identity. It is not necessarily political. One thinks of the familiar nostalgia for "roots"' ... (Hobsbawm 1992: 5). No wonder, most of the attendees in these gatherings had something in common in terms of their self-understanding: they were doing all this for the sake of their children whom they would like to assimilate their cultural values and rituals lest they become thoroughly secularised and anglicised. They invest in these events not simply because they have plenty of leisure time to kill. True, these forums help them with networks and minor social gains and benefits. Yet, the advancement of their sectional interest as an ethnic minority in a plural setting is not their sole preoccupation. Nor is the urge to act as a pressure group to present its demands to the local government their preeminent agenda. Despite the fact that their attempt to forge a regional/ethnic identity has to be negotiated with the everyday state and the host community in terms of a unified and palatable articulation of an ideal migrant community (like sugar in water as the metaphor goes), they are hardly unconstrained by the basic structural features of the originating society be it caste or community. One sees this in the functioning of voluntary associations mentioned above. Be that as it may, these cleavages are not of the order which would derail their essential quest of belonging to an imagined community of Malayalees. The idea of being Malayalee is culturally comforting and helps them sentimentally cherish the bountiful memories of the land they come from. It helps them belong to a community, and it helps them define others out of the same community. It makes them 'us' in relation to 'them', and not necessarily *against* them. Such an understanding of everyday ethnicity at work helps us as well: we stop associating ethnicity with ethnic conflicts and ethnic violence all the time.

References

Baruah, Sanjib. 1994. "Ethnic Conflict' as State-Society Struggle: The Poetics and Politics of Assamese Micro-Nationalism', *Modern Asian Studies*, 28 (3): 649–71.

Brubaker, Rogers, Mara Loveman and Peter Stamatov. 2004. 'Ethnicity as Cognition', *Theory and Society*, 33 (1): 31–64.

Chandra, Kanchan. 2006. 'What is Ethnic Identity and Does it Matter?', *Annual Review of Political Science*, 9: 397–424.

Driver, Edwin D. 1982. 'Class, Caste and Status Summation in Urban South India', *Contributions to Indian Sociology*, 16 (2): 225–53.

Driver, Edwin D. and Aloo E. Driver. 1982. 'Social Class and Voluntary Associations in Urban India', *Sociological Bulletin*, 31 (2): 133–54.

Dushkin, Lelah. 1980. 'Caste Associations in Bangalore', *Economic and Political Weekly*, 15 (37): 1551–57.

Edelman, Marc and Angelique Haugerud. 2005. 'Introduction: The Anthropology of Development and Globalisation', in Marc Edelman and Angelique Haugerud (eds), *The Anthropology of Development and Globalization: From Classical Political Economy to Contemporary Neoliberalism*, Oxford: Blackwell Publishing, pp. 1–74.

Fuller, C.J. and V. Benei (eds) 2000. *The Everyday State and Society in Modern India*. New Delhi: Social Science Press.

Ghai, Yash P. (ed.) 2000. *Autonomy and Ethnicity: Negotiating Competing Claims in Multi-ethnic States*. Cambridge: Cambridge University Press.

Gregory, Jancy. 2002. 'Ethnic Affinity of the Kerala Migrants in Mysore: A Dialectic Process of Nativisation and Localisation', *Man in India*, 82 (1–2): 193–201.

Gupta, Dipankar. 1982. *Nativism in a Metropolis: Shiv Sena in Bombay*. Delhi: Manohar.

Glazer, Nathan. 1987. *Affirmative Discrimination: Ethnic Inequality and Public Policy*. Cambridge, Mass.: Harvard University Press.

Hobsbawm, Eric J. 1992. 'Ethnicity and Nationalism in Europe Today', *Anthropology Today*, 8 (1): 3–8.

Israel, Milton and N.K. Wagle (eds) 1993. *Ethnicity, Identity, Migration: The South Asian Context*. Delhi: South Asian Books.

Jain, Ranu. 1987. 'Jain Oswal of Calcutta as an Ethnic Group: A Socio-Historical Perspective', *Man in India*, 67 (4): 383–403.

Jenkins, Richard. 1997. *Rethinking Ethnicity: Arguments and Explorations*. London: Sage Publications.

Katzenstein, Mary, 1979. *Ethnicity and Equality: The Shiv Sena Party and Preferential Policies in Bombay*. Ithaca: Cornell University Press.

Kumaran, K.P. 1992a. *Migration Settlement and Ethnic Associations*. New Delhi: Concept Publishing Company.

——. 1992b. 'Ethnic Minority Associations and their Sociocultural Functions', *Man in India*, 72 (2): 141–52.

Kurien, Prema. 1994. 'Colonialism and Ethnogenesis: A Study of Kerala, India', *Theory and Society*, 23 (3): 385–417.

——. 2002. *Kaleidoscopic Ethnicity: International Migration and the Reconstruction of Community Identities in India*. New Brunswick: Rutgers University Press.

Lewandowski, Susan. 1980. *Migration and Ethnicity in Urban India: Kerala Migrants in the City of Madras, 1970–1970*. New Delhi: Manohar.

——. 1991. 'Voluntary Associations and Keralite Ethnicity in Madras', in M.S.A. Rao, C. Bhat and L.N. Kadekar (eds), *A Reader in Urban Sociology*, New Delhi: Orient Longman, pp. 277–302.

Mathew, K.S., Mahavir Singh and Joy Varkey (eds) 2005. *Migration in South India*. New Delhi: Shipra Publications.

McElreath, Richard, Robert Boyd and Peter J. Richerson. 2003. 'Shared Norms and the Evolution of Ethnic Markers', *Current Anthropology*, 44 (1): 122–30.

Nair, K.S. 1978. *Ethnicity and Urbanisation: A Case Study of the Ethnic Identity of South Indian Merchants in Poona*. Delhi: Ajanta Publications.

——. 1979. 'Ethnic Identity in the Indian Urban Setting', *Eastern Anthropologist*, 32 (1): 13–23.

Punekar, V.B. and E. Haribabu. 1980. 'Caste Associations in Urban India', *Man in India*, 60 (1–2): 72–82.

Rao, M.S.A. 1981. 'Some Aspects of Sociology of Migration', *Sociological Bulletin*, 30 (1): 21–33.

Rowe, William L. 1973. 'Caste, Kinship and Association in Urban India', in Aidan Southall (ed.), *Urban Anthropology: Cross-cultural Studies of Urbanization*, New York: Oxford University Press, pp. 211–49.

Sabharwal, Gopa. 2006. *Ethnicity and Class: Social Division in an Indian City*. Delhi: Oxford University Press.

Sandhu, Jasmeet. 1984. 'Caste Associations in a New City: Chandigarh', *Eastern Anthropologist*, 37 (1): 75–80.

Sharma, R.N. 1984. 'Intra-Ethnic Groups and Urban Adjustment: The Case of North Indian In-Migrants in Bombay', *Nagarlok*, 16 (3): 25–35.

Subramanian, Narendra. 1999. 'Ethnicity and Pluralism: An Exploration with Reference to Indian Cases', *Canadian Journal of Political Science*, 32 (4): 715–44.

Weiner, Myron, Mary F. Katzenstein with K.V. Narayana Rao. 1981. *India's Preferential Policies: Migrants, the Middle Classes and Ethnic Equality*. Bombay: Oxford.

Weiner, Myron. 1978. *Sons of the Soil: Migration and Ethnic Conflict in India*. Princeton, NJ: Princeton University Press.

9

The Naga Club

Reconstructions from the Spectrum of Socio-oral History of Ethno Genesis, Ethnicity and Resultant Political Permutations

I.L. AIER

The Naga Club for an introductory explanation was a formation of people representing various Naga tribes of the then Naga Hills. The club membership cut across a variety of occupations of government and mission school teachers, office clerks, village headmen and freemen. It is reported that most of them possessed a level of education of being literate in vernacular and in English. Most of them had exposure and thereof awareness of the vast socio-cultural variations of British India and for some, even of Europe, having been indentured into the Labour Corps of the Ist World War (Horam 1998: 34). All the members shared common bond of concern for the welfare of the people vis-à-vis the colonial administration which to the Naga tribesmen, were alien intruders and an imposition. Being driven with a sense of mission, for the welfare of the Naga tribesmen and in particular their future perspective, as we understand now, the Naga Club was formed at Kohima in the year of 1918 (Ao 1993: 171).

At the time of the Naga Club formation, it is worth noting that the Ao, Angami, Sema, Lotha, Rengma, Chang, Sangtam, Konyak and even Katcha Naga tribes and countries (country – as per tribal perception and description) had been annexed in stages and designated as 'Naga Hills' from 1879 on (Ao 1993). House tax annually was long levied as far back as from 1877 to defray the cost of administration by colonial power. Schools had been established both by the administrations and Christian missions from 1878. And Christian proselytisation had begun by 1876 by Rev. Clark in the Ao country (Aier 2006: 44–53).

Colonial Experience and Naga Ethos

The domination over the Naga tribals and annexation of their lands to the imposition of administrative-political control led to several developments. To the Naga tribesmen, the village is the basic unit of society (Horm 1978). In fact, in their perception in the traditional frame, it is accepted as a sovereign republic. Colonial control in consequence meant that the villagers and its citizens lost their age old existential independence. Added to this, paying tax to foreign authority only confirmed their loss. It amounted to slipping their moorings and being sent adrift in a larger water, where they would encounter other Naga tribesmen, friend and foe, in similar distress. This phenomenon progressed into larger configurations of more encounters and commiserations of common plight and seeking each other. Having been dislodged from their age old traditional latitude of sovereign independence to being collectively identified and called as Nagas for various reasons (not discussed here), the various tribes found a common link to nurture and foster, consciously or unwittingly, a common sense of destiny. This ostensibly established a fact and conviction that they all share a common enemy, who had vanquished them and are now trampling over their lands and country which are geographically contiguous to each other.

In fostering a common sense of destiny in the light of being opposed to alien colonial presence, the subject tribesmen began to rear a larger common sense of collectivity – of being one people; in fact the making of a Naga community. This was much spurred on by many commonalities of socio-cultural construct beginning from ancestral origins, myths, folklore, beliefs, rituals and many other practices. In this, it is further observed that colonial policy of 'non-interference' indirectly played a role in the sense that local power arrangements and customary practices were left untouched which much reinforced the commonalities and similarities among themselves. This to the Naga community was also taken as a case of non-surrender to colonial subjugation and thus the future of possibility of emancipation or liberation from colonial control as a community (Aier 2006: 46).

The colonial presence, like a torch lighting the darkness, further heightened Naga community's sense of the presence of other people that were unlike them in many ways. The people of the plains of Assam, Manipur and further west in the larger British-Indian mainland did not share similarities to that of the Naga community. They overtly became conscious of habitat/territory difference, in addition to language, customs and practices and religious beliefs and practices. Here, ever since 1876, Christian proselytisation had replaced the pagan-animistic religion, which all the more strengthened Naga tribal solidarity. This also further sensitised them to other religious particularly Hinduism and Islam, which in the first instance established their sense of fundamental difference with that of the others. Thus, placed against a different dimension as seen by themselves only enlarged their sense of solidarity and destiny.

Naga Ethno Genesis

The Naga community being hill-men by geographical placement naturally felt a physical gulf with those inhabitants of the plains, in a sense of distance. Added to this was the language difference which, except for a few on both sides of the hills and plains engaged in trade and commerce, was for all practical purposes unknown to both sides. The obstacles created by not knowing the immediate neighbour's language aside, was the polyglot world on the far western side, which to the Naga community was mysterious, awe and fear inspiring. Added to it, the schools on the hills taught in vernacular and English, which now understood, served as a barrier or wedge to maintain the distance between the language/dialects of the tribals and those of the Assam plains and beyond to the enunciation of 'those,' 'them' and 'us,' and 'we,' mentally and socially widening the gulf.

It is common man's claim that history divides or unites men in tracing these roots, ancestry and lineage. If that be so, the Naga tribal experience to this stage, (that is, from late eighteenth to early nineteenth century) in their understanding was sufficient reason and justification to erect that imaginary wall of division with those inhabiting the plains and beyond to the west. Included in it were experiences of being identified as different for being organised around a common religion, (that is, having become Christians) in contrast to other prevailing religions. All of these experiences combined led to providing the Naga tribesmen a sense of solidarity, security in each other's presence, a sense of oneness – in fact the emergence of an ethnic group identity, much vaunted by ethnocentric history, emotional upsurge of consciousness as to the alter represented by the British and other non-tribal communities in their geographical and socio-cultural vicinity. In all this, we sociologically observe a heterogeneity of diverse-discrete tribes bonding into a homogeneous identity of being one group.

The above analysis very closely shares resemblances with the process of ethnic group formation with that of the contributions about ethnic formation by Anthony D. Smith (1986: 21–46). He presents six major considerations as commonly present in ethnic group formation:

1. A common myth of descent.

2. A shared history.
3. A distinctive shared culture.
4. An association with a specific territory.
5. A sense of solidarity.
6. An organised religion.

An exercise of superimposing and interfacing the six above considerations to the case of the Naga tribesmen draws out the following understandings:

(1) A common myth of descent. There is a widely prevalent belief among the Naga tribesmen although without credence and substance that long before, the Nagas lived in foreign land, (i.e., present day mainland China) where they were born to common ancestors. Being helpless to dominant superior force, they were enslaved to labour in the building of the Great Wall of China. After many years, with their kinship members proliferating, they fled south toward present day Myanmar.

(2) A shared history. From a common ancestry, begins their shared history of slavery and runaway slaves in another land, where they divided into smaller groups and went their separate ways to separate settlements and experiences, respectively. With the passing of time, they developed their respective dialects and an identity although similarities in languages and sense of common origin sustained on. Having attained identity as a tribe/community on their own respective merits, they moved further to the west and founded a large settlement called Khezakhonoma, where the various tribes settled (Alemchiba 1970). Some, it is claimed, settled at a place known as Maikel. In these settlements, they gave themselves names to identify respective tribal groups. Eventually, each group in turn migrated to settle and proliferate into more population and villages in their present places of habitation. Their history further shared more commonness when the colonial forces all brought them under its control.

(3) A distinctive shared culture. Out of their claimed common descent and shared history, it becomes obvious that they would share common and similar cultural practices. It is these elements that rendered matters inevitable that they could without difficulty in merging into an ethnic group identity.

(4) To this, is that they all share, even today, association with their specific age old territory which is further characterised by physical proximity. This has all the more strengthened and reinforced sense of ancestry, history and culture to inevitably form an ethnic group.

(5) A sense of solidarity is easily observed right from their common ancestry to date. To the time of the formation of the Naga Club, the

sense of solidarity apparently had become one committed conviction as is with ethnic group existence to develop later course of their destiny.

(6) An organised religion in Christianity ostensibly solidified them into the Naga ethnic group, to be much identified as different by other communities in the vicinity.

All the above is much reinforced as plausible within a spectrum of process by what Frederick Barth discusses. In fact, the points of his proposal and contributions from the field serve as a mirror to Anthony D. Smith's contention (1964: 9–58). Of particular pertinence is that of the matter of ethnic group boundary and that of its maintenance that Barth extols about, which is a social context of the rules of relationship with people falling under the spectrum of inclusion and exclusion. On these matters, Naga ethnic group identity have sustained itself by strict adherence to the maintenance of that boundary, which is invisible, yet felt as a fact of being led by it, of identification of the self to others.

Naga Ethnicity and Consequent Political Permutations

The above preceding lines have tentatively attempted, a reconstruction of the Naga Community out of discovering a common level of plight, of the various discrete Naga tribal groups, having been dominated and been made subjects of British colonial India. This Naga community of the then Naga hills in this scheme of discussion is identified as a bona-fide ethnic group, in line to Narroll's definition of an ethnic group (1964).

Being mentally traumatised by ever growing consciousness of the foreign control over them, added to the turmoil of having lost their former independence to the extent of paying tax, the Naga tribesmen's only option was to show their resentment in many ways as possible led by in particular the Naga Club, highlighting socio-cultural, historical differences and the location of their habitat formed a sharp point of statement. Another was that of their hostile relationship with the people of the Assam and Manipur, much projected in dire futuristic perspective and of their apprehensions of being swamped, deprived and dominated by non-hill men. In the Naga Club then was posited a symbol of Naga ethnic movement, reflecting a common identity, solidarity and destiny.

Through the Naga Club, under the show of ethnicity in particular to the colonial rules, was sustained Naga tribal solidarity and on the other, made known their inner decisions of never to be mixed up or bound together in any way with the communities on the plains of the region. In these ways, Naga tribesmen were sensitively aware of colonial intentions and policy. The then British – India Government constituted the Indian statutory commission, with the objective of initiating a national reforms scheme under the chairmanship of John Simon, commonly known as the Simon Commission.

In January 1929, the Simon Commission visited Kohima to ascertain the minds and position of the Naga tribesmen vis-à-vis the proposed constitutional scheme. The Naga club submitted a memorandum, the contents bristling of Naga ethnicity of differences, apprehension and their utmost desire to be left alone as before, in the event of British departure.[1]

The letter to the Simon Commission, it is believed, had a desired effect of impressing upon the British administration that the Naga tribesmen on the hills had transcended their earlier savage head hunting mentality and of ignorance and isolation to a higher awareness of their reality and that of a future for themselves and by themselves. More than this, the letter had the impact of letting the colonial administration know that the Naga tribes did not identify with the people of the plains of Assam and Manipur and, therefore, were ethnically different and, therefore, to be left to themselves in the event of British withdrawal from that area.

Such expression of Naga tribal ethnicity eventually gained a significant recognisation, that as a measure of taking it into consideration Naga tribal desires, as is now felt, the constitutional Act of 1935 decided to keep the Naga Hills district outside of the purview of the new constitutional provision and declared it as an excluded area. This measure on the part of the colonial administration is seen as a measure of protecting Naga right and feelings and a recognisation of their ethnicity. In fact in this, as a measure of evaluation, we could describe it as the maturation of Naga ethno genesis and of its process.

Just a few years later, the Second World War broke out and the Naga tribesmen felt the devastation and loss created by the Japanese invasion of the Naga Hills. The Naga people valiantly supported the British forces particularly during the Battle of Kohima to halt the Japanese advances. Lives were lost, the town devastated with no relief and rehabilitation coming to the Naga public. No reward was given to anybody, which was very much due (Ao 1993). Such insensitive treatment did not go without hurting Naga sentiments. It grew to the point of adding political colour to Naga ethnicity that it was not only Hindus and Muslims that were prejudicial to the Nagas, but also that of the colonial masters.

Naga ethnicity led by the Naga Club, it would seem, was rapidly replaced by Naga political speak of independence. In as much as there were benign colonial administrators concerned for the welfare of the Naga tribesmen, the overall feelings of the larger Naga public was of seeing the colonial power at Delhi and London as not trustworthy, as I now reported. Political speak of self determination, independence instantly began to supplant the points of Naga articulation of their concerns and anxieties. Acutely feeling the pulse, the benign administration at Kohima initiated the formation of the Naga Hills Tribal Council in 1945, in a bid to contain the new Naga political speak and provide a sense of control of their situation through the council. It was well intentioned, but Naga political aspiration like wildfire had already swept across every Naga habitat to be free, as it was the expression then.

Inevitably the Naga Hills Tribal Council, originally meant to control Naga political articulation and a sense of control of their destiny by organising relief and rehabilitation work, was converted into the Naga National Council (NNC). When A.Z. Phizo took over as the fourth president of the NNC, Naga political cause was set to move for independence, which is still an ongoing impasse between the Government of India and the various Naga outfits contemporarily giving continuity to the movement.

By the time of the NNC's emergence, not much data could be traced as to the role of the Naga Club and that of its members. But it is arguably seen that without the Naga club and its role of igniting the minds of the Naga tribesmen of their reality and sense of destiny, Naga politics as it is today may not have been existent.

Note

1. The contents of the memorandum are reproduced below:

   To,
   The Indian Statutory Commission
   Camp India
   Memorandum on Naga Hills

   Sir,
   We, the undersigned Nagas of the Naga Club at Kohima, who are the only persons at present who can voice for our people have heard with great regret that our hills were included within the Reformed Scheme of India without our knowledge, but as the administration of our hills continued to be in the hands of the British Officers we did not consider it necessary to raise any protest in the past. Now we learn that you have come to India as representatives of the British Government to enquire into the system of working of the Government and the growth of education that our hills may be withdrawn from the reforms. We never asked for any reforms and we do not wish for them.

   Before the British Government conquered our country in 1879–1880 we were living in a state of intermittent warfare with the Assamese of the

Assam valley to the North and West of our country and Manipuris to the South. They never conquered us nor were we ever subjected to their rule. On the other hand, we were always a terror to those people. Our country within the administered area consists of more than eight tribes, quite different from one another with quite different languages which cannot be understood by each other, and there are more tribes outside the administered area which are not known at present. We have no unity among us and it is only the British Government that is holding us together now.

Our education, at present, is poor. The occupation of our country by the British Government being so recent as 1880 we have had no chance or opportunity to improve in education and though we can boast of two or three graduates of an Indian University in our country, we have not got one yet who is able to represent all different tribes of our languages much less one to represent us in any Council of a province. However, our population of the hills numbering 10,210,000 is very small in comparison with the population of the plains district in the province and any representation that may be allotted to us in the Council will be negligible and will have no weight whatever. Our language is quite different from those of the plains and we have no social affinities with either Hindus or Muslims. We are being looked down upon by one for our 'beef' and the other for our 'pork' and both for our want in education which is not due to any fault of ours.

Our country is poor and it does not pay for its administration. Therefore, if it continues to be placed under the Reformed Scheme, we are afraid that new heavy taxes will have to be imposed and in the long run we shall have no share in the land of our birth and life will not be worth living then. Though our land at present is within the British territory, Government has always recognised our Private Rights in it, but if we are forced to enter the Council the majority of whose members are sure to belong to other districts. We also fear the introduction of Foreign Laws and Customs to supersede our own customary laws which we now enjoy. For the above reasons, we pray that the British Government will continue to safeguard our rights against all encroachments from other people who are more advanced than us by withdrawing our country from the Reformed Scheme and placing it directly under its own protection. If the British Government, however, wants to throw us away, we pray that we should not be thrust to the mercy of the people who could never have conquered us themselves, and to whom we are never subjected; but to leave us alone to determine for ourselves as in ancient times.

References

Aier, I.L. 2006. *Contemporary Naga Social Formations and Ethnic Identity*. New Delhi: Akansha Publishing House.

Alemchiba, M. 1970. *A Brief Historical Account of Nagaland*. Kohima: Naga Institute of Culture.

Ao, Tejenyuba. 1993. *British Occupation of Naga Country*. Mokokchung: Naga Literature Society.

Barth, Fredrik. 1970. *Ethnic Groups and Boundaries*. London: George Allen and Unwin.

Horam, M. 1975. *Naga Polity*. New Delhi: B.R. Publishing Corporation.

Horam, Ringkahao. 1998. *The Genesis of the Naga Political Movement*. Imphal: MBC.

Narroll, R. 1964. 'Ethnic Unit Classification', *Current Anthropology*, 5 (4): 234–43.

Smith, Anthony D. 1986. *The Ethnic Origins of Nations*. Oxford: Basil Blackwell.

10

Development and Conflict

The Legacies of Forest Management Policies in India: A Case Study in Khasi and Jaintia Hills

REKHA M. SHANGPLIANG

The forest wealth of India has always been perceived with coveted eyes by the authorities who managed it. The ruling paradigm of forest management policies of the government has ever been biased in favour of harnessing of the forest resources for development of the country as against the people whose livelihood depended on it. The policy decision of the authorities has continued to be based on two faulty premises – that a developing country cannot afford the luxury of preserving forest for the sake of ecological balance and that the high potentialities of forest resources need to be utilised for national development purposes. This attitude of the government having been stretched too far has led to the rise of conflict of interest and people's resentment against the alienation of their rights over natural forests. The colonial government found the forest of India to be potential source of revenue and converted large areas of natural forests into 'Reserved forests' restricting the local people from entering into and using any forest product thereof. The National Forest Policy, 1950, on the other hand, enunciated that 'the domestic and agricultural needs of the people should, in no event, be permitted at the cost of national interest'. It specifically said: 'The accident of a village situated close to a forest does not prejudice the right of the country as a whole to receive the benefit of national assets'. Thus, the concept that the forest is meant for the broader interest of the country as a whole, as against the domestic use of the forest dwellers or, in short, the maxim of 'Forest for revenue and development' that has been adopted by the British as well as the national government of India in management of natural resources, has been mainly responsible for the rise of conflict of interest between the government and the people whose livelihood depended on forest.

This paper makes an attempt at focusing on the forest management policies of the government and their impact on the life of the people bringing about socio-economic development and conflict in Khasi and Jaintia Hills ever since the colonial rule.

The British forest policy was primarily oriented towards earning revenue and to achieve this end the government introduced the first forest act of India The Indian Forest Act 1865 gave legal authority to the government to interfere with the rights of the local people and freely use their forest products. The ultimate objective of this Act was to preserve and protect the natural grown forest under the cover of law and to harvest their products, like timber and other products of revenue and trade, for the benefit of the government. The Indian Forest Act of 1865, the first forest Act of India, was then replaced thirteen years later by the Forest Act of 1878 which was more stringent and comprehensive. The provisions of the 1878 Act were to serve as a model not only for India but for other British colonies as well, but, while some officials within the colonial administration were sharply critical of the new legislation, calling it an Act going against the customary usage of forest by Indian people.

According to the 1878 Forest Act, forests were categorised into three types – Reserved forest, Protected forest and Village Reserved forests. These three classes of forests were deemed to be the most commercially valuable and, hence, susceptible to sustained exploitation. Overall state control of reserved forests was sought, which involved either the relinquishment or infringement of people's claims and rights, although limited access was granted. Legally, provisions were open to public to contest the reservation of forests, though rural communities had little experience with legal procedures and illiterate villagers were often unaware that a survey and demarcation was in process for reservation of forests. Protected forests were similarly state controlled, but some concessions were granted, conditional to the reservation of commercial tree species, when they became valuable. Protected forests could also be closed to fuel wood collection and grazing, whenever it was deemed necessary to do so. As demand for timber increased in the country and it was found that the state had limited capability to meet the requirement, the protected forests were upgraded to reserved forests. The Act also provided for constitution of third category of forests called the Village forests – though according to Gadgil and Guha (1992), this was not done by the colonial government over most part of India.

The framework of the 1878 Act was designed basically to cater to the strategic imperial needs at that time – the supply of large scale timber for the railways. Some of the provisions of the Indian Forest Act 1878 ensured the following objectives:

1. The state could demarcate valuable tracts of forest needed especially for railways purposes.
2. Retain enough flexibility over the remaining extent of forestland to revise its policy from time to time.
3. Monopoly right was established by a legal sleight of hand, which sought to establish that the customary use of the forest by the villagers, based not on 'right' but on 'privilege' and that 'privilege' was exercised only at the mercy of the local rulers (the British were then the local rulers).
4. There were provisions for demarcation of 'Reserved' and 'Unreserved' forests with a list of reserved trees being drawn. Persons were to be notified to record their claims over land and forest produce in the proposed reserved and unreserved forests.

The tribals in the North-East, on more than one occasion, expressed their resentment and protested against the government policy of alienating them from their forests and primary source of livelihood. The history goes back to the British rule when the Garos rose in revolt against the conversion of their jhum lands into reserved forests and restricting them from entering and using the land. The most immediate consequence of the Indian Forest Act of 1878 was visible in the discontentment of the forest communities who now totally lost control over their own habitats. The forest Act 1878 evolved a sharp reaction from the simple and straight-forward Garo community who rose in popular revolt in an attempt to restore their traditional rights to freely roam about their forest habitats. The government, however, arrested their leader one Sonaram Sangma and imprisoned him for a short time. This led the Garos to file a public petition on 9 February 1906 signed by more than one lakh Garos to Lord Minto, the Viceroy and Governor General of India. The petition accused the government stating that their ancestors had enjoyed the privilege of living in the forest in Garo Hills, made use of the forest products, sold them for their benefit besides cultivating their land and having the rights of pasturage, but the government has deprived them of this age old privileges. The objections of the people was, however, summarily over-ruled by the British government.

Post-independence Forest Policy

The government changed in 1947 after the British left India, but the forest policy did not change. The Government of India continued to follow more or less the same forest laws. The Indian Forest Act 1927 and the Assam Forest Regulation 1891, the two major forest laws, continued to be applied in the whole state of Assam, including Khasi and Jaintia Hills district. In 1952, the Government of India declared a new forest policy viz, National Forest Policy, 1952, which envisaged (1) maintenance of environmental stability through preservation and restoration of ecological balance, (2) conserving the natural heritage of the country by preserving the remaining natural forests with the vast variety of flora and fauna, (3) checking soil erosion and denudation in the catchment areas of rivers, lakes and reservoirs, (4) increasing sustainability of forest/tree cover in the country and (5) meeting the requirement of fuel, fodder, minor forest produce, small timber for the rural and tribal population. But, unfortunately, the government did not come up with new forest laws to achieve the objectives laid down therein and the high ideals held out by the National Forest Policy remained merely a rhetoric.

In 1952, the Autonomous District Councils were constituted in the hill districts of Assam under the sixth schedule of the Constitution of India which took up administration and control of forests under their jurisdictions. In the district of Khasi and Jaintia Hills the existing forest areas were bifurcated between the state Forest department and the Khasi and Jaintia Hills Autonomous District Council. With this division of forests, all reserved forests, government forest, existing parks and gardens remained with the state forest department, while the rest of the forest areas of the district went under the management of the District Council. The Khasi and Jaintia Hills Autonomous District Council promulgated its own Forest Act under the title 'United Khasi and Jaintia Hills Autonomous District (Management and control of forest) Act, 1958 but the objectives of the Act remained, more or less, dittoed the previous Acts. It classified the forests under the District Council as, Protected forests, Unclassed forests, Village forests and Private forests and sought to control and manage them with the meagre fund allocation received from the Centre and the state government. The forest areas that came under jurisdiction of the District Council being larger than it could manage with its small Forest staff they became merely a source of revenue earning. The Protected forests, the legacy from the state Forest department, being rich in timber value, were exploited it to the point of its denudation by the District Council.

After the state of Meghalaya was carved out of Assam in 1972, the state Legislative Assembly adopted the Assam Forest Regulation 1891, under the title Meghalaya Forest Regulation (Application and Amendment) Act, 1973. This Act empowers the government to constitute a reserved forest at any land at the disposal of the government in a manner provided therein. But so far no reserved forest could be constituted in Khasi Hills or Jaintia Hills as there was no land at the disposal of the government in these districts. It also deals with constitution of village forests and to frame rules related to it. Thus, it is seen that the existing forest laws enacted by the colonial rulers are merely adopted and continued to be followed by government after government without any change in the basic policy or in the pattern of forest administration. Neither the state government nor the District Council showed any intention to preserve and protect forest for the sake of environment and ecological balance and for future generation.

Forest for Development

With the implementation of a series of Five Year Plans by the Government of India since 1952 onwards, the nation got into rapid strides along the path of progress and development. There was rapid growth in agriculture, industries, health and sanitation, literacy and education, and so on, leading to socio-economic development and better standard of living of the community. The government aimed at harnessing all the resources of the country for all round economic development. The forest was found to be one of the potential natural resources for industrial and infrastructural development. Timbers were liberally used in construction of buildings, bridges, furniture and other structures. Forest based small and cottage industries like saw mill, veneer mill, carpentry workshop, and so on, grew up all over the country pushing up the demand for various qualities of wood. Large scale bamboo groves were denuded to meet the demand of paper-pulp for burgeoning paper mills. Thus, there was a paradigm shift in the basic forest policy of the government from the colonial 'forest for revenue' to the national 'forest for development', both being equally destructive of the forest resources and detrimental to the people who live in close communion with nature. The high ideals held out by the National Forest Policy were flouted away; every possible element of the forest was harnessed in development activities; pristine forest wealth was exploited resulting in large scale destruction of forest cover. To cite a concrete example, the FSL, in monitoring the forest cover of Meghalaya on a two-year cycle found that the total forest cover of 15,633 sq km in 1999 was reduced to 15,584 sq km in 2001, showing a net loss of 49 sq km. The following paragraphs will give us an account of the impact that have been made upon the social and economic life of the common people due to destruction and alienation of forest from them.

Socio-economic Impact

Before the advent of the British, the people of the Khasi and Jaintia Hills lived peacefully in perfect harmony with forest. The forest was a well loved home which they never exploited for their profit except for their home consumption, instead they preserved it as store-house of their livelihood. They believed the forests as the sacred abodes of gods and spirits and looked at them with a sense of reverence and awe and never dared to disturb the sanctum-sanctorum of the place. They took away from the forest what is barely needed for their livelihood and let the flora and fauna grow and flourish in their solitary habitats. This was true, more or less, of all the tribal societies of the North-East.

The colonial forest policy was, therefore, the first assault on the traditional life of the tribal people of the North-East in general and the Khasis and Jaintias in particular. There were, primarily, three colonial forest Acts which had decisive impact on the socio-cultural and economic profiles of the tribals – Indian Forest Act VII of 1865, Indian Forest Act 1878 and the Forest Act 1927. The first Act 1865 declared a certain forest areas as Protected forests and excluded the people from their benefits; the second Act 1878 came as a more concrete law which conferred the government with the right to constitute Reserved Forests on 'any forest land or waste land which is the property of the government'. This Act not only debarred the local people from entering into and removing any forest produce from the reserved forest and protected forests but also permanently alienated them from the land itself. This had a far reaching affect on the livelihood of the people in more than one way. First, agriculture being the main stay of the people, the land constitutes primary factor of their economy. Secondly and more significantly, land, for the hill people who grow their food by jhum cultivation, means a natural resource available in abundance for shifting cultivation changing from place to place. The Khasis carry out jhum or shifting cultivation which is locally called '*Thang Shyrti*'. It is a forest based method of cultivation followed by them since time immemorial. This type of cultivation, despite its many demerits and adverse opinions, has come to stay in Khasi society even to this day. This is mainly because of their peculiar land tenure system. The land tenure system in Khasi and Jaintia Hills recognises two types of land – *Ri-Raid* or community land and *Ri-Kynti* or private land. Every member of the community has the right to carry out cultivation anywhere on the community land, at his will and free of cost, as long as he wants. In case, he abandons the land for a consecutive period of three years and shifts to some other land, the land occupied by him will revert back to the community and becomes Ri-Raid land. A community with this system of social economy was, therefore, affected more than anybody else, by the British forest policy which appropriated their land of jhum cultivation.

The land and the forest, the two most crucial factors of village economy over which the people enjoyed irreversible rights were increasingly appropriated by the British government as the demand for timber increased. The proprietary rights, thus, established by the colonial rulers through promulgation of laws, permanently deprived the people of their traditional rights. The following extract from Indian Forest Act VII of 1878, cleverly crafted to suit the colonial interest, clearly reflects the commercial intention of the government. It runs: 'The local government may, from time to time constitute any forest land or waste land which is the property of the government or over which the government has proprietary rights or to the whole or part of forest produce of which the government is entitled, a reserved forest'. Needless to say, 'the British rule in India, like other western empires elsewhere in the developing world could be regarded as an elaborate system of resource extraction and allocation, determining who was to have access to nature's wealth.'

As the implementation of Five Year Plans progressed in the country, more lands were required for multifarious development purposes. Large areas of land were utilised for construction of a network of roads and communication, establishment of institutional buildings, extension of townships, industrial sites, stadiums and airports, and so on. These lands were, undoubtedly, acquired by government at the cost of either agriculture or forest lands. The construction of irrigation canals, dams and reservoirs for hydro-electricity uprooted many families from their hearths and homes. In Khasi Hills, an area of 4,000 acres of cultivated and home-stead land was submerged under reservoir for hydro-electricity by constructing a dam across Umiam river. In Garo Hills, an area of several thousand hectares of land has been acquired by government for setting up a Bio-sphere Reserve. A new airport was established in Garo Hills and the existing air-field at Umroi, in Khasi Hills was up graded by acquisition of large areas of land. These hill areas, before they were acquired by government, were forested land used by villagers for jhum cultivation. It is, thus, evident that a considerable chunk of agriculture and forest land was diverted by government in the name of national development programmes which contributed to severe impact on the socio-economic condition of the people who depended on the land for their subsistence.

The Government of India passed Wild Life (Protection) Act in 1972 which was a step forward towards the strengthening of conservation of flora and fauna of the country. Long ago, during the British rule one such legislation existed by the title Wild Birds and Animals Protection Act,

1912. The new Act passed by the Government of India provided much needed security to the birds and animals, many of which were on the verge of extinction, but at the same time it went directly against the interest of the common people by diversion of more lands for extension/creation of Wildlife Sanctuaries, National Parks, Tiger Reserves, and so on.

The Forest Conservation Act, 1980 was considered as a significant piece of legislation in so far as it sought to ban irrationale conversion of forest lands to non-forest purposes, as we have seen large scale conversion in the foregoing paragraphs. It also aimed at imposition of compensatory afforestation in lieu of forested land diverted on unavoidable circumstances. Undoubtedly, this was a step in the right direction which sought to provide legal protection to dwindling forest. This Act, however, was not subservient to the needs of the people as it infringed the traditional rights of the tribals by restraining them from using their community lands for jhum cultivation, which is traditionally done in forested land. It also restricts them from cultivating tea, coffee, spices, rubber and horticultural crops. Because the Act defines these crops as 'non-forest crops' and bans cultivating on any forest land. These are the crops which grow well in the hill areas, because of climate and hilly terrain, and primarily the hill people cultivate them. It will, thus, be seen that the tribal people living in the hills, like Khasis, Garos, Nagas and Mizos are gradually being marginalised by the government through bringing in various forest laws. The Government of India seemed to be more conscious about the degradation of forests rather than being concerned about the livelihood of the people who traditionally depend on it. For, no forest law so far enacted by government provides for the safeguard of the rights and interest of the people who are the real protectors of forest.

In 1988, the Government of India declared a revised National Forest Policy 1988 with the view to increasing, substantially, the forest cover in the country and to maintain the environmental stability. One of the significant objectives of the policy was to meet the requirement of fuel, fodder, minor forest produce and small timber for the rural tribal population. In order to implement this policy, the Ministry of Forest and Environment, in June 1990, issued a circular to all forest departments of states to launch Joint Forest Management (JFM) programme for revival, restoration and development of degraded forests along with participation of the people. A number of states, including Meghalaya followed the instruction of Central government and started the JFM programme in various districts. The programme has achieved some degree of success in building up non-timber forest resources in the most degraded forests adopted by the Forest Management Committees. The Forest Management Committees involve all the households in the village as members of its general body of the Committee, where the decisions are jointly taken and afforestation activities are done with their collective labour. The Joint Forest Management (JFM) programme, however, could not mitigate the people's livelihood problems arising out of the loss of their forest habitats. The prolonged application of development oriented government policy in the realm of natural resource management resulted in inevitable impact on the forest community whose livelihood depended on forest. Thus, the larger section of the people living in the rural areas continued to be marginalised by the forest policy and administration adopted by government.

Judicial Activism in Forest Administration

The greatest impact on the livelihood of the forest community was made by the Supreme Court Order of 12 December 1996 imposing complete ban on felling trees from any forest, irrespective of ownership and doing trade in timber. The Apex court intervention in forest operation originated from a PIL case, viz – TN Godavarman VS. Union Government of India, 1995 in which the Supreme Court suspended felling of trees in all forests irrespective of whether it belonged to government or any private person, except in accordance with the working plans of the state government formally approved by the Central government. The Supreme Court also interpreted the term 'Forest' as all forested lands disregard of their classification and nature of ownership. Prior to this order, the term forest implied only the government forest whether it covered any tree or not, while lands with significant cover of tree were not regarded as forests and the people were free to cut down trees from anywhere grown in their lands. Because of this lacunae in the definition of forest, large areas of forest belonging to private owners did not fall within the purview of the Forest Conservation Act, 1980 and they were being severely deforested by their owners without any restriction. In Khasi and Jaintia Hills, unlike any other parts of India, great majority of forests belong to community/clans and private individuals on which the state Forest department or the Autonomous District Councils have no control. Nearly one-third of the total forest area of Meghalaya is owned by community/clan or private individuals. Before the Supreme Court Order, 1996, these proprietors of private forests caused large scale felling of trees from their forests to make quick bucks which led to near denudation of forests.

The Supreme Court Order, 1996 not only brought about a grinding halt on the felling of trees heralding a new era of security to flora and fauna, but also had a far reaching impact on the livelihood of a large section of the working class people engaged in the forest industry. The impact was felt more severely in the hill areas of Khasi and Jaintia Hills where the tribal economy was traditionally based on forest. A large community of people beginning from those who worked in the forest operation and transport of logs to those who were engaged in saw mills, veneer mills, factories, carpentry work-shops and building of houses were virtually thrown out of employment as a result of this judicial activism. The Supreme Court Order banned forest operation but did not order for providing alternative source of income to those who lost their jobs. In fact, the entire natural resource management policy of the government lacked livelihood focus for those who depend on forest. There was also lack of community involvement in policy process. Many issues primarily concerning common man and their livelihood related issues do not get reflected in the government policies.

A survey was conducted by the Department of Botany, North-East Hill University, under the guidance of S.K. Barik and V.T. Darlong to study the impact of government resource management policy on the livelihood of forest poor which had taken up nine villages in five districts of Meghalaya. It was found that in all the nine villages, forest dependence was high due to the practice of shifting cultivation, timber trade and NTFP (Non-timber forest produce) collection. In one particular village named Mawthoh of West Khasi Hills district, they found that there were 20 households with 150 persons. 63 per cent of the village area was under forest which were entirely owned by private individuals, 31 per cent was agricultural land and 6 per cent was kitchen garden. All the households were dependent on forest for their livelihood. After the Supreme Court Order 1996, a few families turned to charcoal making, some other to agriculture and kitchen gardening. Before the Supreme Court Order, income of the village from forest timber business was ₹ 1 lakh per year which came down to zero as a result of the judicial order. Due to impact of the Supreme Court Order the income from agriculture increased to ₹ 40,000, from kitchen garden ₹ 10,000 and from mining labour to ₹ 20,000 per year. Some of the families shifted to charcoal making, bee-keeping, etc.

References

Darlong, V.T. 2002. 'An Overview of Forest Policies and Legislations vis-à-vis Forest Resource Management in North-East India', in B. Datta Ray and K. Alam (eds), *Forest Resources in North East India*, New Delhi: Omson Publications, pp. 102–32.

Gadgil, Madhav and Ramchandra Guha. 1992. *This Fissured Land: An Ecological History of India*. Delhi: Oxford University Press.

Indian Forest Act, 1878. Government of India Press.

Kannan, K.P. 1982. 'Forest for Industry's Profit', *Economic and Political Weekly*, 23 (2): 235–38.

Nongbri, Tiplut. 2003. *Development, Ethnicity and Gender: Select Essays on Tribes in India*. Jaipur and New Delhi: Rawat Publications.

Shangpliang, Rekha M. 2010. *Forest in the Life of the Khasis*. New Delhi: Concept Publishing Company Pvt. Ltd.

Sinha, A.C. 1993. *Beyond the Trees, Tigers and Tribes: Historical Sociology of the Eastern Himalaya Forest*. New Delhi: Har-Anand Publications.

The United Khasi and Jaintia Hills Autonomous District (Management and Control of Forests) Act, 1958 and Rules, 1995. Shillong: Khasi Hills Autonomous District Council.

Tucker, Richard P. 1988. 'The Depletion of India's Forest under British Imperialism: Planters, Foresters and Peasants in Assam and Kerala', in Donald Worster (ed.), *The Ends of the Earth*, Cambridge: Cambridge University Press, pp. 45–53.

11

The Politics of Collective Muslim Identity in Modern India

ESITA SUR

Modernity, in words of Kant, is associated with the spirit of Enlightenment, which on the whole is an idea as well as a cultural impulse, the rule of secular reason. So modernity speaks for the rational self and the constitution of selfhood or identity and it involves the process of identification of individual with the collectivity and society. But in the modern era, the identification with primordial categories like religion, caste, gender, ethnicity reveals the greatest paradox of our times that the idea of ethnic groups, communities was returned at the very time when the processes of capitalist globalisation and liberalisation had been firmly set at place. So the relationship between modernity and ethnicity calls for a special attention. Ethnicity is a sense of ethnic identity, which has been defined by De Vos as consisting of the 'subjective, symbolic or emblematic use' by 'a group of people ... any aspect of culture, in order to differentiate themselves from other groups' (Brass 1991: 2). An ethnic group that uses cultural symbols in these ways is a subjectively self-conscious community that establishes criteria for inclusion into and exclusion from the larger group. Ethnicity or ethnic identity not only involves subjective self-consciousness but a claim to status or recognition and in this case the role of objective cultural markers like language, customs, religion or race becomes very important in constituting the ethnic identity.

So the reproblematisation of the relationship between ethnic community identity and modernity has become a central concern in the theoretical debate on modernity and ethnic identity.

Sociologists like Durkheim believed that modernity can be defined by a movement from the mechanical forms of integration, characterised by ascriptive values and an immediate identification of individual with the collectivity, and these are characterised by the contractual relations (Denalty 2000). He also believed that the recovery of the sense of community could be compatible with the requirements of individualised era as the challenge for the modern society. On the contrary, Max Weber said that modernity exhausted the possibilities of cultural meaning. For him, culture provides individuals with the resources for meaning but societies which undergo the process of rationalisation, loses the possibilities of cultural meaning. It means that the process of modernisation prioritises the self of the individual which may go against the collective will.

But it must be mentioned that the very logic of modernisation itself reaffirms the need for a community identity and culture. This is primarily a modern phenomenon that emphasises the formation of identity based on a central organising principle of ethnicity, religion, language, gender, or caste positions. And it is a sort of compelling remedy for anonymity in an otherwise impersonal modern world. It is, thus, said to be a 'pattern of belonging, a search for comfort, an approach to community.' So it can be argued that the quest for community has been inspired because of the failure of the social. While the society has been associated with the aspects of modernity like rationalisation, individualisation, industrialism and disenchantment, then community feeling has been successful in expressing the emotional demands and needs for solidarity, trust and autonomy.

However, the complex social changes and the imbrications of various forces, factors and events in this modern world have rendered such production and recognition of such identities problematic. This is to say that any search for an '*authentic self* or *identity*' is not an innocent possibility rather it involves negotiating 'other', often overlapping and contested, heterodox or multiple '*selves*'.

In this context, while addressing the Muslim identity as a collective identity, it is important to mention that after independence Indian State has tried its best to blend the individual as well as community identity under framework of liberal democracy. The state has not only guaranteed citizenship rights but also ensured minority rights and identity. So, the state has never intervened in the private domains of the community on the ground of maintaining the minority identity and culture. So the argument of the paper is that the development of collective Muslim identity is not only a product of primordial attachments but the active involvement of the state in nurturing and manipulating this identity plays an important role to protect this collective identity.

That is why the question of identity construction and identification of Muslim community with the society becomes very significant in a sense that in this modernising society, identification of the Muslim community still occurs with the religio-cultural identity, but not as a deprived disempowered group of people (a more secular identity based on socio-political and economic factors) both by the inside agency and outsiders. So the process of identification of the individual with a particular identity of community, religion, ethnicity, social group is important both for Muslims and non-Muslims to contribute to the formation and construction of a collective identity of a group (Islam 2009). So the dominant construction of secular/communal binary has remained central to address Muslim identity in modern India. This is one of reasons for which Muslim question has been caught in the trap of religious-cultural space in this modern secular society and the role of the state as well as religious elite cannot be overlooked to construct the dominant discourse of projecting the Muslim community as merely a religious community.

So the paper will try to address a few questions like 1) why does community and ethnic identity still matter in this era of modernisation and globalisation? 2) How does post-colonial State deal with the formation of Muslim collective identity? 3) Apart from the primordial factors what are other factors which contribute to the development of the collective identity? And lastly 4) What is the role of the modern state to shape Muslim identity? So the paper will try to provide a critical examination of relationship between Muslim collective identity and modernity.

Muslim Identity as Collective Identity in Post-Colonial India

A pervasive myth within modernist self-understanding is that modern conditions destroy every collective formation and unleash different forms of individualism (Bhargava 2010). On this view, collective identities and communities cannot survive the modernist onslaught. But a glance at the process of modernity reveals, however, that while it undermines some kinds of groups, it simultaneously generates others. The most obvious example of a group made possible and supported by modern-processes is the nation and other sub-national groups and communities. The Partition of the Indian sub-continent left a Muslim minority in India. The constituent assembly, set up in December 1946, rejected the political majority-minority framework on the ground that special representation rights in India had begun the awful habit of treating Hindus and Muslims as distinct political entities. This rejection of a political majority – minority framework was entirely consistent with the acceptance of a social majority-minority framework (ibid.).

So Muslims were recognised as a distinct cultural and religious group and were given a constitutionally guaranteed right to the survival and renewal of their own cultural resources, a right to their languages and its scripts, a right to maintain their own educational institutions and a right to freedom of worship. They have also right to their own personal laws, that is, laws pertaining to family, marriage, divorce, maintenance, inheritance, child custody and adoption. In this way Indian state has made Muslims a distinct cultural community.

Muslim Personal Laws as the Maker of Ethnic Muslim Identity

The right of the Muslim Personal Laws has remained a very significant issue in India. The Muslim Personal Laws has become an integral part of the identity and culture of the Muslim Community. It goes without saying that Muslim identity is wound up with the existing personal laws. Since Independence, Indian State has tried to protect the identity and culture of the minority groups by not intervening into their private domain, especially in personal laws. This is one of the reasons which has given rise to the self-legislating Muslim community where religious leaders had played a significant role to define Muslim identity. It is due to the fact that the application of the personal law is often a complex matter and the interpretation of the Sharia is the monopoly of Ulemas. This is one of the principal mechanisms through which Ulemas and mullahs maintain their control over Islamic Society. Religious leaders have conveyed the message to Muslims and secular Muslim political elites that any attack on the Muslim Personal Laws is basically a threat to Muslim identity. That is why, question of reform of Muslim Personal Laws has been a crucial issue in India.

This attitude was very much clear in Shah Bano Case (1986). While all other Indian women may claim the legal right to spousal support after divorce, Muslim women may not. While other women criminally prosecute their husbands for bigamy, Muslim women may not. According to this act, a divorced Muslim woman is entitled to: (a) a reasonable and fair provision of maintenance within the period of Iddat. (b) two years of maintenance for her children. (c) Mehr and all the properties given to her by her relatives, friends, husband and husband's relatives. If these are not given to her at the time of divorce then she can apply to the Magistrate to direct her husband to follow the order. The government's response to this Act rested on the need to provide protection of minority identity defined in terms of religious and cultural terms. The government argued that it was against imposing a single pattern on all. The government argued in favour of differentiated criteria of citizenship as against universalistic criteria. It is important to mention that differentiated citizenship is mainly concerned with the inter-group equality, not with intra-group equality. That is why it leaves many structures of discrimination untouched. It also asserted that the impetus for change must come from within the Muslim community. So the government championed community rights, which gives priority to community's self-defining and self-determining character. But some opposition MPs argued that the bill benefited only the affluent sections of Muslim society. Saifuddin Ahmed said 'in the villages mehr is generally a very small amount as little as ₹ 3.50 along with the plastic and chemical ornaments'. In his opinion the bill looked after the interests of well-off of section of the community (Jayal 2002).

Indian State very deliberately never intervened in the private sphere of minority community. It is not only because of preserving their culture and identity but also for maintaining its own vote bank. The state could not guarantee the right to maintenance after divorce because the Muslim fundamentalists perceived it as an intrusion into their culture and religion. Muslim religious leaders and ulemas issued a *fatwa* (proclamation) that guaranteeing maintenance right was against the teachings of Islam. Within few months the whole issue took the form of communal agitation claiming that Islam was in danger. Modern Indian State never intervened in the reform of Muslim Personal Laws. The basic question was that the State could intervene to provide equal rights to women of one community, that is majority community and then what was the ground for not doing the same for others? There are two problems behind this issue. First is Indian interpretation of secularism on the basis of which Indian State devised policies premises on a 'principled distance' between the government and religion. Second is the conflict between the claims of cultural communities and women's rights of equal citizenship. The State never tried to reform Muslim Personal Law because for the Indian State equality of citizenship is important but the political leadership realised that respecting religious sensibilities was more important. That is why on religious ground the state does not intervene in reforming Muslim Personal Law. Reform in Muslim Personal Laws is definitely necessary but as Zoya Hasan argues that the process of reform is very complicated. In spite of reforms it is unlikely to radically improve the status of Muslim women by giving them equal and improved access to important social goods such as educational and employment (Hasan 2000). Because of these reasons personal laws remain one of the cultural identity makers.

Muslims as a Religious and Legal Community: A View from Within

Apart from Muslim Personal Laws, Urdu language as a marker of cultural identity and the role of religious elites remain important issues to be addressed. The conception of Muslim community held by the Ulema is generally religious and cultural in nature. In modern India, religious leaders assign much importance to religion and the primary symbol of Muslim identity is Islam itself in which adherence to the Sharia is an indispensable aspect. Urdu has also been included in the Ulema's definition of the Muslim community as a cultural symbol. As it is quite visible that the interpretation of the holy *Quran* is the exclusive preserve of the Ulemas, so in many ways it tends to violate principles of gender justice, equality and liberty of individuals and these are integral part of modernist paradigm. Religious leaders on several occasions have interpreted the verses of the *Quran* like polygamy, triple talaq, inheritance in such a manner that it has gone against Muslim women's rights also. It is also important to say that the autonomy of the community and the use of this by its protector have gone against the interests of its women. Because, for the preservation of Muslim identity and integration of community as cohesive and organic entity, ulemas have given excessive importance to Islamic norms and strict adherence to the *Shariat* (Lateef 1990).

In the words of Pereira, 'the major problem with reconciling Islamic tradition with today's understanding of universality, equality and women's human rights is that conceptions of Shariaalong with accepted notions of what Islam is supposed to hold, are steeped in misogyny' (2002: 80). It has several implications for Muslim women. As strict adherence to the *Shariat* and Islamic norms not only has strengthened the community control over Muslim women but women have also become crucial symbols of community identity and markers of traditions and culture. Through this process, the independent selfhood has been rolled back from the public domain to the interior space of the household and then further pushed back into the hidden depths of an inviolate, chaste, pure, female body. Not only this when strict adherence to *Shariat* is demanded, then at the same time pluralism in matters pertaining to the *Shariat* has affected rights of Muslim women.

As Imtiaz Ahmed has argued, 'where Islam clashed with the local beliefs, it is ignored and local councils which interpret Islam for benefit of their constituents merely reflect their version of its percepts (see Moinuddin 2001: 8). The way rights of Muslim women are explained in the *Quran* and the way it has been interpreted by religious leaders, shows that what Islam has given to women, male-dominated society has taken away. As interpretations on verses on polygamy, triple talaq, veiling is not free from influences of patriarchal power, tradition and culture. As Maulana Umar Ahmed, a noted commentator on the *Quran*, said that the *Quran* does not permit more than one marriage except with orphans and widows. The issue of triple talaq is also integrally related to this issue of polygamy. Muslim jurists of all schools believe that it is the exclusive preserve of man to pronounce divorce in one setting. But it is an inference not a divine rule. World renowned Egyptian Islamic scholar, Allama Yusuf al-Qaradawi has shown several instances of women who appeared before the Prophet without the veil. Islam also does not prevent women to work outside home, provided they can maintain their modesty. So in several cases this verse has been misinterpreted. In this case community leaders have exercised their full autonomy to confine the boundaries of Muslims including primarily women (Engineer 1999).

Muslim Collective Identity: A Responsibility of the Modernising State?

After Independence, Indian Constitution (Articles 25 and 26) guarantees freedom of religion. According to this, the Constitution guarantees every citizen's right to freedom of conscience and freely to profess, practice and propagate religion. But Partha Chatterjee (2000) argues that under this brand of secularism, the Indian State has also been allowed to intervene in religious matters to achieve the 'modernist' purpose of socio-religious reform.

That is why, by invoking the principle of liberty, the Indian State has carried out extensive reform of Hindu Personal Laws and of the administration of Hindu temples. The Hindu Code Bill was enacted in 1955 and the Indian Parliament went through the immensely complicated local and sectarian variations of Hindu law and laid down a single code of personal law for all Hindu citizens. Many of its new provisions involved gross departure from traditional brahminical principles, for example the new code legalised inter-caste marriage, sanctioned divorce and prohibited polygamy and gave the daughter the same right of inheritance as the son.

But when it comes to Muslim Personal Laws, then the Indian State did not make an attempt to reform personal laws and fulfil its modernising project. For example, in Shah Bano Case (1986) the verdict given by the Supreme Court was not materialised to protect Muslim Vote banks. That is why; Islamic fundamentalists have no quarrel with the ideal of modern secular state. For this reason, it gives rise to the real possibility of the Hindu right locating itself quite firmly within the domain of modernising state and using arguments for interventionist secularism to promote intolerance and violence against minorities (Chatterjee 2000).

It is important to say that the rebirth of Hindu nationalism under the NDA regime had profound impact on the Muslim community. A rising tide of Hindu orthodoxy had two antagonistic sides, that is, the reconstruction of Hindu identity and 'other' Muslims identity. Stereotypes about the Muslim community such as the practice of polygamy and non-observation of birth control measures lending to Muslim demographic explosion and disproportionate rise in Muslim population in India, sympathy and support for Pakistan on critical issues affecting Indo-Pak relations facilitated the rise of Hindutva ideology in India. All these manifestations of this new trend included *EkatmataYagna* and *RamaJanakiRathaJatra* in 1984 sponsored by the VHP and aimed at protecting and preserving India's national integration. Apart from this, the demand for restoration of Hindu temples converted into mosques by Muslim rulers in the past and clamour for building a temple at *Ramjanmabhoomi* (the birth place of lord Rama) in Ayodhya where a mosque constructed by Babar stood in place of an earlier temple were also raised (Basu 2009).

On 6 December 1992, the mosque was destroyed. In the months preceding the demolition, the BJP, the RSS, the VHP and the Shiv Sena had called for the construction of a temple on the site of the mosque as integral to their struggle to achieve Hindu rule in India. Over 1,50,000 supporters converged in Ayodhya, and, using hammers and pick-axes reduced the mosque to rubble. The police did not intervene. The incident sparked violence across the country in which at least 1,700 people were killed, thousands were injured, and an unknown number of women and girls were raped. The majority of the victims were Muslim (Bose 2009). The focal point of the violence was the city of Bombay, the capital of Maharashtra. For the ten days following 6 December, much of the violence took place between the police and Muslims protesting the destruction of the mosque. Police fired on demonstrators, entered and burned Muslim homes. Hindus also marched in support of the destruction of the mosque. In the latter days of the violence, members of the Shiv Sena attacked Muslim households alongside the police. During this time, the Sri Krishna Commission was established in response to the violence in Bombay. The Commission's report, presented to the government of Maharashtra in February 1998, more than five years after the violence took place, determined that the attacks were the result of a deliberate and systematic effort to incite violence against Muslims. It singled out Shiv Sena leader Bal Thackeray and Chief Minister Manohar Joshi as responsible for this massacre (Narula 2009). The Shiv Sena-BJP-led government refused to accept the Commission's recommendations, and instead labelled the report 'anti-Hindu'. The campaign to build the Ram temple is on-going and continues to raise the spectre of further violence in the country. The recent revival of the campaign in 2002, corresponding to BJP election losses in key states, centred on the 15 March 2002 deadline set by the VHP to bring stone pillars to the site in order to initiate the temple's construction. In the weeks preceding the violence in Gujarat, Hindu activists had been travelling to and from Ayodhya on the Sabarmati Express train. On 27 February 2002, following weeks of rising tensions between Hindu activists and Muslim vendors at the train station, a Muslim mob attacked Hindu activists riding in a train car of the Sabarmati Express. Two train cars were set on fire, killing at least forty eight people, including women and children. Between 28 February and 2 March 2002, a three-day retaliatory killing spree by Hindus left hundreds of Muslims dead and thousands homeless and dispossessed throughout Gujarat, marking the country's worst religious bloodletting since the Bombay riots a decade earlier (Bose 2009).

Apart from this, the era of economic reforms after 1990s has benefited a large section of the nation's population, but it has also generated a growing dissatisfaction among the rest of the people left outside the economic mainstream. And, among them, it was the Muslims who were the worst hit. The Sachar Committee Report (2006) shows that despite the economic boom talked about in India, today one finds that Muslims in India had to bear the brunt of the so called 'competitive' forces unleashed by liberalisation. Internal and external liberalisation has brought with it considerable cost in terms of unemployment and displacement of workers who have lost their jobs to competitive companies that import products. For instance, the import of silk particularly from China (which devastated the indigenous silk industry), combined with the increased production of ready to wear garments, resulted in a huge loss of work, jobs and trade for tailors and weavers, the majority of whom were Muslims in the country. Muslims by and large are engaged in the unorganised sector of the economy which rarely enjoys protection of any kind and, therefore, the adverse impact of liberalisation has been more acute on them. In fact the poverty has increased during the phase of economic reforms. 84.5 per cent of Indian Muslim households spend not more than ₹ 20 per day and ₹ 609 per month. Only 2.2 per cent Indian Muslims who are regarded as high income category by the report spends ₹ 2,476 or ₹ 93 per day. So, there is no doubt that the era of economic reforms has aggravated the marginalisation of the community. And this new economic diversity and disparity revived old fears and created fresh anxieties.

After 1990s, the revival of Hindu nationalism as well as economic reforms has made Muslim identity more vulnerable as well as marginalised. The Hindu revivalism has not only led to the reconstruction of the Hindu identity that is exclusivist but also constructed the identity of Muslim as 'others'. So the modernising project of the Indian state has not been able to eliminate influences of collective identities. Rather the role of the state itself becomes very important in nurturing the ethnic identity of Muslims. Even, to a great extent, the character of the Indian state has been dubious in nature. Because the state has failed to provide socio-economic resources to this marginalised group and that failure was supplemented by delegating autonomy to community leaders to manage their own affairs. So the modernising state itself has pampered several ethnic and other groups for its own survival.

Conclusion

So it is quite clear from the above discussion that the phenomena of ethnic politics amongst communities divided on the basis of religion, language and region has indicated incompatibility of world views on various issues, including the models of modernisation. Particularly in post-colonial societies like India, ethnic identities are not only product of primordial attachments but also structures. In India, we find that despite adoption of a liberal democratic polity after independence, communities and collective identities have remained active and continue to claim recognition. So it is quite clear the Indian polity has consistently tried to negotiate the allegiance to a liberal (individual) spirit and the concerns and consciousness of community. This process has recognised a wide array of autonomous and largely self-governing communities. It has sought to reconcile itself as an association of individuals and a community of communities, recognising both individuals and communities as bearer of rights.

That is why many scholars believe that a material basis for the enunciation of identity claims has been provided by the post-independent state and its structures and institutions. In other words, the state is seen as an 'active contributor' to identity politics through the creation and maintenance of other structures which define and then recognise people in terms of certain identities. There are economic, political as well as ideological structures which also form ethnic identity. So the process of modernisation and ethnicity has an integral relationship which cannot be ignored easily.

References

Bhargava, Rajeev. 2010. *The Promise of India's Secular Democracy*. New Delhi: Oxford University Press.

Brass, Paul R. 1991. *Ethnicity and Nationalism: Theory and Comparison*. New Delhi: Sage Publications.

Bose, Anuja. 2009. 'Hindutva and the Politicization of Religious Identity in India', *Journal of Peace, Conflict and Development*. Retrieved from: www.peacestudiesjournal.org.uk2, February 13.

Delanty, Gerard. 2010. *Modernity and Postmodernity: Knowledge, Power and the Self*. London: Sage Publications.

Chatterjee, Partha. 1998. 'Secularism and Tolerance', in Rajeev Bhargava (ed.), *Secularism and its Critics*, New Delhi: Oxford University Press, pp. 54–57.

Engineer, Asghar Ali. 1995. *The Qur'an, Women, and Modern Society.* New Delhi: Sterling Publishers.

——. 1995. *Problems of Muslim Women in India*. Bombay: Orient Longman.

Faegheh, Shirazi. 2009. *Velvet Jihad: Muslim Women's Quiet Resistance to Islamic Fundamentalism*. Gainesville: University of Florida Press.

Hasan, Zoya. 1994. *Forging Identities: Gender, Communities and the State*. New Delhi: Kali for Women.

Hasan, Zoya and Ritu Menon. 2005. *Unequal Citizens: A Study of Muslim Women in India*. New Delhi: Oxford University Press.

Hossain, Anowar. 2008. *Muslim Women's Struggle for Freedom in Colonial Bengal, 1873–1940*. Kolkata: Progressive Publishers.

Islam, Maidul. 2009. 'Posing the Muslim Question in India: A Leftwing Perspective', *Journal of Humanities and Social Science*, 6: 123–32.

Jayal, Gopal Niraja. 2002. *Democracy and the State*. New Delhi: Oxford University Press.

Lateef, Shahida. 1990. *Muslim Women in India: Political and Private Realities: 1890s-1980s*. New Delhi: Kali for Women.

Narula, Smita. 2009. *Overlooked Danger: The Security and Rights Implications of Hindu Nationalism in India.* Retrieved from: www.indianmuslims.com, March 4.

Sachar Committee Report. 2006. *High Level Committee Report on Social, Economic and Educational Status of the Muslim Community of India*. New Delhi: Akalank Publications.

12

Modernity of Traditional Polity in India's North-East

G. AMARJIT SHARMA

Despite works (for instance, Rudolph and Rudolph 1967; reprinted in 2010) that show that modernity and tradition are not necessarily dichotomous, and that modernity incorporates and transforms tradition, there is still a sense of discomfort, the moment one thinks of the association between modernity and tradition polity. This was expressed during the discussion of earlier draft of this study at a seminar on modernity and ethnic processes in India held at North Eastern Hills University, Shillong (organised by Sociology Department, NEHU, 14–16 March 2012). This reservation could be empirically contextualised to the existing layers of tension (on territorial and cultural identities) among the communities in North-East India. The roots of tension could be assigned to the loyalties many of us give to various insulated ethnic politics and thereby, the sceptics urging many of us to leave ethnic identity (understood as anachronistic element of tradition) behind and march forward. However, I retain this title as major theme of my study.

Let me deal briefly with this problem of association. The existing tension between ethnic groups should not lead one to approach the problems of identity with discomfort or hatred; rather, one should also look at the modern solution or usefulness that various agents have found in traditional moorings of society and polity. This means tradition does not always cater to sectional interests, but also at times has provided models that have helped mediation of disputes among the communities or of an inclusive historical political life in the region. No doubt, there are problems associated with these traditional models, which one should still debate; it is also true that people now transform and contextually use them to deter new inter-communities tensions in our society. This element of reflexivity, or reasoning with one's own society, not always with others, is also the part of our modernity that can be celebrated instead of sidelining identity assertion as an anachronistic exercise. This study emphasises this aspect of tradition in our modern context.

To clarify our position further, there is a need for a prior engagement with other levels of our understanding of modernity and democracy: one, by looking at newer understanding of modernity; second, by engaging with modern democratic polity that stands on the principle of membership of individual on 'secular times' and explaining the problems with such understanding of 'secular polity'. Modernity as a singular and homogenous process has been at the root of western modernity. Such process looks at traditional authority and religious worldviews as things of past where reason cannot access; individual has to pass through middlemen or authority who could be priest/church. This leads to the tendency of reading political/social development in non-western societies as things lying within the domain of tradition, yet to be modern. Now it is important to listen to what Sudipta Kaviraj (2010: 16–18) has argued that modernity is not singular and it does not necessarily follow a homogenous sequence of events. This means there could be differential routes of modernity. This is because of three reasons. One, coming of modernity is a massive alteration of social practices, yet this alternation does not occur in a sense that earlier society was unfamiliar of these practices. These new practices retain traditional practice as well, not occur on 'clean slate'. Secondly, the plurality of process constitutes modernity. Thirdly, modernity is reflexive in nature; collective actions are regularly monitored and reformed in response to our own perceived failures or in search of effective solution. Hence, because of these reasons modernity cannot either be just repetition of West or ending of practices prevailed in our past society. This, hopefully, clears the ground laid by the sceptics on the association between the traditional polity and modernity.

Now, it is legitimate to say that nature of modernity in our society does not mean ending traditional ways of relating each other but the incorporation or enhancement of tradition as the functional aspect of our present political acts. This unpacking of our own understanding of modernity also leads to another important clarification on the modern democracy and religious worldviews or schemes of life and territory. The idea of modern democratic polity that stands on the principle that one becomes member of modern polity because there is equal opportunity for all to get access to the polity without any middlemen like kings or priests. But this has been found problematic because of failure to recognise the positive side of or functionality that certain religious worldviews give to certain group of people (for some discussion, Bhargava 1998; reprinted in 2010: 1–28). A legitimate democratic polity is also one that gives space to such functional/reforming/transforming scheme of religious worldviews.

With these clarifications, let me proceed to the empirical specificities of my study. This study analyses modern political practices of the valley-dwelling Meiteis in the state of Manipur in North-East India that invent a cultural core around an ancient political centre to establish affinity with the surrounding hill ethnos. This invention of a core must be seen in the context of movements for separate territorial rights of major conglomerates of hill tribes such as the Nagas and Chin-Kuki-Mizo. The Nagas have been fighting for sovereign territorial rights and of late they have entered into peace talks with the Government of India. One of the implications of such peace talks has been the possible integration of the 'Naga inhabited areas' of Manipur to Nagaland. To the larger plain-dwelling Meiteis, this possibility is seen as a major threat to their age-old perception of an organic political life.

It is in this context that the idea of a cultural core emerges so as to keep intact what has been assumed to be the organic political life of the people in the hills and valley of Manipur. But the invention of a cultural core is a form of political practice that locates a ritualistic centre as a way of managing not only the political upheavals in the hills of Manipur, but also an increasingly indeterminate social life among various communities. It is a quest for a type of sociality, an organic political life which is expected to deal with increasingly indeterminate territorial and social boundaries. Such an act of invention has historical precedents, and must not be seen as something created new; it is not a rupture with earlier practices. The idea of 'core' as something that pulls together surrounding communities is an age old idea and practice. Hence, in the process of modern politics, the civilisation of the ancient Meitei state system is reborn, though in different political circumstances. The quest for a type of sociality, considered here as a form of political practice that helps to evolve a core cultural system, has carried historically transmitted patterns of meanings embodied in symbols and imprints of the pre-modern state order. This order doesn't distinguish society from state. State in this order was a social body; the idea of organic human body serves as a model of the pre-modern state.

Key argument I am putting forward in this study is that there are not only different routes of modernity but also *differential ways of using tradition*; it is not merely that tradition gets itself transform in modern context. For instance, we must say specifically that the carrier that traditional institutions (for instance, caste) takes in modern democratic polity is not same with that of carrier taken by the traditional core polity (Kangla) in Manipur. Latter type differs because of the function it performs and the type of historical structure it is responding to. It's not just because that one is a social institution (caste) and other a organic polity (Kangla); the invention of or transformation Kangla in modern context occurs *within* modern state; more specifically, it stands as the domain of practices that shows the limits of existing democratic polity: failure to give legitimate solution to existing problems of ethnic politics. Kangla as the core polity questions the forms of democratic polity found in India's North-East and questions the use of democratic polity in giving solution to identity and territorial contestations. Modern democratic polity is perceived as one that does not promote unity among ethnic diversities. Rather, democratic polity is perceived as a threat to the existence of historically unifying aspects of society. This is shown in our study in the last part of our study. To many, the secularising project of government that seeks to convert Kangla as heritage site has ended the lived relationships that various socio-religious groups and political bodies in the valley of Manipur have with the traditional polity and its centre.

Kangla as Core of Life and Territory

Kangla is the ancient capital of Manipur, located at the heart of the urban areas of Imphal, the current capital of Manipur. Kangla has been the site of several contestations both in early and contemporary histories of the state. The Assam Rifles had been stationed there since the establishment of the British rule in the state. In 2004, the 'naked women' protest took place in front of it after Thanjam Manorama was 'raped and killed' by Assam Rifles, which led to huge public agitations. The transfer of Assam Rifles from Kangla after this episode has been interpreted by many as an act that gives 'voice to voiceless', an act that is supposed to return the faith of people. There have been stakeholders to this area that include public associations in general and various other socio-religious groups that attempt to conserve it for reasons having to do with inter-ethnic harmony and territorial integrity of Manipur. In June 2001, when the Indo-Naga peace talks were extended 'without territorial limit', which in principle brought Naga-populated areas of Manipur into a greater Nagaland, many of these groups launched political agitations in Imphal against any incursion into the territory of Manipur, and eighteen people were killed in police firing. These groups are against the integration of 'Naga inhabited areas' in Manipur into Nagaland. In many of these developments, it can be discerned that Kangla increasingly occupies the centre, at least of the political imagination of the plains Meiteis. In the mind of a local historian (Arambam 2001), 'June uprising' had re-opened old questions in a new context. To him, in the historical past, plains Meiteis had been taking a politically centrist position in the midst of surrounding ethnic communities; but now when there have been demands for separate homelands and self governing ethnic territories among the ethnic Naga and Kukis, and when the Indian state has adopted policies that may weaken already divided societies, the question arises if the Meiteis can continue to take such a 'centrist position'.

The critical question, however, still remains as to what sort of centre does Kangla provide to the people in Manipur today. To the state government, it occupies a historical site, a site of tourist attraction. But, to several other sections of the society, it is a centre that serves as the vital core of the communities and their territory. Its importance can be seen both in the realms of sacred and secular performances. The question is why it acts as the centre of politics in recent times. There is a historical background to Kangla as understood by the Manipuri people; of Kangla serving as the functional centre in historical times. But the legitimacy of its divine origin lies behind this historical function. Both its historical emergence as a functional political centre, from where acts of governance were executed, and its divine origin have been major aspects of its *relevance to contemporary* politics. But the critical issue is whether political power was subordinated to ritualistic significance or vice versa. We are saying that it is the ritualistic significance of the centre which is being reinvented. But it is essential to know that the reinvention of Kangla is more in the sense of building an organic political community, than a mere celebration of the powers of the pre-modern state, in which the ritualistic elements are heavily present.

Our historical argument traces meanings of 'political community' as it had existed in the pre-modern state order, which contemporary Meiteis have reinvented to address current fragmentation along the territory and ethnic lines. This is where our treatment of historical materials is different from the ways in which Sudipta Kaviraj (2010) treats the historical state and society. Our historical argument is not to locate the state, or to find out if state existed 'on behalf of society', but to locate a sense of political community relatively distinct or autonomous from the state in the traditional order. We hope to arrive roughly at a consideration of state as a temporary entity and political community as a permanent entity across time and space.

Like in many pre-modern states, polity formation in early Manipur started with attempts to establish a centralised polity. Establishment of such a polity follows geographical imperatives. The valley consisting of relatively fertile areas had been the seat of state power and hills had been marginal players to it. However, the valley was not the site of settlement in the early historic periods of Manipur. It had been known as a place full of water bodies not suited for human settlement. Over the course of time however, settlements shifted from hills towards the centre of the valley. Politically, the shift of settlements from the hills towards the centre of the valley did not reflect the evolution of smaller groups into a larger sovereign political unit; rather, these groups during the course of migration established independent principalities at different places at the drier areas of the valley.

The state, despite having a rough constitution and division of labour among occupational groups, departments and religious bodies, was least present the further it was from the central portion of valley. There were chiefs who were not completely under the state, despite the latter's expansionist policy. Despite apparently similar origins (of similar ancestors), the principalities fought each other to establish one kingdom. This came into being with emergence of the rule of the Ningthouja dynasty over the rest (roughly in 50 A.D.) at the central area of valley (Kangleipung). To the contemporary Meiteis, the birth of this dynasty is the birth of their 'nation'. By around 50 A.D. there were seven principalities including the Ningthouja group of people. The establishment of this rule has also been considered as the establishment of the rule of Meiteis. Ningthouja were known originally as the Meiteis. With their control over the rest of the principalities, the nomenclature Meiteis came to be generalised as the name of the entire groups of people settled in the valley. By the fifteenth century, this process of establishing one rule under a group, with the exception of one group called Moirang till the eighteenth century, was relatively complete. But what is important for our context is that it was the emergence of the Ningthouja dynasty as the strongest ruler (ruling from the central valley) that marked the emergence of core of the Meitei state – Kangla.

Kangla also meant the first area of human settlement in the valley after the flood ended. In another sense, it also refers to the seat of power of a princedom or principality. It is also believed that there were many Kanglas, meaning the centre of each principality. However, with the establishment of the Ningthouja dynasty there emerged one Kangla, the present Kangla. It is at this juncture that the importance of not merely a spectacular but also a ritualistic state emerged. The state at the centre had developed not only at the level of administrative structure; it also had evolved a set of terminologies that made sense of this presence of the state.

Several vernacular texts of the Meitei throw up a range of terms which could be the derivatives of Kangla, and expand the meanings and representation of Kangla. Terms such as Kanglei, Kangleipung, and Kanglei Sana Mayol broadly refer to city, public place and centre of a territory; it referred to the areas around the palace where the king and his royalists resided, and where the work of administration was carried out. In other meanings, Kangla refers to the capital of a state where people come to claim justice (Kangla Wakatpa); suggests that justice be given at the capital (Kangla Liwa Setpa or Kangla Laiwa Paring Tamba); the place where at the time of war, a huge drum was beaten to announce war to the people and to mobilise an army (Kangla Yaipung Thinba); officials or rules coming to the palace (Kangla Thoungharakpa) (Khelchandra 1978: 20). The centre also means the Kangleipung, the elevated portion of earth where there was also the centre of power.

Largely, the above meanings came after Ningthouja rule was established. But the presence of the state needed to be instilled at areas far away from the centre. Here emerged the ritualistic significance of the centre and state itself. The power of the state had to be subservient to the ritualistic significance of the state. Our argument is that even the spectacular state with its pageantry could not survive unless it rested on ritualistic arguments. This also means that the kind of political community that emerges in contemporary politics around such a centre is basically subordinated to the ritual meanings of the centre,

Kangla has been interpreted as the sacred core of life and territory of the Meiteis, who inhabit the valley of Manipur. It represents a sacred scheme that arranges sites which are as abodes of cosmic as well as territorial deities (umang lais, the forest deities as well as ancestral deities, maikei ngakpa lais, the deities that guard different territorial corners). It is not completely an imaginary space, but also a physical space. It is materially an ancient palace, the fort. Though politically, it represents a political hierarchy with the capital as the centre where the King is seated, spiritually it is the source of ancestral lines for the Meitei. The spiritual and material meanings together constituted Kangla as the political centre in early Meitei polity. Unlike the sacred complex, it is not just a religious site, but also has been understood as the centre of an organic political life. One finds such parallel concept in tantric Hinduism and Buddhism; it is the concept of mandala. In the Indo-Tibetan tradition mandala comprises a centre (manda) and enclosed element (la) (Tambiah 1985: 259). Similarly, the concepts of Maung in Thailand and Nagara in pre-colonial Indonesia may be cited. Maung had emerged in 13th century Kingdom of Sukhothai that marked emergence of a Thai polity. It signifies kingdom, country, province, town, capital and region. It also signifies centre-oriented cultural and territorial spaces, typically standing for capital, town, or settlement with the surrounding territory over which it exercised jurisdiction (ibid.: 259). To this model, the centre ideologically represents the totality and embodies the unity of the whole. The capital of the kingdom is the starting point for the performance of annual cosmic rites of regeneration and purification. Here is the significance of regular ceremonies, like the festive tradition cited in the present work, which signifies the centre-oriented polity. Broadly, the concept of territory designed with Kangla at the centre is somewhere closed to the 'exemplary centre': Negara, the theatre state in nineteenth century Bali. The 'exemplary centre', according to Geertz

(1980: 13), was the expressive nature of the Balinese state for 'it was always pointed not towards tyranny, whose systematic concentration of power it was incompetence to effect ... but rather towards spectacle, towards ceremony, towards the public dramatization of the ruling obsession of Balinese culture: social inequality and status pride. It was a theatre state in which the kings and princes were the impresarios, the priests the directors, and the peasants the supporting cast, state crew, and audience.'

There has been revival of such notion of centre, with certain exceptions informed by its own context, in contemporary Manipur, which points to the renewed importance of traditional moorings around the pre-modern political order in the construction of a meaningful political community in the present. To understand this order, it is essential to know how Kangla has been defined within the cosmological thought processes of people. Vernacular Meitei texts speak of how heaven and earth were created. Kangla in this thought process represents the vital connection between heaven and earth in various ways. The concept of seven layers of earth (Thon Taret Thonlamei) as found in the vernacular texts is particularly relevant in this context. It talks about how earth was lifted from the water through various creatures. This appearance on the surface of water is represented by a shape of python (Paphal). This Paphal represents among many of its representations a territorial identity and the centre of it is represented by the point where the head bites the tail. It is written that there were 365 forms of Paphal. This particular form of Paphal that has head biting tail is the most common form (Bahadur 2005: 106).

Pre-modern state, it is believed, had its centre at the centre of the Paphal where the head and tail of the python bite each other. The state was believed to be in order as long as its centre was located at the centre of the Paphal. The social belief was that Paphal represents a religious symbol that protects one from evils. For the state it would have been considered as protection from enemies. Men Surung, located inside Kangla, the palace, was the sacred site representing Paphal, where coronation of the King took place.

Kangla, according to vernacular texts, represents spatially within its premise several important cosmic locations – the place of origin of sacred deities such as the important Umang Lais, the deities of lineages, the places of tutelary deities-the Marjing, Thangjing, Koubru and Wangbrel. It represents the sacred geography; the microcosmic representation of the macro features of the land. The concept of Kangla also provide a biological homology of the physical state functioning like a human organism, where Kangla (historic capital of Manipur) occupied the navel, the hollow in the belly left by the detachment of the umbilical cord. In the bio-physical structure of the state, the Koubru hills in the north-west, the early settlement area in pre-historic times, is regarded as the head, the three river Iril, Imphal and Nambul are regarded as the main arteries of the body, and the Loktak Lake as the pelvic zone. The Drain at the Chindwin beyond the 'Sugnu Nungthong' (Stone Door of Sugunu) was regarded as the rectum. Kangla, therefore, occupied a strategic area in the body structure; which was the energy receptacle in the human organism. It was the seat of the placenta, the vital connection that gives life-blood to the child (Lokendra 1991: 60).

What can be arrived from the above analysis is that the sovereign power of the state (King) was subservient to the ritualistic significance of the state and the cosmic arrangements. It can at least be said at this moment that a sense of political community apparently existed beyond the temporality of the administrative aspects of the state. Now we are coming to the spectacular enactment of the core state and ritualistic sense of political community in festive practices that emerged in the 19th century.

Enacting Core, Festive Community

In this section, we look at how the festive practices enacted the core Meitei state, and helped to evolve a pre-modern political community around those practices. Up till now, it is argued that state had to subordinate its powers to an aura of divinity around the centre of polity, which was what established the legitimacy of the authority of state in the eyes of its subjects. This section shows that there were complementary practices that attempted to make the surrounding chiefs and people feel part of the political community. This does not deny that there were other purposes of festive practices; festive practices were also meant to restore peaceful life, for fruitful agricultural harvest, and freeing from calamities and sins. We attempt to make the point that festive practice had enabled the state to be more participative in nature, deriving its legitimacy not merely from the ritual characteristics of the centre. Here we make a difference between the spectacular characteristics and participative characteristics of state. Kaviraj (2010) had argued that pre-modern state was seated in the middle of segmentary societies and it was basically spectacular and ceremonious in nature. But he was silent on participative nature of the pre-modern state.

Festive practices around the centre of the state apparently formed a populist domain, a secular space, while ritualistic practices served as the sacred domain. Festival apparently made it easier for the people to become part of the state. Rituals and its rules might have been inaccessible as well as not easily understandable. Festive practices on the other hand, while not lacking in sacredness or ritual, gave a relatively wider space to accommodate people.

Among many state festive practices, Mera Haochongba, the festival that celebrated hills and valley affinity around the core state was particularly important as far as construction of political community was concerned. This is because it attempted to deal with the surrounding communities including the hill dwellers, after state formation was relatively accomplished in the fifteenth century in the valley areas.

In order to understand the meanings and importance of Mera Haochongba in its historical context, I will use the unpublished work, written in the vernacular language, of a scholar specialised in the archaic literatures, B. Kulachandra Sharma.[1] Kulachandra's work is based on his readings of the 'original' sacred literatures of the Meiteis (Puyas) which are not only inaccessible, but also unknown to the larger masses.[2] Kulachandra located the festival in its historical context in the following ways. Mera Haochongba was the festival of hillmen and valley dwellers organised by the core Meitei state (King and his functionaries). The core state was represented by the presence of the King (Meidingu), his nobles (Agam Athou) and heads of various departments (Loishangs). But 'festival' was also meant in a broader sense as the event organised by the valley dwellers for the hillmen. Mera refers to the month in Meitei calendar (which falls either in October or November in English calendar). However, the month of its organisation was decided in consultation between hill and valley dwellers. It could be Hiyangei, the following month of Mera in Meitei calendar. No specific date and month were decided and written down in the past. Hao refers to the chiefs (Khullakpa) of the surrounding villages and neighbours.[3] Chongba refers to dance. According to Kulachandra, Hao is the Tai language, which in the Chinese language is Hou. Hou was the *honorary title* given to the heads of the clans and tribal groups in imperial China under the Yin dynasty.[4] Kulachandra has also interpreted the hill people as the guest (Mithunglen) and the valley dwellers as the host (Thoubu) of the event.

What is significant about the term Hao in the above usage is that in pre-modern state and society the term tribe was not used. But today Hao would mean broadly the tribes. Also significantly the meaning of Hao was employed to mean only the chiefs of the surrounding villages. This could also mean that Hao was not strictly limited to the hills, but could be referred to the chiefs in the villages of the valley. As the meaning of the festival (Mera Haochongba) referred to the hills (Ching) and tam (valley), Hao apparently referred to the chiefs in the hills and valley surrounding the core Meitei state. But the festival, despite participation of the valley dwellers (chiefs), was taken as the event specifically meant for the hill people organised by the valley dwellers (especially the core state). The festival also could be interpreted as the merry-making ceremony of the chiefs from the hills at the core Meitei state, showing loyalty as subjects of the state. In the meanings of the event, the festival also gives a sense of generalising the societies of the hills and valley by taking the King, chiefs of the hills and the heads of departments as key representatives of these societies.

Kulachandra Sharma further writes on the goals of Mera Haochongba in the historical context. The goal was to build unity between the hillmen and valley dwellers.[5] But Kulachandra was not actually clear on what sort of unity was meant by this. It seems to me that 'unity' was not the consolidation of some already established rule over a territory and known subjects of the core state, but more of a projection of unity to cover up the geographical limits of the state, the distance of the hill people from the core state. The festival was, to Kulachandra, to invent unity between the brothers, hillmen as elder brother (Chingmi Mayamba) and valley dwellers as younger brothers (Tammi Manao).[6] He sees the festival as serving two needs: one, the need for governing the hills (leigaklon); the other, to maintain social affinity (Khunailon) between the hill people and valley dwellers. But these needs were driven by the historical juncture the core state confronted in early nineteenth century, when this festival is believed to have begun (Kulachandra argued that it emerged in 1847).

The historical juncture of this time was well put by Kulachandra: 'the history (Puwari) of Manipur was a sequence of warfare (sa lal)'. King (Meidingu) Garibniwaz (1709–48) invaded Burmese territory consecutively for seven years.[7] By early nineteenth century, after the reign of Garibniwaz, the core Meitei state had been under seven years (1819–25) rule of the Burmese (Ava). The post-Burmese occupation period required the consolidation of the core state and the need was urgently felt to pull its surrounding hill people around the core. More significantly, to Kulachandra Sharma, constant Burmese invasions and seven years occupation also raised the importance of 'Manipuri Jatis' and identities of these Jatis (Jatisingi saktam).[8] However, I suggest that the 'Manipuri Jatis' at this point of time were not concrete groups of people who felt the necessity of defending their identity as 'Manipuri'. It is unlikely that a group of people or even chiefs of villages in the hills and valley would be in a position to respond to the external threat of the Burmese invasion. Rather, the idea of 'Manipuri Jati' is more likely to have been an idea developed at the core of the Meitei state in order to develop a sense of a broader community. This community was, however, to be built around the threat perceptions of the Burmese from the eastern side, and not in the modern sense of a community of equal participation in the affairs of the state.

According to Kulachandra Sharma, this sense of community was mainly along the vertical geographical axis – hillmen and valley dwellers – rather than horizontally, along inter-subjective intra-group relationships. The chiefs represented the villages of the hills and valley at the core of the state both in spheres of administration and cultural practices. Two senses of community are then apparent: one along the vertical geographical division and the other, among the chiefs of both the hills and the valley. Mera Haochongba offered the potential of displaying these senses of community and also reinforcing them at the core Meitei state.

Another feature is the practice of hillmen called Tangkhul Potlak during the festival of Haochongba. Tangkhul was the looting of specific items sold in the market in the capital of the Kingdom on the day of Haochongba, under the eye of the King. This practice is mentioned in the text called Mashil: 'in looting markets the items to be looted are vegetables, betel nuts, fish, pottery products, banana leaves, flowers. The items which should not be looted are wood, rice, salt, cotton, clothes, and utensils. If these are looted, they are punishable' (Singh 1997: 5–6).

This practice of letting the Tankhuls, a group of hill dwelling people, to take specific items from the market in the heart of the core state on the day of the festival cited here was the practice different from the usual raids of the surrounding hill dwellers in the valley on various occasions: looting and flight of the raiders. Several such raids have come across in the history of the land. But, to the general public today, the above practice called *Tangkhul Potlakpa*, that means literally the snatching of items sold in the market by the Tangkhuls, is very much considered part of the tradition of inter-group harmony. This practice is a permitted activity that constitutes part of the festive mood of the day. But one may also question why only Tangkhuls. The Tangkhuls have been parts of both the popular myth of brotherhood between the Meiteis and Tangkhuls and more importantly in the creation myths of the valley dwelling Meiteis. It is important to cite here that without the performance of Tangkhul in the ceremony of the famous ritual performance *Lai haraoba* (literally Pleasing of Gods) of the Meiteis, the performance is considered incomplete. Perhaps, the festive practices that also had formed the constitutive parts of the larger ritual performances and worlds of the valley dwelling Meiteis reflect the necessity of prioritising the attentions of major community like the Tangkhuls while building the larger collective consciousness.

Another important tradition of the festive practice cited here is that of giving gift on the day of festival. As per this tradition, many of the surrounding chiefs brought the specific items growth in their villages as gift to the King. But this tradition has been much debated at present for it is often confused with the tribute-paying practices, which shows the continued loyalty of the subjects, subservient to the King. In other way, it has been interpreted as a form of feudal practice. But interestingly this gift giving has been transformed at present as a way of showing affinity between the valley dweller Meiteis and the hill dwellers. The transformation will be better seen in later part of the paper.

Colonial Modernity, Passing of Tradition

The core Meitei state and political community evolved around it, however, encountered colonial modernity in late nineteenth century and twentieth century, that brought changes in the idea of state and sense of community. Colonial modernity will be discussed around two key points: one, ways in which colonial administration transformed the structure of state; two, how did the colonial administration dealt with cultural activities. While doing this analysis, I am also differing from general argument among the local scholars who treat the subject of religion in twentieth century as a separate one from the colonial modernity. It is rather, within the colonial modernity that the religious practices of the Maharaja as well as splitting of hills and valley along religious lines should be understood. This analysis also falls in line with argument elsewhere that colonial modernity was ambivalent by nature of its practices; it is within this ambivalence that major strands of politics of people since nineteenth century till contemporary times have been defined in Manipur.

The Anglo-Manipur war of 1891 that led to the defeat of Manipur heralded a new era in the politics of Manipur. The major changes were witnessed during the times of political agent Major Maxwell and Raja Chura Chand. The first crucial change was the change brought in the monarchical rule. The second occurred in the sphere of economy. The third was in the cultural sphere. After 1891 war, though direct annexation of Manipur was much debated among the colonial officials, it was decided in favour of continuation of state of Manipur as an indirect British dominion in Manipur. This was evident in the Sanad of the British Governor General in Council given to the state of Manipur, according to which the rights of the Manipuri Raja was solely derived from the Government of British India.

Other major changes were made in the sphere of economic policies. The system of paying manual service to the state was abolished. This is called lallup, a system of men's service for 10 days of every 40 days to the state, which previously existed under the pre-colonial Meitei polity, which was termed as forced labour under colonial terminology. As per order of the Government of British India, Maxwell announced the abolition of lallup in 1892. This is where the benevolence of the colonial dominion was constructed. Maxwell felt that the system of lallup was mainly borne by people of poorer classes and Brahmins, and other well to do people were free from it; the Raja did not properly feed those who gave the services. He also was in favour of abolition as it was considered burdensome to the women. For when the men failed to give service under lallup system, the Raja demanded cash compensation which was borne by the women who were active in trading activities. After lallup was abolished, it was substituted by house tax of ₹ 2 per annum, and citizens as taxpaying subjects of state emerged.

However, the service rendered by men to the state still continued to exist in another form. Under this system called pothang, villagers provided compulsory labour in repairing road, schools, and transport of officials' baggage. The policy of pothang was apparently designed as temporary measure, as Maxwell said that compulsory labour could not be completely abolished as the development of communication required such labour.

Colonial rule also brought changes in the structure of core Meitei state that pulled together surrounding chiefs in the hills. The hills were brought under the direct control of British administration and the King was given indirect rule over hills. This means that there was a clear split between the core Meitei state and the hill people. By 1919, major administrative changes were brought in; hills were put under direct administration of the president of the Manipur State Darbar and the Political Agent and were divided into three administrative sub-divisions headed by sub-divisional officers. The hill people became taxable subjects of the colonial state. However, hills were still vast geographical areas where administration could not be carried out regularly. This gap was intended to be bridged in several ways. One way was by depending on the erstwhile intermediaries of pre-colonial core state, the Lambus. Secondly, other ways of dealing with the hills was the practice of making official tours in remote hill areas. Thirdly, the gap was bridged by following the policy of least interference with the customary practices of the hills. Lastly, there was a policy of enlisting hillmen as labour (Pothang), though it was abolished in large parts of valley, both for the administrative purposes as well as external policy of war of the colonial state.

On the whole, the British largely helped in splitting politically the subjects in hills and valley. I do not suggest that the pre-colonial core Meitei state was successful in building up a close political community. But it did succeed in the construction of symbolic allegiance of the many surrounding chiefs in the hills and valley around the core, especially through the festive practice of Mera Haochongba. I differ from the argument of John Parratt (2005: 13–14) that there was 'effective control of hills' under pre-colonial rule of Meitei Kings and 'a fair degree of autonomy' was possible under them, and that this was ended by the British administration in the hills. I suggest that the core Meitei state was equally absent in hills in terms of regular administration. But the core Meitei state was able to generate loyalty and coherence through a centre 'stuffed' with ritual, to which the surrounding chiefs were subservient. The spectacular and ceremonious nature of core Meitei state was crucial in ensuring this loyalty, but its participative nature state was also projected through the festive practice of Mera Hoachongba. Unlike the splitting of hills and valley under the British administration, the core Meitei state was intended more to pull together the hillmen, particularly after the Burmese threats in the eastern side of the core state.

The splitting of hills and valley was also deepened by religious activities in twentieth century. These religious activities, however, cannot be delinked from colonial modernity that apparently distinguished state administration and religious sphere. This leads to our discussion on two other aspects of colonial modernity: one, on how much the Meitei Raja was given autonomy in the sphere of religion; secondly, how much the hills was allowed to be converted into Christianity. The British virtually took control over all administrative activities and the sphere of religion was apparently left free for the Raja of Manipur to deal with. This was related with the declining legitimacy of the King as sovereign head of state, as he was no longer appointed according to the wishes of the native people and the government. The British exercised the right of approving the rightful heir as the Raja of Manipur. Raja Chura Chand, who ascended to the throne in 1891 as per the wishes of the British, was an extremely unpopular King especially in twentieth century Manipur. This decline in authority was attempted to be restored through monopolising the spheres of religion: one was through enforcement of religious duties: compulsory religious services for sections of society as well as charging religious taxes on some of the pre-Hindu religious practices and duties; and secondly, control was exercised through a class of Brahmins.

It was especially under colonial modernity that Hinduism became a major factor. John Parratt (ibid.: 19) wrote on the expanding social base of the Raja of Manipur among a new class of Brahmins and how the Raja used Gauriya Hinduism as means of asserting his authority. According to Parratt, under Raja Chura Chand, the old sections of Brahmins of his predecessors were rejected and a new section institutionalised into a body called Brahma Sabha.[9]

It was through this body of Brahmins that the Raja of Manipur exercised his authority. This class of Brahmins with Raja's patronage started dictating the religious affairs of the Meitei society. They appointed Brahmins in each community and village to conduct religious ceremonies and rites according to Hindu customs. As a result, temples and mandaps came up in several areas. For all the religious functions performed by them, fees were taken (ibid.: 19). There was also the practice of treating a person Mangba (polluted) and Sengba (purified). The authority to treat any one as Mangba was exercised by the new Brahmins patronised by the Raja. From the little available information I come across, it is found that the religious power to treat a person in this way was decided according to Hindu Shastras. Colonial intervention was inclined towards formating legal procedures to treat a person as polluted (Mangba) and punish those who did not follow such procedures, rather than to curb the practice.

A class of Brahmin scholars pursued the thesis of Vedic origin of, or connections with Manipur, which led to the labelling of hills as non-Hindu space. It was P. Atombapu Sharma, who was patronised by Raja Chura Chand, who authored the thesis of Vedic connections with Manipur. For him Meitei civilisation is Vedic in origin. He locates Manipur in the Hindu epic of Mahabharata and also brought into being the narrative of arrival of Arjun in Manipur, who married a Manipuri woman.

The valley, thus, became the fertile ground for the Hindu religious practices. However, it is difficult to arrive at the point when Christianity became a parallel religious force in the hills. Moreover, in the hills, the pace of Christian conversion in nineteenth and twentieth century was slowed down because there were resistant hill people. The contrast between Hinduism and Christianity became evident only in independent Manipur since the 1960s, especially after there were movements for separate territorial identities of hill tribes. This will be dealt later in the study. But for the moment it is important to say that hills were not Christianised at the time when a class of Brahmins under Brahma Sabha emerged in the valley. Still it can be stated that the hills became the space of survival of Christianity. Hills, however, showed diversity in religious practices. There were rebellions based on the indigenous beliefs system. It is the identification of the core with orthodox Hinduism in twentieth century Manipur that contributed to the emergence of counter cultures and politics in the hills in the latter phases of its history.

Post-1949 Hill Politics

Post-independence Manipur has witnessed diverse political trajectories. At the time of Indian Independence Manipur had a constitutional monarchy with a Constituent Assembly that established adult franchise in 1948. This Assembly gave representation to three broad categories of population: valley Meiteis, Muslims and hill tribes. But after Manipur was forcibly merged into India in 1949 there emerged mixed reactions from the people in the valley and hills. The Manipur State Congress (the erstwhile Manipur Nikhil Mahasabha) for instance, was in favour of including Manipur as part of free India while others opposed the merger of Manipur with India. Eventually, Manipur became a full-fledged state in 1972. But the hills, despite heterogeneous voices due to diverse social and geographical settings, have evolved a dominant politics that challenges the territorial integrity of the state. Of these voices, the dominant one asserts the historical existence of hills as different political entity/entities. This was basically premised on the colonial officials' reasoning and colonial practice that treated the hills as separate administrative zones. Major voices of hills politics have been that of the All Tribal Union, the voice of Nagas that seeks to integrate parts of Manipur to Nagaland, and that of the Kuki-Chins that have the vision of merging the Kuki, Chins and Mizos in North-East India and Burma.

In recent years, these diverse political upheavals in the hills have been taken over by the demands for separate territorial identity for the hills. Two types of territorial identities can be observed in such demands: one, a 'tribal state' for all the tribes of Manipur; two, states for trans-state tribes such as Greater Nagaland (incorporating 'Naga Inhabited Areas' of Manipur with Nagaland) and Kuki-Chin-Mizo grouping across the Indian states of Manipur, Mizoram and Myanmar.

The All Tribal Students Union Manipur (ATSUM) demands a separate tribal state out of hill tribes of Manipur. Their arguments are laid out in their publication entitled *Territorial Rights of Outer Manipur* (2000) where the hills have been equated with tribal areas and valley as that of the Meiteis/Manipuri. The ATSUM claims to represent and speak for the interests of all the tribes in the state. The institution that forms the base of the 'tribal state' is the Chieftainship. For them 'the chiefs are lords of the hills' and the chiefs had never been under the control of the Maharaja of Manipur in pre-colonial times. There is an assumption of tribes constituting 'independent and sovereign nations' till the advent of British. The chiefs, though despotic, are considered to have governed their lands according to their customs without any interference from 'outside'.

Thus, ATSUM has reservations about the merger of Manipur to India, on the grounds that when the Maharaja signed the agreement, the tribal chiefs and their territories were outside that agreement, as the Maharaja of Manipur was not a tribal representative who had authority to act on their behalf, and the tribes were not his subjects (ibid.: 23). While many valley Meiteis too have reservations about the merger, their reason is that they believe the Maharaja was forced to sign the merger document with the Government of India.

But hills politics is diverse and the ATSUM's project of creating a tribal state falls apart once it is known that tribes who are known as Nagas demand a separate territorial identity for themselves. The Naga project still remains the challenge to the valley Meitei's imagination of core state. The Naga project in Manipur challenges the historical, geographical and social settings of Manipur.[10]

The Naga project of integration has been built on a series of engagements not only with the geographical and social linkages in one form or other with the valley society of Manipur, but also with state reorganisation of India in 1960s. In 1960, the Naga People Convention entered into the sixteen-point agreement which established the state of Nagaland that included the Naga Hills and Tuensang Area of what was then Assam. This had divided the Naga civil society into moderates and extremists, the latter not accepting the union of Nagaland with India. However, the idea of integrating Nagas in the contiguous states/union territories of India gained momentum in the 1960s in both Manipur and Nagaland.

This idea of a contiguous and compact Naga inhabited area maintains a distance from the valley society of Manipur. It is with this campaign that the religious labelling of hill people as Christians and valley dwellers as Hindus/Sanskritised becomes relevant. This distinction was not evident in the early twentieth century, that is, in the colonial period, despite the advent of Christian missionaries in the hills and royal patronage for a class of Brahmins and Hindu religious practices in the valley. But in post-independence hills politics, the Naga project of integration of the 'Naga inhabited areas' in Manipur into Nagaland constructed a religious contrast between hills and valley. The argument of hills as the domain of Christians and valley as that of the Hindus has been the key factor in the Naga project.

The United Naga Council Working Group (UNCWG 2002) claims that the name 'Manipur' is a sanskritised name and the Meiteis are the 'Hindu dwellers of the plain'. This understanding matches a school of thought among Meiteis who believe in the connection of Manipur with the Vedic age and with Arjuna of the Mahabharata, as discussed earlier, but it is not an uncontested interpretation. There have been critics of this thesis among the Meiteis, not only from the revivalist Meiteis, but also from scholars.

The UNCWG says that the nomenclature 'Manipur' was never found in the oral traditions or recorded history of the early Meiteis. Their understanding is that before the Meiteis were converted into Hinduism (Vaishnavism) in the eighteenth century Manipur was known by different nomenclatures among the Meiteis and by other neighbouring countries.

In other literature, the essentialisation of valley society as Hindus has extended to other places in the region. Medom (2002: 33) said that the Hindu society comprised the Meiteis from the Imphal valley and Assamese in the Brahmaputra valley. He considered these societies as linked by their history and emotions with the 'rest of the Hindus in the heartland of India'. This narrative has put Meiteis and Assamese in the same religious group. As a result, this narrative has treated Meiteis (and Assamese) as the regional 'religious other' with whom Nagas believed that they do not share cultural and geographical affinities. Another implication of this narrative is the geographical enclosure from outside, of Manipur into the valley.

In Search of Affinity, Recovering Tradition

The Manipur Cultural Integration Conference (MCIC) published a volume *Ching Amasung Tamgi Mari* (hills and valley relationship) in 1976. This was the product of discussions held under a civil organisation called Ching

Tam Luptin, which used MCIC as the publisher of the volume. Though this volume was published much earlier than the recent upheavals in the hills, its contents are in fact used as the fundamental arguments among many valley dweller Meiteis. The volume discovers affinity between hills (Ching) and valley (Tam) dwellers, an affinity sought to be reflected in the revival of pre-colonial festive practices by the Ethno-Heritage Council (HERICOUN).

HERICOUN has re-invented Mera Haochongba in the contemporary political context of Manipur. This organisation prefers to use the name Houchongba instead of Haochongba. This is because Hao at present is a derogatory term. But I will continue to use Haochongba for historical reasons. HERICOUN at present organises this festival annually in the month of October. The tradition of Haochongba, as I have observed, is an attempt to recast the symbolic aspects of the centre-oriented polity to culturally pull together the hill and valley dwellers around the cultural core, Kangla. Some of the important features of the festival are as follows: re-enacting Kangla through the public procession and introduction of living King, as the 'living ritual core' of the lives of people in Manipur; symbolic representation of Kangla as the core of public life, periodisation of history to locate a time in the past when there was unity among the hills and valley dwellers; aesthetic correction of past 'wrongs', which means an attempt at collective level to forget and minimise any sorts of tyrannical rule in past of the core state vis-à-vis the subjects through re-interpretation of the festive practices and participation of various groups as the ways of showcasing shared cultural ties of the people around the core state; and lastly, showcasing the myths of brotherhood between the present tribes and Meiteis.

On the morning of Haochongba, the King and his royal guards and members, dressed in traditional dresses, move in public procession to the Kangla. This festive form is a theatrical display of the bygone era when the Meitei King was protected by his royal guards and advisors. The priests and priestess, Maiba and Maibi, who are still accepted as part of Manipuri society, are experienced ritual functionaries for the day. The Maiba Loisang (house of the priest) and Maibi Loishang (house of the priestess) are located at the complex of the Sana Konung (Royal Palace), where the procession concludes. This ritual procession has become more elaborate with increased media reportage.

The pomp and elaborate ceremony with which the procession of the King and his royalists proceeds from the Royal Palace to Kangla and then returns after the rituals, is witnessed by large numbers of spectators on the streets of Imphal. One can interpret this public display of the symbolic powers of the king and the involvement of both the media and local people as an attempt to transform the physical sites of Kangla and Royal Palace into a repository of faith and belief – Kangla as the site where ancestral spirits live and the Royal Palace as the residence of the ancient Meitei Kings, bearing the legacies of monarchy. In addition, there is an attempt to historicise the whole event and these physical sites together. Such an attempt to historicise can be seen in the statements of another organising committee Lainingthou Sanamahi Temple Board (sister organisation of Ethno-Heritage Council):

'The inhabitant of the hills and valley of Manipur are to feel and co-exist as brothers and sisters, originating from the same place and living in the same country though they have been divided owing to different historical and religious factors ...'

A similar attempt is seen in the words of the organisation HERICOUN who, along with the Sanamahi Temple Board, organises this festival:

'To connect the present generation with the past, history needs to be opened .... The blood relation between the people in the valley and those of the hills even if forgotten by our own people, there are proofs of this linkage in the history. The only festival that has been with us which cannot be separated from the existing ethos is Houchongba.'

The attempt to historicise the physical sites and actualise the imagined hills-valley affinity is also an attempt to legitimise the claims of the anti-Hindu revivalist groups who attempt to own what they believe to be pre-Hindu sacred spaces, and who see the hills-valley affinity as pre-Hindu legacy. Sanamahi is a household deity, now transformed into a religion whose 'Other' is Hinduism. As a result, the history of Manipur is periodised into pre-Vaishnavite and post-Vaishnavite. Periodisation becomes an important means to identify the coming of Vaishnavism. Traditionally, Maiba and Maibi Loishangs (house of priest and priestess) functioned under the Manipur King. However, after Manipur was merged to India there were changes in the functioning of the Loishangs. Presently, these Loishangs are located next to the Govindaji Temple. Whether they come under the Sanamahi Temple Board or Govindaji Temple Board is a point of contestation between the Hindu Meitei and non-Hindu Meitei. In fact, both the boards come under the Government of Manipur. Despite this contestation over the control of the Loishangs, the priest and priestess serve both in the Hindu and non-Hindu rituals.

The arrival of Vaishnavism is taken as an event that disrupted the imagined ethnic harmony among the dwellers of hills and valley. Most of the songs presented in Mera Haochongba festival at Palace Compound express the discontentment of the people with Hinduism, as it is believed to be the only factor that divides hills and valley in Manipur. Nongkhreng Eruppa is identified as an event in which Meiteis were forced to convert to Hinduism. It is also believed that Meiteis were then allowed to reconvert through the intervention of the then titular King of Manipur, Okendrajit, on another occasion called Nongkhreng Parei Hanba (6 October 1974). The authenticity of these events is supposedly established through the intervention of an ancient Meitei sacred book called Puyas. According to Sairem Nilabir, a Meitei scholar, in Puyas the meaning of Nongkhreng Parei Hanba is 'freeing from the binding of an oath' (through which Meiteis were converted to Hinduism), thus enabling reconversion to Sanamahi beliefs (Nilabir 1991: 123–24).

Sarangthem Ongbi Tharongoubi Devi, an artist who performed in the festival of Haochongba organised in the year 2005, narrated that after the Nongkhreng Eruppa 'we forgot the land is ours ... bringing divide between two brothers (hill and valley) who are sons of the same mother.' She felt that pre-Hindu religious beliefs have been 'corrupted' because of the arrival of Hinduism in Manipur. This cultural performance that traced the event of Nongkhreng Errupa as a particular moment in the history of Manipur, clearly demonstrates that Haochongba is a part of the broader Sanamahi revivalist movement.

Recalling of specific events like Nongkhreng Irrupa in a festive practice has important implications. It is worth knowing that the practice of recalling is itself 'social' and 'artful' (Tonkin 1992). Though the act of recalling may be the same among different sections, there may be differences in interpretation of these past events: this is what marks the politics of recalling. As far as the recalling of the Nongkhreng Irruppa during the Haochongba is concerned, it has one more added meaning: the unity between the hills and valley has been disturbed after Hinduism reached Manipur.

The song Nongkhreng Irruppa during Haochongba is a key part of the ritual. The English translation of a section of the song presented in the Haochongba festival in 2003 at Sana Konung, the Royal Palace located in Imphal, may be cited:

> Highlanders, lowlanders,
> All descendents of fathers and grand fathers,
> All the beloved servants of the almighty,
> Let us dance 'Hou' today,
> When the month of Mera comes,
> Hou Ha Hou, Hou Ha Hou.
>
> Let us wake up today,
> Fortify the boundaries,
> Face the enemy,
> Confluence at the goal,
> Let us go back to the origin,
> Hou Ha Hou, Hou Ha Hou.

The song is clearly not merely a stable text to be read or performed. It is very much a medium through which an understanding is constructed every time it is recited, and it can also be considered 'as a site of social action where identities and relations are continually being reconfigured' (Guss 2000: 7–12). The appearance of the song Nongkhreng Irruppa during the Haochongba and its underlying anti-Hindu tendency signifies the discursiveness of the cultural performance. What is represented as forced conversion of the Meiteis to Hinduism (according to the Sanamahi devotees) in Nongkhreng Irruppa is believed to be undone through the celebration of the event called Nongkhreng Prei Hanba (reconverting to Sanamahism through spiritual dip in water with a branch of a tree called Nongkhreng).

Modernity of State, Secularising Kangla

In this section, we will look at how the state has planned to transform the cultural core into a heritage park and how this affects existing belief systems as well as the spatiality of the centre. I hope to show the moments of disjuncture between the project of cultural core and the project of city modernisation. This disjuncture also raises the issue of how re-invention of the core can be sustained without the material foundations of such a core: what happens when Kangla, the cultural core, transforms into a 'heritage park'? City modernisation changes the materials as well as the structure of urban space. The sites and spaces within Kangla fort will be structured as the objects of the tourist gaze. The City Development Plan (CDP) for Imphal city and other projects (road projects for internal and inter-state connectivity) have different consequences for Imphal city in terms of the city as cultural space. This could be termed as nationalisation of the physical space of the city. Nationalisation of the city could be interpreted in two ways: one is the way in which the cultural manifestations of ethnicity, religion and region in the city is subordinated to the larger identity of national citizen; another is the co-optation of these manifestations as heritage objects. This reminds us of Holston and Appadurai (2003: 296) that despite exclusionary and conservative practices in the history of its evolution, 'nation-states have sought to establish citizenship as that identity which subordinates and coordinates all other identities – of religion, estate, family, gender, ethnicity, region, and the like – to its framework of a uniform body of law'.

In this process, the city forms not only as a strategic arena for the development of citizenship, but also an arena where citizenship is contested. In Manipur, Imphal city also forms an important arena for civil society organisations to define the cultural rights of the people in Manipur. The sacred sites in the city are being reclaimed in different ways in this process.

Nationalisation of city has been occurring through the CDP and other national projects, (e.g., roads). This not only results in treating the city as an economic unit, but also in the production of a different meaning for the city's physical spaces through the plan documents. It is in this process that both the Union and state governments have produced different notions of space. This can be best illustrated by the ways CDP and other plan documents visualise the holy places and historical monuments/archaeological sites in Imphal city. The Concept Development Plan, which forms an important part of the City Development Plan specifically deals with the restoration and reconstruction of Kangla.

These plan documents have acknowledged that Kangla belongs to the people of Manipur. The state archaeology department has conducted field surveys inside the fort. Now Kangla fort is protected under the Manipur Ancient and Historical Monuments and Archaeological Sites and Remains Act, 1976 (as Amended and Rules 1979). It has been kept under the care of the Kangla Fort Board constituted under Kangla Fort Act, 2004. The Concept Development Plan for Kangla was prepared under Nalini Thakur, who was the chief consultant. The Concept Development Plan consists of the following works: restoration and reconstruction/development of 'important historical monuments and sites'; development of 'important holy places'; reusing of 'important/beautiful European type buildings/bungalows as museums & offices'; plantation of trees especially medicinal plants and indigenous trees to make Kangla a bio-diversity centre/ecological park and to provide fresh air to the inhabitants of Imphal city; 'to preserve/protect important historical places & memorials'; 'to convert open spaces in Kangla as recreational centres since Imphal has no big park'; 'to construct an aquatic pond and unity park with model houses of different ethnic groups of Manipur', and lastly, 'to keep a small force to protect Kangla from encroachment'.

Of these, the works of restoration and reconstruction of historical monuments and sites, and development of holy places, have become issues of tension between the state archaeology department and different religious bodies. The state archaeology department (Department of Art and Culture, Government of Manipur) has identified two categories of places: one is termed as 'Important Holy Places of Kangla', and other, 'Important Historical Monuments/Sites of Kangla'.[11] Together twenty-nine holy places and nineteen historical monuments/sites are identified. Brief descriptions of the location and specific histories of the holy places and monuments/sites are packaged in a systematic manner.[12] Interestingly, the present researcher was told during a visit in Kangla that the state archaeology department on some occasions uses the map of Kangla drawn by the British (Manipur was conquered by the British in 1891) as a reference for locating sacred places/monumental sites. For instance, the map given in the book written by Mrs Grimwood: *My Three Years in Manipur*. In this map, there is not a single holy place; there are spots in the map marked as polo ground, citadel, *basti* (place of living for villagers), palace, and so on.

The holy places are identified as the mound (pung), dwelling house (yumjao), hills (ching), stone (yai), pond/lake (pukhri/pat), stream (khong) and cave (surung). The location of any one of these places is identified through the measurement of distance from one of the holy places located near it, with Khudup (a yard) as the unit. Another way of identifying the location is through the word pheidom (plot of land). The state archaeology department has the view that the physical space of Kangla comprises nine pheidoms. It has adopted the above given names of the holy places as markers of identification of the physical locations and specific stories associated with the places/sites. It is local belief that between the periods of the kings Meidingu Nongda Laren Pakhangba and Meidingu Garbinawaz, there had existed traditions of making the mound, constructing of King's dwelling house, constructing of markets, digging and cleaning of rivers, making of storage house (kei), erecting stone monoliths.[13]

Such activities of restoration and conservation, however, have produced various mutually contesting claims from various religious groups, and also contestation between the state archaeology department and the latter. These religious groups continue to have living association with several sites inside Kangla fort. For instance, there is a demand from a few religious organisations to place in the erect position, a stone monolith believed to be sacred inside Kangla Fort, which is currently flat on the ground. Again, an organisation called the Leihou Nunghou Shangland (with its office located at Imphal East District) submitted a memorandum to the Chief Minister of Manipur requesting identification of one hundred and forty Kangla Laipham (sacred abode of gods/goddess) inside the Kangla Fort.[14] This organisation has provided as evidence of existence of these sacred places inside Kangla, a puya (sacred text) called Pakhangba Laihui, along with maps of Kangla that locate the sites of sacred places. Interestingly, the Religious Committee (a body under the Kangla Fort authority that is concerned with religious matters inside Kangla Fort) discussed this demand as an issue of authenticity in one of its meetings. The Vice-Chairman of the committee (Shri Yumnamcha Budhichandra) contested the authenticity of the text Pakhangba Laihui cited by Leihou Nunghou Shangland. The committee sought re-examination of the book through consultation with other Manipuri scholars.[15]

An officer in the office of state archaeology stated in an interview with me that so far forty-four holy/sacred sites had been identified inside Kangla. But he denied that all the other sacred places as mentioned by the above organisation could be identified inside the present Kangla. He also gave the opinion that the boundary of Kangla in ancient times was much larger than the present one. As a result, the rest of the sacred places might exist outside the present boundary. The officer also felt that such demands were unscientific (the sacred places cannot be excavated through scientific methods), and belonged to the domains of faith and belief. In another interaction, archaeologist Dr K. Indrani Devi of the state archaeology department narrated an incident in which a person in Imphal sought the help of the state archaeology department to excavate a site which he thought of as sacred because in his dream he saw a sacred relic of god Pakhangba there. She informed me that the state archaeology department rejected it because it was merely a matter of belief.

I came to know that even while the Assam Rifles was still stationed in Kangla Fort, there were priests and priestesses who developed personal relationships with the chief army officer to get access to some of the sacred places. They still occupy those areas even after the guardianship was given to the state archaeology department.[16]

In another case, where similar contestation developed between the state archaeology and religious organisations, an organisation called Malem Kanba Lup Machin Manao urged the Kangla Fort Board to change the place and position of a stone monolith, which is claimed as lying near Kangla Uttra, 'so as to uncover, clean and construct the Holy Place of worship and thereafter to pray and worship in unanimity by each and every section or organisation of the people to bring peace, happiness and prosperity to the land of Manipur and the world as a whole.' This organisation attempted to establish a relationship with the place where the stone monolith is, by offering its own self-authenticated facts (of the position and place of the stone monolith). For instance:

'It is revealed that at this place of 'Kangla Mein Tongpham' there existed the 'Main Phambal' the Holy Place of the Meitei God, LAIYINGTHOU LEIMAREL (Shidaba Shidabi) believed to be the supreme creator and ruler of the universe ...

And that, at this same place of worship, there stood one 'Uyung Nungphal' which is also known as 'Kangla Nungyungbi' as a deity or monument .... And it is submitted that the 'Uyung Nungphal' as it may be interpreted, is nothing but a flat and tall stone standing as pillar (flat monolith). It is further submitted that the Meiteis when believing a stone as a deity, it is never placed flat on the ground but it is always kept erected and worshipped.'[17]

The importance and sacredness of the stone is proven through its connection with the coronation seat and the God Lainingthou-Leimarel. Perhaps, the organisation feels that this sacredness associated with the stone and the place where it is believed to stand, needs to revive because it can bring healthy life to the present society. The site (including the stone) has also become more important to the organisation because it is where

King Khagemba took pledge to bring healthy life. Despite such claims about the position and location of the stone, the state archaeology department does not appear to conclude that there is anything sacred about the stone.

There is another case of tension with regard to the restoration work of the Govindaji temple at Kangla. I had witnessed a debate on one routine visit to Kangla, between an official of state archaeology and a person who claimed that he was a follower of the Sanamahi religion. The Sanamahi follower was not happy with the amount of money and restoration work carried on at the site of Govindaji temple inside Kangla, because he felt that Kangla should be the place of pre-Hindu Meitei sacred places. He even claimed that there is a structure of a temple of Pakhangba, the first king of Meitei Kingdom, *beneath* the Govindaji temple. However, the state archaeology official refused to hear all these arguments. His only argument was that the state archaeology department would take up the work of restoration and reconstruction on those monuments, which have existed since the times of British. That the state archaeology department uses the British period as a reference point is also demonstrated by the map of Kangla in an official publication, which is from a book by Mrs Grimwood mentioned earlier.[18] His argument was that restoration and reconstruction works could only be done when there are material evidences on the monumental sites. This 'evidence' appeared to mean the broken material remains of monuments or some traces of buildings, either in maps or any findings on the ground.

In fact, the Manipur Ancient and Historical Monuments and Archaeological Sites and Remains Act, 1976 [Section 2 (a)] defines historical monument as 'any structure, erection or monuments or any tumulus or place of interment, or any cave, rock-structure, inscription or monolith, which is of historical, archaeological or artistic interest and which has been in existence for not less than one hundred years' and it includes the following: the remains of an ancient monuments, site of an ancient monument, portion of land adjoining the site of an ancient monument as may be required for fencing or covering in or otherwise preserving such monument, and the garden, if any, appurtenant to such monument, the means of access to and convenient inspection of such monument (but these do include any ancient or historical monument declared by or under law made by Parliament to be of national importance).

Following the above definition, it appears that the site where Govindaji temple is located appears to pose fewer problems for the state archaeology department than sites such as the coronation seat of Meitei Kings and other such sacred sites, because these places are more shrouded in mythology, and less amenable to 'scientific' archaeological evidence.

Conclusion

It may be said that the cultural core around the centre of traditional polity is a modern politico-cultural space around which a certain form of sociality among people is being constructed. This sociality constitutes a form of political life and a modernity of the traditional polity and centre. There are attempts to bring into being certain organic relationships among communities; an alternative political life to what is otherwise understood as an increasingly indeterminate territory and society at the periphery of India. This form of political life is invented around historical experiences that the society and polity of the state of Manipur had undergone in the past. Thus, the tradition acts as a model that gives direction to politics in the present. The sacred centre, Kangla, in the political life enacted around it represents a political community that makes power subservient to the ritualistic significance of centre.

The politics around the core produces continuous anxiety for the plain dwelling Meiteis if they fail to play the traditional role vis-à-vis hill dwellers. It is at this moment that the politics around the cultural core shows tendencies of cultural/historical conservatism; the refusal to begin conceptualisation of political life from the experiences of people of its own periphery. It is important to note that this is debated and discussed among the same community. Many sections of Meiteis consider the politics of building a cultural core around Kangla to be feudalistic, historically orthodox and showing tendencies of religious fundamentalism. Nevertheless, the study shows that the form of political life around the sacred centre Kangla shows the possibility of one kind of alternative political life among many alternatives that people at the margin may have imagined so far. This shows that people in the margin of India continue to find ways to live through several forms of alternative political life despite violence, state oppression and inter-ethnic conflicts. On the other hand, it is equally important to note that the search for alternative political life through the cultural core has to be pursued in the face of state planning and the state project of nationalising the city landscape. The process of urban planning has impacted on the lived association that the people of Imphal and of Manipur in general have with the sacred/historical sites. Once the sacred becomes the site of 'heritage', lived associations are diminished and museumised. One may say that there is the modernity of traditional polity on the one hand and on the other, the modernity of state. The previous one attempts to build a specific modernity in the public imagination that reinvent tradition in the light of contemporary politics of ethnic identities and later attempts to museumise tradition.

Notes

1. B. Kulachandra Sharma lives in Imphal, Manipur. He may be considered as a scholar unaffiliated to as well as untrained in University but is a socially accepted traditional scholar. Tradition is considered locally to a large extent safeguarded at the hand of the scholars like Kulachandra Sharma. It is also largely believed to be stored in the archaic literatures, Puyas. He is one of the few scholars surviving today who can read and transliterate these ancient literatures.
2. The ancient literatures, Puyas, are unreadable for lack of knowledge of the scripts to larger social members of Manipur, for these were written in ancient script (the existing Manipuri language use Bengali scripts). These literatures are considered to be at the hands of few traditional scholars. I have known four such popular scholars in Manipur. The literatures are, however, transliterated into modern Manipuri language (of Bengali script) and available in bookstalls for popular usage.
3. But at present Hao would also mean in commoner language broadly the hill dwellers or the tribes. More importantly though Kulachandra takes Hao and Hou as same meaning of different language speaking people, at present both are treated differently: Hao refers to tribe/the hillmen, which is derogatory and Hou is the sound produced during dance. Many would prefer Hou instead of Hao as the latter is found derogatory to contemporary society of Manipur.
4. The Meiteis, who are the plain dwellers of Manipur, are Tai group of people. The Tai groups of people were believed to migrate to the present part of North-East India in general and Manipur particularly from the Southwest China in historical times.
5. The myth of brotherhood between hillmen and valley dwellers has been popular in the region and much of it was used during colonial conceptualisation of the hills and valley in Manipur.
6. The Meitei state and Burmese state were also occasionally entered in matrimonial alliance. King Charairongba, father of King Pamheiba (Garibniwaz), gave his daughter to Burmese King on signing peace pact between them on the promise that she would be given the status of head queen. But she was not given such status. As a result, Charairongba had the intention of taking revenge for such act of the Burmese King. Early records give the information that the invasion of Garibniwaz was also partly driven by this episode.
7. I feel that the meaning of Jati here is limited to the sense of grouping of people, not the Jati under the Hindu caste order.
8. Darbar came into being after 1891 defeat of Manipur at the hands of British and Meitei King was the president. It was reconstituted in 1907.

'The Raja', a term given by the British to the Meitei Kings in twentieth century, was previously the president of the Darbar, but after 1907 it was reconstituted and ICS officer became the president. There were five unelected members nominated by the Political Agent and the Raja.

9. There were also anti-Brahma Sabha Brahmins, who were members of the Nikhil Manipur Mahasabha. Nikhil Manipur Mahasabha was previously called Nikhil Manipur Hindu Mahasabha and it was patronised by the Raja of Manipur. The first session of Nikhil Manipur Hindu Mahasabha was held in Manipur with the King as the key architect. Attempts were made to popularise Manipuri language and Hindu religion not only in Manipur, but also to places outside the state. But the body became political party in 1930s with the aim of bringing a 'responsible form of government' that questioned the institution of Monarchy. It was this turn that not only deleted the term 'Hindu' from its name, but also made Nikhil Manipur Mahasabha a political party. The Raja, thereafter, refused to give royal patronage to this political party. The members of the party resigned from the offices of the state. But Nikhil Manipur Mahasabha though went beyond Hindu subjects and went on supporting the interest of the hillsmen, it continued to say for rightful Hindu tradition in Manipur; its programmes included educating the Brahmins.
10. For the sake of analysis I will focus on the Naga integration movements from the side of Manipur. Naga movement has quite a long history in the North-East region of India and particularly in the present state of Nagaland. Later on, Manipur also became the centre of the movement. Since the present focus of the study is the construction of the cultural core in the valley of Manipur as a historical response to the challenges from the surrounding hills since historical times I deliberately give more emphasis on the movement of Nagas as seen in Manipur. This does not mean I will ignore the implications of the movement in the state to the neighbouring state of Nagaland and to the region at large.
11. The State Archaeology has published a book on Kangla as part of the 'restoration and reconstruction' of this historic fort. It is in this book that descriptions of the holy places and historical monuments/sites of the historic fort are given. See Singh, Bheigya and Singh (2006).
12. Detailed history of such place-making tradition is given in a work by Hemchandra (1996).
13. Memorandum was found in the office of state archaeology during a visit by the present researcher.
14. Minutes of meeting of the Kangla Religious Committee held on 17 July 2007 at the office of state archaeology department.
15. This information was gathered during a discussion with an official of the state archaeology.

16. The paper containing this statement of the organisation *Malem Kanba Lup Machin Manao* was found in the office of state archaeology during a visit by the present researcher.
17. These self-founded facts or 'revealed facts' of the organisation *Malem Kanba Lup Machin Manao* are quoted from an application given by this organisation to the Kangla Fort Board, Government of Manipur. The present researcher had collected this application during a visit to the office of the state archaeology.
18. Part of this book was used in this paper.

References

All Tribal Students Union Manipur (ATSUM). 2000. *Territorial Rights of Outer Manipur*. Manipur: ATSUM.

Arambam, Lokendra. 2001. 'On Ethnicity, Conflict and Development in Manipur', *MRFD Bulletin*, 1 (4): 1–13.

Bahadur, Mutua. 2005. *Illustrated Manuscripts of Manipur*. Imphal: Mutua Museum.

Balibar, Etienne. 2002. *Politics and the Other Scene*. London: Verso.

Bhargava, Rajeev. 2010 (1998). *Secularism and its Critics*. New Delhi: Oxford University Press.

Chatterjee, Partha. 2004. *The Politics of the Governed: Reflections on Popular Politics in Most of the World*. Ranikhet: Permanent Black.

Chaube, S.K. 1973 (reprinted in 1999). *Hill Politics in Northeast India*. Delhi: Orient Longman.

Das, Rajat Kanti. 1985. *The Manipur Tribal Scene: Studies in Society and Change*. Delhi: Inter-India Publications.

Devi, L. Kunjeswori. 2007. *Archaeology in Manipur*. New Delhi: Rajesh Publications.

Eaton, Richard M. 1997. 'Comparative History as World History: Religious Conversion in Modern India', *Journal of World History*, 8 (2): 243–71.

Geertz, Clifford. 1973. *The Interpretation of Cultures*. New York: Basic Books.

——. 1980. *Nagara: The Theatre State in Nineteenth Century Bali*. Princeton, NJ: Princeton University Press.

Gills, Preeti (ed.) 2010. *The Peripheral Centre: Voices from India's Northeast*. Delhi: Zubaan.

Guss, David M. 2000. *The Festive State: Race, Ethnicity, Nationalism as Cultural Performance*. California: University of California Press.

Heller, Agnes. 1991. 'The Concept of the Political Revisited', in David Held (ed.), *Political Theory Today*, Cambridge: Polity Press, pp. 330–43.

Hemchandra, Chanam. 1996. *Kangleirol* (An Account of Different Places of Manipur with Important Historical Events). Imphal: Ching-tam Press.

——. 1998. *Meihourol Salai Khaiba*. Imphal: Ching-tam Press.

Holston, James and Arjun Appadurai. 2003. 'Cities and Citizenship', in Neil Brenner et al. (eds), *State/Space: A Reader*, London: Blackwell Publishers, pp. 296–308.

Hudson, T.C. 2007 (first published in 1908). *The Meitheis*. Delhi: Low Price Publications.

Kaviraj, Sudipta. 2010. *The Imaginary Institution of India*. Ranikhet: Permanent Black.

——. 2010. *The Trajectories of the Indian State*. Ranikhet: Permanent Black.

Khelchandra Singh, N. and L. Ibungohal Singh. 2005. *Cheitharol Kumbaba*. Imphal: Manipur Sahitya Parishad.

Khelchandra, N. 1978. *Ariba Manipuri Sahitya Itihas* (History of Old Manipuri Literatures). Imphal: Manipur Sahitya Parishad.

Lukacs, Georg. 1971. *History and Class Consciousness: Studies in Marxist Dialectics*. London: Merlin Press.

Manipur Cultural Integration Conference (MCIC) 1976. *Ching Amasung Tamgi Mari*. Imphal: MCIC.

Mao, John. 1990. 'Manipur: A Cultural Region', Thesis submitted to the Manipur University, Department of Anthropology.

Nabakumar, W. 2005. 'Communalism and Ethnic Divide: An Anathema to Secular Society', Paper presented in the National Seminar on 'Indigenous Tribal Religions of the Northeast', sponsored by the Centre for the Studies in Civilization, New Delhi, at Imphal, Manipur, 21–23 March.

Nilabir, Sairem. 1991. 'The Revivalist Movement of Sanamahism', in Naorem Sanajaoba (ed.), *Manipur: Past and Present, the Ordeals and Heritage of a Civilization*, Delhi: Mittal Publications, pp. 122–41.

Parratt, John. 2005. *Wounded Land: Politics and Identity in Modern Manipur*. Delhi: Mittal Publications.

Parratt, Saroj Nalini. 1980. *The Religion of Manipur: Beliefs, Rituals and Historical Development*. Calcutta: Firma KLM Private Limited.

Reid, Robert. 1983. *History of the Frontier Areas Bordering on Assam: From 1883–1941*. Delhi: Eastern Publishing House.

Rudolph, Lloyd I. and Susanne Hoeber Rudolph. 2010 (first print 1967). *The Modernity of Tradition: Political Development in India*. Delhi: Orient Blackswan.

Saha, R.K. 1987. 'State Formation among the Meitei in Manipur', in Surajit Sinha (ed.), *Tribal Polities and State Systems in Pre-colonial Eastern and North Eastern India*, Delhi: K.P. Bagchi & Company, pp. 214–41.

Seaton, S. Lee and Henri J. M. Claessen. 1979. *Political Anthropology: The State of the Art*. The Hague, NY: Mouton Publishers.

Sharma, B. Kulachandra. 2009. *Meitrabakki Maningtamba Leipakna Hourakkhiba*. Imphal: B. (O) Dima Publications.

Shimray, R.R. 1985. *Origin and Culture of Nagas*. Delhi: Mittal Publications.

Singh, Karam Manimohan. 1989. *Hijam Irabot Singh and Political Movement in Manipur*. Delhi: B.R. Publishing Corporation.

Singh, Khuraijam Bijoykumar. 2005. 'Sanamahi Movement among the Meiteis of Manipur: A Sociological Study of a Socio-Religious Movement', Ph.D. Thesis, Centre for the Study in Social Systems, Jawaharlal Nehru University.

Singh, L. Bhagyachandra. 2008. *A Critical Study of the Religious Philosophy of the Meeteis before the Advent of Vaishnavism in Manipur*. Imphal: L. Momon Devi.

Singh, Manikchand Konsam. 2007. *Sang Pannaba Mashil, Konsam Ongbi Jamini Devi: Imphal.*

Singh, N. Khelchandra, Sapam Bheigya and S. Rupoban Singh (eds) 2006. *Kangla* (The Ancient Capital of Manipur). Imphal: State Archaeology, Department of Art & Culture, Government of Manipur.

Tambiah, Stanley Jeyaraja. 1985. 'The Galactic Polity in Southeast Asia', in Stanley Jeyaraja Tambiah (ed.), *Culture, Thought, and Social Action: An Anthropological Perspective*, Harvard: Harvard University Press, pp. 252–86.

Tonkin, Elizabeth. 1992. *Narrating Our Pasts: The Social Construction of Oral History*. Cambridge: Cambridge University Press.

United Naga Council Working Group (UNCWG). 2002. *The Naga Perspective: Issues Relating to the Territorial Integrity of Manipur*. Manipur: UNCWG.

13

Modernity and Ethnic Identity Formation of Rajbangshis

NANDINI BASISTHA

Modernity is highly ambivalent and increasingly global. But we can scarcely enjoy the melodies of modernity without simultaneously experiencing their maladies. It combines benefits with disasters – both positive and negative consequences. Modernisation generally leads to a post-traditional, post-medieval historical period of capitalism, industrialisation, secularisation, and rationalisation. But, consequently, it also helped in ethnic identity formation, which generally leads to politics of separatism. Now the question is when and how the identity gets politicised. Three contending theories seek to identify the causal conditions that produce political mobilisation of group's identity. For the *developmental perspective*, which regards community or ethnicity as a primordial sentiment, ethnic political mobilisation occurs when states fail to integrate ethnic groups into the national mainstream, thereby widening the socio-cultural and politico-economic gap between the ethnic group and the rest of the nation. In contrast to this view, the *reactive ethnicity perspective* regards the infiltration of ethnic homeland by members of the dominant cultural group (and not its isolation) and the 'cultural division of labour' that is caused by the allocation of valued roles and resources to the dominant group as the main cause of ethnic political mobilisation (Hechter 1975). A third approach, the *ethnic competition perspective*, argues that the process of modernisation sparks ethnic political mobilisation when dominant and subordinate groups are forced to compete with each other for the same rewards and resources. Somewhere all reasons are inter-connected and inter-dependent. However, without going to the debate on the appropriateness of the aforesaid theories, I want to concentrate on the effect of modernity on the process of ethnic identity formation of Rajbangshis.

Identity formation is not a one-day event, which can be done just switching on one's idea in one direction. It takes several years as it does with the case of Rajbangshis. Literary, the word 'Rajbangshi' means the 'Royal Community'. They are, actually, descendents of the medieval Kamata and Koch kingdom. Established by Prithu in twelfth century, Kamata kingdom comprised the tract of land bounded by the Karotoya in the west, the Brahmaputra in the east, the Dooars in the north and the Padma-Brahmaputra basin in the south. The last Kamata king, Nilambar (1480–1498) expanded the kingdom to include the present Cooch Behar districts of West Bengal and the undivided Kamrup and Darrang districts of Assam and northern Mymensing in Bangladesh as well as eastern parts of Dinajpur district. Sometime after the fall of the Kamata kingdom, indigenous 'Koch' ruler, Biswa Singha established Koch Kingdom in the same tract. Despite several attacks from Mughals and British, these Koch-Rajbangshi rulers maintained their separate political identity and independence up to 1949. Every ethnic identity formation needs a historical past. Here Kamata-Koch kingdom helped in this regard.

But, in the meantime, the social identity of Rajbangshis faced a crisis. Although Hindu Brahmins christened 'Kshatriya' status to the Koch ruler Biswa Singha, Rajbangshis got 'Tribal' or low-caste status in the British Census. After the marriage of King Nripendra Narayan with Suniti Devi (the daughter of Brahma Samaj-founder Keshab Chandra Sen), the Koch royal family, however, drifted gradually away from caste rigidity and caste-based identity. Moreover, they felt pride in introducing themselves as Koch (Debnath 2007: 44). But Rajbangshis are not happy in their low status. So, under the leadership of Rai Saheb Panchanan Barma, educated and affluent Rajbangshi intelligentsia had started *Kshatriyaisation movement*, which eventually acted as the base of the various ethno-political movements of Rajbangshis (Barma 2007).

Although this movement started with the declared aim of caste upliftment, we cannot fully ignore effect of modernisation behind such moves. This movement is actually a consequence of the modernisation process of British officials and king of Cooch Behar. Generally we can identify three markers of modernity – industrialisation, democracy and nationalism (Riggs 1998). The first two are a direct effect of state policy while the third one originated from the Western education and literature.

In North Bengal, British officers had started tea plantation vis-à-vis tea industry. This led to commercialisation of agriculture. As labourers, several ethnic groups started to settle in the Rajbangshi-dominated areas of Assam and the whole of Northern part of Bengal. In Assam, the Rajbangshis started to be mixed up with the Assamese people and left their separate identity. But, in Bengal the case was different.

Often described as 'Ethnological Museum', North Bengal became a multiethnic and multicultural region. Along with the aboriginals of this area, there migrated a large number of ethnic groups, e.g., Bengalis, Nepali, Mech, Rabha, Oraon, Munda, Santhal, Malpahari, Madhesi, Toto, Kharia, Jugi, Khen, Pan, Paliyya, Deshi, Nasya Seskh (Muslim) and so on, in addition to the so-called higher caste people. All of these groups have preserved their ethnic identities and languages. In fact, here, demography encompassed ethno-linguistic identity issue, the religious composition, and the historical heritage of the princely state. Its strategic location can be blamed for that. The North Bengal is bounded by Assam and Bangladesh in the east, Sikkim and Bhutan in the north, Nepal and Bihar in the west and river Ganga afterwards South Bengal in the south.

Large scale migration from Bangladesh (former East Pakistan or East Bengal) to North Bengal greatly changed the demographic scenario of the region. In competition for eco-socio-political rights, Rajbangshis get outnumbered by the immigrants, especially Bengalis. There is no denying the fact that the Cooch Behar royal family was always in the grip of the outsiders and all privileges were exercised by non-Rajbangshi people.

Having acquired modern education, many Rajbangshis got influenced by the nationalistic notion. Soon they realised about their condition and started movement for betterment. Here we can specially refer to the name of Panchanan Barma. First 'graduate' Rajbangshi, 'Thakur' Panchanan Barma failed to secure any post other than that of a 'Hostel Superintendent' and, for his criticism of the Royal family, he was declared unwanted in Cooch Behar. Being treated ignominiously, he jumped into the Kshatriya movement begun by predecessors, like Haramahan Khajanchi and Harikishore Barma. Thus, to survive in the new colonial socio-economic structure, in which British counted them as semi-tribal, Rajbangshi gentry forced to start movements for their lost power and status.

To regain the lost social status of the Rajbangshi community in Hindu society, 'Thakur Panchanan' established Rangpur Kshatriya Samiti in 1910. Very soon it acquired the status of a central association of the whole Rajbangshi community. To achieve its immediate objective, Samiti intensively incorporated Brahmanical values and practices for a purified social image. Moreover, Samiti took various initiatives to unite Rajbangshis. This includes bringing out a monthly journal called '*Kshtriya*', in which many provocative writings were published against the Bengali upper-caste hegemony and advised the community members to sever all socio-political ties with these castes. Even the intellectual sections henceforth discontinued their association with the literary organisations of Bengalis.

However, such social uplift movement organised by the Kshatriya Samiti not only consolidated caste solidarity among the common Rajbangshis but also created consciousness of a separate identity among the educated youth of the community in particular (Sarkar 2006).

But, often it was said that the movement got confined to a particular section of the Rajbangshis, who were mainly land-owners, jotedars and autochthonic population. The leaders of the Kshatriya movement were equal to other caste Hindu Bhadraloks in matters of education, profession, dress and manners and felt quite acutely the odium of belonging to a low caste in Hindu society due to their low social origin (Mukhopadhyay 2009). So, the rural poor, who constituted the bulk of the Rajbangshi peasantry, were unable to identify themselves fully with those people of their community who belong to the high strata of the society. Thus, the class solidarity of the Samiti got fractured under the weight of class contradictions, and ultimately the Samiti failed to crystallise a distinct 'social identity' for the Rajbangshis.

The leaders of the Samiti, however, later realised that just adoption of the sacred thread and upper-caste practices could not help in raising the social status of the Rajbangshi masses whose economic condition was extremely bad. Then they started looking for being accommodated in the government-approved institutional arrangement of 'protective discrimination', especially in matters of education and employment. To avail this, they were ultimately granted 'Scheduled Caste' status in Bengal. Therefore, the social movement of the Rajbangshis, which initially began for achieving a superior status in the caste hierarchy was ultimately reduced to a mere real politic for getting reservation in government services, which later on created certain confusion in the question relating to the identity of the Rajbangshis. The offshoots of Koch-Rajbangshis got different status in different provinces, like 'Other Backward Classes' in upper Assam, 'More Other Backward Classes' in lower Assam, 'Scheduled Tribe' in Meghalaya, and simple 'Backward Classes' in Bihar. This led to a fragmented identity of this ethnic group at the all India-level.

Another vehicle of modernisation, viz., process of democratisation through electoral system, drifted towards consolidation of Kshatriya Samiti's political identity. Though the Kshatriya Samiti started its way mainly as a social organisation, it began to partake in national politics from the second decade of the twentieth century. The Samiti gave candidates in all the four elections held in Bengal Legislative Council from 1920 to 1929 under 1919 Act and achieved striking electoral success. The Samiti placed their candidates against the all-India party candidates because they considered the Indian National Congress (INC) and the Communist Party of India (CPI) as associations of the upper caste Hindus. The candidates of the Kshatriya Samiti won in the Assembly election of 1937 and 1946 against the candidates of the INC and CPI. The elected candidates formed the *'Independent Scheduled Caste Party'* in 1938 along with Scheduled Caste representatives of East Bengal. But, against the background of the constitutional negotiations continuing since the appointment of the Simon Commission, the Kshatriya movement became involved in the issue of political and economic reforms and improvement of ritual and social status was given the back seat. Actually this movement dried up with the death of Panchana Barma in 1935 and merger of its leaders with Congress and mainstream politics.

However, from the election results, it should be clear that Kshatriya movement had considerable influence on the political life of Jalpaiguri and its neighbouring districts of Rangpur, Dinajpur and Cooch Behar although it did not gather momentum in the princely state of Cooch Behar as any kind of movement was not allowed there. The only exception was *Hitasadhani Sabha*, under which we can see the rise of second stream of Rajbangshi-led movement.

According to some historians, Hitasadhani Sabha was established in 1918 for the development of the indigenous (*deshi*) people of Cooch Behar (Varman 2008: 85). But this student-oriented party was banned by Prince Nityendra Narayan in 1921. In 1942, Cooch Behar Legislative Council was formed in response to the persistent clamour for responsible government in the princely states throughout the country. After contesting election primarily on the issue of awareness and rights of the Rajbangshi people and winning all the seats, aspirations of the Rajbangshi members got a big fillip. King's administration was so long run by the educated, non-Rajbangshi, upper-caste Hindus and there was no Rajbangshis although the king himself belonged to the same caste (Dakua 2007: 54). The participation in administration through this democratic medium raised hope amongst the commoners that *deshi* people can capture the power of administration at last and they can achieve the ultimate goal of being administered by themselves. So they started movement against the *Bhatias (*outsiders).

In mid 1940s, Hitasadhani Sabha was, formally, established by *deshi* (Rajbangshi Hindus and Muslims) elites and jotedars – like Satish Chandra Singha Sarkar, Khan Chaudhury Amanatulla, Gajendra Narayan Basunia – for the Hita (good) or welfare of *deshi* people. Although the exact date of its foundation is not known, its presence felt in the historic meeting of 19 May 1946 in the field of Rashmela of Cooch Behar. The communications were not so developed at that period. Still the people came by bullock's carts or on buffaloes, by bicycles and on foot (Barman 2007: 73). In a state of around five lakh people, this meeting was attended by around two lakh people. Here, the Sabha-leaders raised the proposal of keeping Cooch Behar under the Central government of Indian Dominion for the interest of the development of the local people.

Although political activities were illegal in Cooch Behar, it got registered by the Cooch Behar dynasty. On 26 July 1948, Radhakanta Sarkar wrote about Hitasadhani Sabha that '... a most reactionary group has been formed, formulated and patronised by the Maharaja of Cooch Behar, to serve his own personal purpose of dominating and ruling the people for his own exploitation to the detriment of the interest'.

In the meantime, it was made clear that India would be free but Pakistan would emerge as a new state out of the divided parts of India. The native states were allowed to join with either of the two states. The King of Cooch Behar was in a 'Horns of Dilemma' to join (Das 2007: 101). The people of Cooch Behar came to learn that the king's going out of democratic ideas would be prevailing in near future. So they wanted to rule Cooch Behar for the all round development through the local representatives of the people as per democratic system. So, Hitasadhani Sabha, along with Independent Scheduled Caste Party raised the first demand of a separate homeland for the Koch-Rajbangshi community. This proposed state, 'Rajasthan' comprised Siliguri, Purnia of Bihar, Goalpara of Assam, north-eastern side of Rangpur, Jalpaiguri and Dinajpur districts. Although the-then princely state, Cooch Behar, was not included in the proposed state, it was supposed that it will be naturally merged with the 'Rajasthan' state, after signing the merger agreement by the existing king. This demand of 'Rajasthan' was popularised by the-then Central Minister Jogendra Nath Mandal in the mass meeting in Darjeeling, Jalpaiguri and Dinajpur on 4, 6 and 7 May 1947.

However, the demand of Rajbangshi people was never taken seriously and Cooch Behar joined the Indian Union as a Part 'C' state. After India's Independence the Hitasadhani Sabha took the name of *Cooch Behar State Praja Congress*. On the question of joining of the native state Cooch Behar the Indian Union, the Sabha demanded for the proclamation of Cooch Behar as a separate state. A part of the Rajbangshi Hindu and Muslim Jotedars of Dooars were also inspired by the Cooch Behar State Praja Congress and they preferred to stay under the umbrella of proposed 'Cooch Behar' state. But their demands were, again, looked down upon.

In spite of the hindrances of the demand of a separate state raised by the Hitasadhani Sabha, their movement did not obliterate completely. On 30 October 1949, the representatives of Cooch Behar State Praja Congress, along with Darjeeling Gorkha League, Sikkim Praja Sammelon and Jalpaiguri Gurkha League assembled at Darjeeling. In this gathering they called for separate state styled as *Uttarakhand Pradesh Sangha*. Malda and West Dinajpur were not included in the proposed Uttarakhand Pradesh Sangha, but Sikkim was there. The demand for the establishment of Uttarakhand Pradesh Sangha was raised before the then Prime Minister Jawaharlal Nehru in 1952 when he came to Darjeeling. But he did not give any importance.

Meanwhile, with the signing of Merger Agreement between Government of India and Maharaja of Cooch Behar in 28 August 1949, Cooch Behar lost its separate existence and, ultimately, joined West Bengal as a mere district on 1 January 1950.

The newly independent India followed Nehruvian model of modernisation where participatory democracy, capitalism and industrialisation were encouraged. But, the new political system of independent India failed to preserve economic and political interest of Rajbangshis. So, after getting united and mobilised by the Kshatriyaisation movement, one group of common Rajbangshis started a movement for Rajbangshi-led homeland in form of a separate state, under the 'Union of India'. This is generally a proletariat movement fought for the socio-political upliftment of the group status. Another group of Rajbangshis, mainly backed by the middle class intelligentsia, started movement in demand of the proper implementation of Merger Agreement 1949 for regaining separate entity of Cooch Behar as a Union Territory under the control of Central Government.

The most important cause of the disgruntlement of the Rajbangshis is the question of land. The newly-formed Congress Government in West Bengal as well as in Delhi failed to introduce land reforms to address the problem of landlessness of those who were capable of tilling lands; and apathetic was the government policy as to deal with the growing menace of refugee influx from East Pakistan. The problem even christened with the fresh immigrants at the time of Bangladesh war (1971) and their illegal and forceful occupation of vested and even some personal waste lands for settlement. The local people are rather aggrieved in this matter and felt helpless as the different political parties support this illegal act of refugees for their petty political gain. In fact, the series of disputes and litigations over land have halted the progress of land reform measures in many parts of the sub-division. The migration of people across different borders and refugee influx leading to growing crisis of land compared to increasing number of population and economic problems thereof following which there bubbled up socio-economic and political tensions.

In addition, the area is also industrially back ward. Amidst of economic misery a large number of cultivators are converting their agricultural lands to small tea gardens. Lack of agro-based industry the presence of which could have propped up the speedy growth of agriculture and industry both and could have absorbed unemployed people in increasing number and which in turn could have prevented the flow of people from North Bengal, in search of jobs, into the Western states of India. Discriminative policies, lack of education and exploitation of common people in the covetous hands of bureaucrats, engineers, doctors and politicians raising the grudge of common people against government officials vis-à-vis governmental system. It is alleged that most of the people in power of the government are not sons of soil and they are not inclined to carry any level of love for the people of the North.

All these, in turn, had evoked discontent amongst the native dwellers; one of its effects is rise of Uttarkhand movement. 'Uttarkhand' as a nomenclature of a separate state in North Bengal was first used in a conference in Darjeeling in 1949. A view in support of the Uttarakhandis for giving the name of Uttarakhand to their movement was that a large number of labourers, working in the tea gardens of Jalpaiguri Dooars, Malda and West Dinajpur were sympathetic towards the Jharkhand movement. To acquire the support of the tea garden labourers, the Uttarakhandis preferred to take 'Khand' from 'Jharkhand' and gave the name of Uttarakhand to their party (Ghosh 2007: 182). Although their movement was popularly known as Uttarakhand movement, they named their proposed state, 'Kamtapur' following long historical tradition. Out of the Uttarkhand movement, the Uttarakhand Party came out after a procrastinating historical process. The prime aim of the Uttarakhand Party was to set apart North Bengal from South Bengal and create a prosperous state Indian state called 'Kamtapur' in order to protect the people of North Bengal from the exploitation of Calcutta-centric capitalist leaders. The Uttarakhandis were determined to create a separate 'Kamta' state out of West Bengal, comprising five districts of West Bengal – viz., Malda, Dakshin Dinajpur, Uttar Dinajpur, Jalpaiguri, and Cooch Behar. In their version, this wider area of 8,384 sq km would be much greater than many Union Territories of India from the point of view of area, population and natural resources. In justification of their movement, they exemplified the creation of several states – like Maharashtra, Gujarat, Nagaland, Haryana, Meghalaya and Andhra Pradesh – according to language and culture. Moreover, according to the Uttarakhandis the name of any part of India can be changed by the amendments of the Constitution. Therefore, according to the Uttarakhandis, their demand of a separate state would be legitimate from all respects. The Uttarakhandis also gave assurances that in their proposed new state the people would reside peacefully irrespective of caste, class, and creed. So, up to that time their movement was not purely ethnic in character. But, in the eighties, the Uttarakhand Party started the Bhatia Khedao movement. They called Bengali refugees and immigrants from Bangladesh as '*Bhatia*' and started agitation against the Burgeoning Bengali settlement in the North Bengal area. From there onwards we can see changing character of socio-political movements of North Bengal.

However, Uttarakhand Party could not make stable organisation in West Dinajpur and Malda and had its influence mainly in Jalpaiguri, Cooch Behar and in the plains of Darjeeling district. But, there also this movement saw decay and gradual dismemberment. In the General Election, held on 10 March 1971, the Uttarakhand Party contested in Maynaguri, Dhupguri, Sadar, Falakata seats of Jalpaiguri District and one Lok Sabha seat of Jalpaiguri (Ray 2007: 119). But their candidates were defeated mainly for the lack of funds. As a result, the party began to split.

In the intermediary period between the decline of the Uttarkhand Dal and the emergence of the Kamtapur movement, an auxiliary organisation named *'Uttarbanga Tapasili Jati/Upajati Sangathan'* (UTJUS) had been formed. They continued 'Bhatia Khedao' movement with a strong mass base in the rural and tea garden areas of Dooars. The so-called autochthonous people, mainly the Rajbangshis, became the torch-bearer of a movement of anomalous type with explicit demands for the redress of their socio-economic and educational grievances, but more with the objective of dormant political design and ambition, including the one against the citizenship of the Bhatias after 1971.

After the liberation of Bangladesh in 1971, a large section of the Bengali refugees coming from Bangladesh were Namasudras. To protect themselves from the flame of the Bhatia Khedao movement, the Namasudras also started to unite themselves to maintain their own existence. All of a sudden, at the time of a big Central Conference of UTJUS, the Bharatiya hoodlums, consisting members of different clubs and the activists of different political parties, opened the Pandora's Box of their brutal force and hundreds of people were injured, even women old and young were not spared. The police took no cognisance of the crime. On the contrary, the Bengali people of Alipurduar gave the account that the leaders of the UTJUS delivered provocative speeches asking the audience to reclaim those plots of lands even of Alipurduar town which once had been grabbed by the immigrant Bhatias. They further added that no plot of land was grabbed; the Bhatias had to buy lands at the prices as were prevalent from time to time. In this chaos of mutual blaming of disrupting peace, the real reason of that unfortunate incident still remains unsearched and a matter of impartial investigation. But this, instead of terrorising, further inspired those Rajbangshis in political involvement who so far maintained aloofness from political involvement. So, from the ruins of this disastrous incident, the full-fledged Kamtapur movement was resurrected.

However, the Rajbangshi-led movements of divergent interests never become too powerful to reach destiny. For becoming numerically stronger, time to time some attempts of joint collaboration have taken place. But these are too fragile. So, never their movement succeeded to fulfill their aim. However, troubles of North Bengal never solved and, so, politics of separatism goes on. Modernity became a catalyst of such movements but root originated from elsewhere.

Note

This is part of my D.Phil. thesis on 'Politics of Separatism in North Bengal: A Fight for Justice', ongoing under the supervision of Prof. Mohd Aslam from the Political Science Department of Allahabad University, Allahabad.

References

Barma, Sukhbilas (ed.) 2007. *Socio-Political Movements in North Bengal: A Sub-Himalayan Tract.* New Delhi: Global Vision.

Barman, Prasenjit. 2007. 'Hitasadhani Movement', in Sukhbilas Barma (ed.), *Socio-Political Movements in North Bengal: A Sub-Himalayan Tract,* New Delhi: Global Vision.

Dakua, Dinesh Chandra. 2007. 'A Journey from Hitasadhani to Greater Kuch Bihar', in Sukhbilas Barma (ed.), *Socio-Political Movements in North Bengal: A Sub-Himalayan Tract,* New Delhi: Global Vision, pp. 56–64.

Das, Parbananda. 2007. 'The Hitasadhanee Sabha and the Tensions of Cooch Behar's with India', in Sailen Debnath (ed.), *Social and Political Tensions in North Bengal Since 1947,* Siliguri: N.L. Publishers, pp. 101–23.

Debnath, Sailen (ed.) 2007. *Social and Political Tensions in North Bengal Since 1947.* Siliguri: N.L. Publishers.

Ghosh, Srabani. 2007. 'Revisiting the Uttarakhand Movement', in Sailen Debnath (ed.), *Social and Political Tensions in North Bengal Since 1947,* Siliguri: N.L. Publishers, pp. 178–91.

Hechter, Michael. 1975. *Internal Colonialism: The Celtic Fringe in British National Development.* London: Routledge and Kegan Paul.

Mukhopadhyay, Rajatsubhra. 2009. 'Social Formation of the Rajbangshis and the Emergence of the Kamtapuri Identity', in N.K. Das and V.R. Rao (eds), *Identity, Cultural Pluralism and State: South Asia in Perspective,* Kolkata: Anthropological Survey of India, pp. 482–91.

Ray, Haripada. 2007. 'The Genesis of Uttar Khand Movement', in Sukhbilas Barma (ed.), *Social and Political Tensions in North Bengal Since 1947,* Siliguri: N.L. Publishers, pp. 116–27.

Riggs, Fred W. 1998. 'The Modernity of Ethnic Identity and Conflict', *International Political Science Review,* 19 (3): 269–88.

Sarkar, I. 2006. 'The Kamtapur Movement: Towards a Separate State in North Bengal', in Govind Chandra Rath (ed.), *Tribal Development in India: The Contemporary Debate,* New Delhi: Sage Publications, pp. 153–65.

Varman, Lalit Chandra. 2008. *Rajyar Dabite Uttarbange Andolon* (in Bengali). Assam: N.L. Publishers.

Index